IN
OBEDIENCE
TO
INSTRUCTIONS

to say, to the past and future generations of our kin and of our speech, that we took up our positions, in obedience to instructions.

T.S. Eliot
from *Defence of the Islands*
1940

IN OBEDIENCE TO INSTRUCTIONS

FANY WITH THE SOE
in the Mediterranean

by

MARGARET PAWLEY

LEO COOPER

First published in Great Britain in 1999 by
LEO COOPER
an imprint of
Pen & Sword Books
47 Church Street
Barnsley
South Yorkshire
S70 2AS

ISBN 0 85052 633 7
A catalogue record for this book
is available from the British Library

Typeset in 10/12.5pt Plantin by
Phoenix Typesetting, Ilkley, West Yorkshire

Printed by
Redwood Books Limited,
Trowbridge, Wiltshire.

For our grandchildren
And especially for mine
Thomas, Jamie, Katie, Natasha,
Lucy and Imogen

CONTENTS

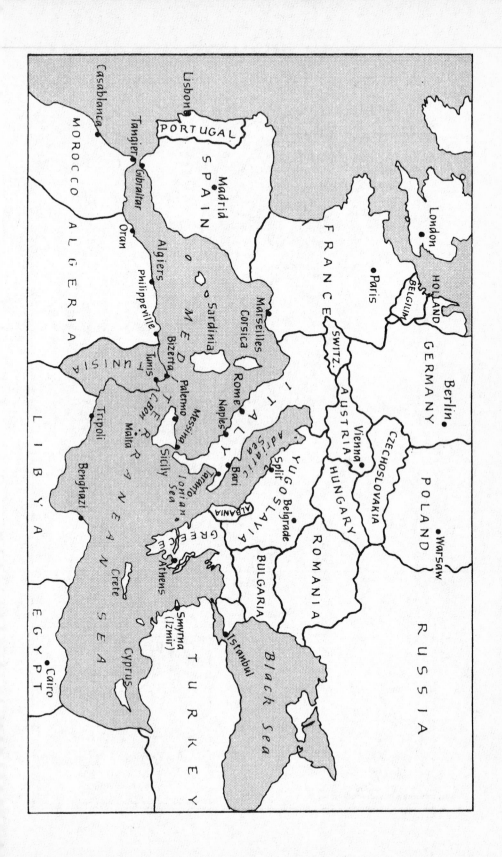

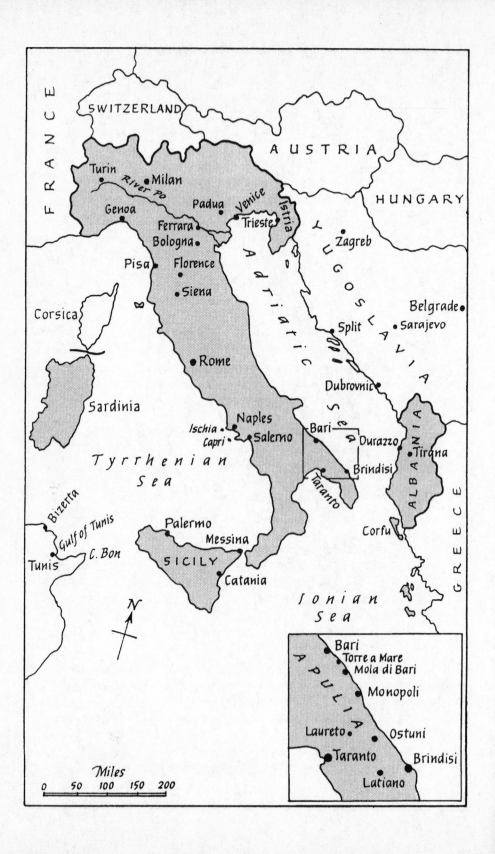

INTRODUCTION

It was not I but Anne Younger (formerly Anne Butler) who originally thought of writing this book. Four years ago she asked me to collaborate with her in an account of our shared wartime experience as members of the FANY Corps, in the organization known as Special Operations Executive, in Egypt and Italy. It had struck her that much had rightly been written on those FANYs who had been infiltrated into occupied France and endured imprisonment in concentration camps and in some cases death, but little had been recorded of the 'back-room' girls: FANY W/T operators, working sets into occupied Europe, secretaries, coders, drivers, administrators, interpreters, intelligence officers, staff in 'holding' houses, who had contributed to the running of SOE in unspectacular capacities. She felt she wanted to relate the events of those extraordinary years for the sake, in particular, of her grandchildren. I was completing a book at the time and, although this was for me a new field, I agreed to cooperate. Anne's health deteriorated over the next months and, despite valiant efforts to survive for the sake of her family, and renewed treatments when her courage never failed her, she died in March, 1996.

In order to decide whether to tackle the job myself, it seemed important to revisit the south of Italy where we had spent most of 1944 and the first half of 1945. Accordingly, during one of my annual visits to friends in Tuscany in June, 1996, I took the train to Rome and then the *Pendolino* across the Apennines to Bari. Several years during the sixties had been spent in Rome with my husband and children, but I had not set foot in the south since I left Bari for Siena in March, 1945, fifty-one years before.

As the express train plunged on through the mountains, so memories rushed back with the names of the railway stations: Caserta, the former palace of the Kingdom of the Two Sicilies, then Allied Force Headquarters, where I had come in September, 1944, on the daily courier plane from Bari to find information to complete a forged document for an agent about to drop into Austria; Benevento, a break in a hitchhike jeep journey back from leave, where the driver put his head under a gushing fountain to stop himself from falling asleep.

At Bari friends of friends in England, the Renzullis, British wife and Italian husband, gallantly agreed to put up a stranger. We spoke of years past and of the memorable massive German air raid on 2 December, 1943. Lindsay Renzulli drove me to Mola di Bari, a fishing village on the shore of the Adriatic. I easily found the narrow house where I lived for nine months. Our headquarters, the eighteenth-century Palazzo Albertonza, was in poor shape and buttressed by wooden poles. I could not get in. In nearby Torre a Mare, to Lindsay's amazement, I searched for a basketball pitch where all ranks, including colonels, played together on many winter afternoons; now the site held a block of pink flats. My journey back to Pisa, its airport, and home to England, was via the railway station at Florence; the indicator directed me to platform one. I settled myself into an empty carriage on an empty train with an hour's wait. To my horror it began to draw out. I quickly assessed the situation; missing my plane, my ticket not transferrable. I threw my luggage out and, as the platform began to recede, followed, remembering the old SOE adage 'Keep your knees together as you jump'. I survived the impact, only mildly shaken, and picked myself up as the train withdrew to some railway never-never land. Recollections had been so vivid that I was led to reactions as they would have been fifty years before. Moreover, I had come to a decision: I would try and recapture those times and write on what the Queen, in the wake of Cleopatra, once called our salad days (only for us there hardly ever were any green vegetables). The book which follows is the result of that resolve.

A few preliminary observations need to be made: first, it has not been feasible to follow a strictly chronological order. The units in which FANYs served in the Mediterranean had their own very unique character and sphere of operations. It was imperative to describe each individually. Overlapping of dates has invariably occurred. Secondly, some of the activities and operations of the units themselves have been described; otherwise the work of the FANY as auxiliaries, back-room girls, call us what you will, would have been un-intelligible. Lastly, FANYs are here referred to by the names by which they were known during the war years, with any subsequent name in brackets on the first occasion a name is mentioned. Contemporary spelling and terminology have also been used: i.e. Jugoslavia, gramophone.

The help that I have received in the writing of this book has been consider-able. It has come in great measure from my contemporaries in the FANY Corps in the shape of reminiscences, letters, calls and hospitality, the loan of letters home an act of particular generosity. To Antonio and Lindsay Renzulli for their hospitality in Bari and to Margaret Olsen who drove me to see our old headquarters in Siena, I am most grateful. And I express my thanks for help of various kinds from former members of SOE: Arthur Brown, Edgar Chavasse, Peter Cooper, James Darton, Sir Douglas Dodds-Parker, George Hollowell, Hilary King, Peter Lee, Glyn Loosmore, Ian Macpherson, William Pickering, Arthur Radley, Annette Street, Fred Tillson, Sir Peter Wilkinson. My particular gratitude goes to Christopher Woods for setting aside time from his own book to give me much valuable information for mine; and to Duncan Stuart, present SOE adviser to the Foreign Office, who has sent me material germane to my subject from SOE files. To FANY HQ, the staff of the Bodleian Library, the Imperial War Museum, the Wye branch of the Kent County Library and to Maurice Kidd, Elizabeth Evans for her exemplary typing of my MS, Mary Hallett and my sister, Pamela Herbertson, my thanks for all you have done on my account. It is my hope that Anne Younger's grandchildren will find events of interest in this book.

MARGARET PAWLEY
Wye, Kent.
1999.

Chapter One

DEFENCE OF THE ISLANDS

In the days of my childhood in Germany in the later twenties the buzz word was Reparations, a term I understood not at all. It was repeated with boring regularity by my British parents and the guests who came to our home in the Rhineland. During my schooldays in England in the thirties the buzz word was Appeasement. What I understood most clearly on that subject was that my father and many of his friends were against it. After September, 1939, the current phrase had become Helping the War Effort. It was in this interest that girls of my generation joined the Special Operations Executive and the FANY Corps; we were given to believe that our country had been ill-prepared for a just war and there was need to make up for this as swiftly as possible.

Those in pursuit of appeasement towards Germany had been guided by two main considerations: the first understandable, the second rather less so. First, with memories of the years 1914–1918 still vivid, that it was essential to avoid a repetition of that war with its appalling slaughter in the trenches and the loss of almost a generation of men. Secondly, and this was, with hindsight, a surprisingly widely held view, that the Nazi régime in Germany was believed to have achieved wonders for that nation in the way of producing order, purpose and economic stability. Moreover, it was considered possible to take seriously a desire for conversations on the subject of peace, expressed by its leader. On the subject of Germany's educational programme in the thirties theorists waxed eloquent: German youth were receiving direction and encouragement. A friend comments that talks along these lines were given, and produced interested reactions, in English public schools; this had been his experience in 1938.

Some visitors to Germany were enthusiastic about what they saw. Typical of this attitude is that expressed by Henry Williamson (author of *Tarka the*

Otter and other books on the natural world) in his *Goodbye West Country*[1]*
which gives a rosy account of a visit to Germany in 1936. He considered
hostile criticism in the British press of German treatment of Jews 'distortion-
ally magnified'; there were no beggars on the streets. 'Everywhere I saw faces
that looked to be breathing extra oxygen; people free from mental fear.' He
wrote of Hitler, 'Here at last is someone who has perceived the root causes of
war in the unfulfilled human ego and is striving to create a new human-
fulfilled world'; the nightlife of Berlin had been cleaned up since the new Party
took over government.

My father did not share these views: Hitler's revoking of the Treaty of
Versailles and the re-occupation of the de-militarized Rhineland in 1936 filled
him with sorrow and foreboding. For the British and French governments to
have acted immediately with a show of force was, he felt, the only possible
course to prevent further aggression; this they failed to do. Hitler himself, it
has consequently become clear, was not in a strong position, but, in spite of
warnings from his military leaders that the allies might retaliate, went forward
successfully. The occupation of Austria in 1938, Czechoslovakia in 1939 and
the attack on Poland later that year followed. By 3 September we were at war
with Germany.

The state of shock was somewhat lessened by the fact that, except to the
initiated, nothing very much happened until the spring of 1940. At school,
there were First Aid classes after lessons given by a doctor who was a parent,
with the headmistress sitting in as a chaperone. A parents' meeting took
place to discuss whether the school, in a vulnerable part of Kent, should be
evacuated; eventually, half of it went to Cornwall, the rest stayed put.
Gasmasks were issued. Gradually there were some changes: the black-out
was one. All windows needed to be covered with thick opaque material and
show not a chink of light which would reveal directions to enemy aircraft.
Schoolchildren were evacuated from congested towns to the country; sign-
posts were removed to mislead possible invaders and a prohibition placed on
the ringing of church bells, which were only to be used to herald an invasion.
Aliens were required to register; young men of twenty to twenty-two years
were called up for the armed services, while older men, veterans of the First
World War, joined the Home Guard, originally named the LDV, Local
Defence Volunteers. Identity cards and ration books were issued. Poisonous
snakes were destroyed in the London Zoo, in case bombing might release
them. A newspaper commented that their keepers were 'visibly affected' as
some had spent twenty-five years with the reptiles and grown fond of them.
(How *could* they?)

* See Notes p. 165.

By 4 September, 1939, soldiers of the British Expeditionary Force had arrived in France, where conditions were quiet. The only sign of enemy activity was in the Atlantic. The British liner *Athenia* was torpedoed on the first day of the war, two hundred miles from the Hebrides, carrying children to so-called safety in America. On 19 September HMS *Courageous* was sunk by a U boat, to be followed by HMS *Royal Oak* on 16 October and some merchantmen. An account of German treatment of Jewish nationals was published by the British Foreign Office, with details of their having been sent to Buchenwald concentration camp, but it was mild in comparison with what later became known.

It was a particularly cold Christmas in 1939 and warnings of fuel shortages made depressing reading. Food rationing began on 8 January, 1940. Loss of merchant shipping was beginning to bite. A crop of trivial and foolishly optimistic songs, such as 'We're going to hang out the washing on the Siegfried Line' (the main German fortifications), caught the popular mood, which was defensive in character. It seemed that British citizens were gritting their teeth against the utter boredom of the situation, the Phoney or Bore War. The evacuation of the British Expeditionary Force from the continent at Dunkirk in May, 1940, was to alter everything.

The German army had been established on the borders of Belgium and France since the previous autumn. On 10 May an attack on the Albert Canal, north of Liège, was the start of a successful German sweep across north-west Europe and the occupation of the so-called neutral countries of Belgium and Holland and of northern France. By 27 May Hitler ordered his army to advance again to within thirteen miles of Dunkirk. Operation DYNAMO, to call on the owners of self-propelled craft between thirty and a hundred feet, had a notable response. With this help, that of the Royal Navy and various ferries, lifeboats and merchant ships, it proved possible to evacuate around 338,000 men, both British and French by 4 June. Photographs of the returning soldiers told a sorry story: wounded, hungry, dirty, exhausted, often without boots and having lost most of their equipment, they poured into English ports. That they had returned at all in such numbers was a matter of triumph, but the fact that it was actually a colossal defeat which had been inflicted on the British army had a powerful effect on the public attitude. The buzz words now were 'the Dunkirk Spirit' and 'Britain Stands Alone'.

The speeches of Winston Churchill harnessed and stimulated a change in national outlook and produced a determination that the war must be won by the people as a whole. A FANY who later served in Italy has written jokingly that she relinquished her studies at Birmingham University and joined the Corps because 'I didn't think they'd win the war without me,' but her intentions were real enough. Another FANY who served in North Africa commented:

> If it is possible to call war just, this was such a one. The reaction of those serving, very many of whom had family members also involved, was not to question what was demanded of us, and this was based on an early understanding that here was no game.

My own attitude towards Germany was never ambivalent during the war. In spite of having been born and raised in that country, I was never aware of myself as other than British. My own birth and that of my younger sister had been registered immediately at the British vice-consulate in Cologne; Armistice day and the official birthday of King George V were celebrated yearly with pomp and ceremony by the British community. During the years 1929–30 when my father was the last British High Commissioner in the allied occupied Rhineland, there was a permanent reminder of my Britishness with the Union Jack on a flagpole in the garden. In 1940 it was good to look back at happy times during my childhood and with affection towards our German governess and lessons with her, but Germany, my birthplace, was never *die Heimat* (homeland), a favoured German concept, as *La Patrie* is likewise a powerful French one – terms that do not exist in English, though loyalty does. A stand against what Naziism represented claimed my loyalty.

Immediately after Dunkirk Hitler pronounced his victory and ordered the flying of flags and ringing of church bells. There existed a very real fear as to where it was his intention, his troops poised immediately across the channel, to go next. Opinion now differs as to how seriously he pursued Operation SEALION, the plan to invade Britain, but the possibility was there. King George VI spoke to one of his ministers on 31 May, 1940: 'Hitler wants to come here'. On 17 June the French government asked for an armistice.

Although the general understanding was that Britain had been unprepared for the war, certain steps had been taken to form two departments which were the precursors of the Special Operations Executive and therefore within the brief of this book. One, which had its origins in the spring of 1938, was an offshoot of the War Office. Originally named GS(R), (R) representing research into irregular warfare, and later known, from the spring of 1939, as MI(R), it dealt with activity which could be carried out by soldiers in uniform. The director was a major in the Royal Engineers (later Major-General) J.C.F. Holland. One of its members was Major Colin McVean Gubbins[2], the future head of SOE, a considerable and enduring supporter of the deployment of FANYs in his organization. He had served with distinction and gallantry in the First World War, showing marked qualities of flair and leadership. Two officers who were to play leading roles within SOE emerge at this point: Peter

Wilkinson[3] and Douglas Dodds-Parker[4] who took part in courses run by Colin Gubbins. Having written a series of pamphlets on guerrilla warfare and sabotage, he was selected on 25 August, 1939, to join the British Military Mission to Poland, sympathy for whose countrymen became a lasting characteristic. Peter Wilkinson accompanied him. During Gubbins' command of the 'Independent Companies', the forerunners of the Commandos, in the Norwegian campaign which followed, he won a DSO.

The second group who prepared for possible hostilities was Section D of SIS, the Secret Intelligence Service, now known as MI6. It was also commanded by a Sapper officer, Major Lawrence Grand, and explored undercover activities by which an enemy could be attacked by other than military means.

The possibility of invasion in the summer of 1940 led to the creation of a new force. It was highly secret and not completely revealed until the late 1950s, that of the Auxiliary, or stay-behind, Units, which were set up to deal with a situation which would exist in England in the event of a German landing and occupation. On his return from Norway Colin Gubbins was informed that the creation of the underground army that would operate in the United Kingdom should such an invasion become a reality was being placed on his shoulders. Britain was to have a resistance movement.[5] It was to be led by him with the rank of Colonel. His first approach was to the Commander-in-Chief of the Home Forces, Field Marshal Ironside, whom he had served as an aide-de-camp in 1919. He was promised the men and supplies he required; in return a weekly progress report was demanded. The only other copy went to Winston Churchill, by then Prime Minister. Within a few weeks and under conditions of great secrecy, an organization of five thousand men and a few women had been formed. Since it was anticipated that a German invasion, if it came, would arrive by sea, the Auxiliary Units became concentrated within an area of thirty miles inland from the coastline, stretching from southern Wales to Scotland.

Colin Gubbins' intelligence and training officers were old friends and colleagues, such as the writer Peter Fleming, Peter Wilkinson and Andrew Croft,[6] the polar explorer who also was to follow him into SOE. Recruits came through recommendations from local people – landowners, farmers and gamekeepers who knew the neighbouring terrain well. They were enrolled into the Home Guard and wore its uniform, but, having signed the official secrets' act, were not absorbed into its normal activity; rather each patrol was provided with a carefully hidden underground hide-out, known as OBs or Operational Bases, disguised from the outside. Inside was sleeping accommodation, cooking facilities, food, radio communications, weapons, ammunition and explosives. It was the development of new forms of explosives to be used against an invading army by Auxiliary Unit patrols that led to

Colin Gubbins' first encounter with members of the FANY Corps, which was to have such far-reaching consequences.

Section D ran a research laboratory which developed forms of weaponry and explosives, located at Aston House, near Stevenage.[7] A new type of plastic explosive had been perfected which it was considered suited the needs of the Auxiliary Units for the blowing of bridges and so on. To solve the problem of packing these devices safely for distribution Colin Gubbins rang a family friend, Phyllis Bingham, who had joined the FANY Corps, to ask for volunteers to undertake this work. She, who later was to become the commander of SOE FANYs, went to Aston House herself in June, 1940, together with Peggy Minchin, a future conducting officer for FANYs who dropped into France; later still, she went out to Italy. Having signed the Official Secrets Act, they packed plastic explosives and detonators into small tin boxes. Some sites of underground burrows for stay-behind patrols are still visible to the initiated, twenty miles from the Kentish coast. The exact locations were a well-kept secret. One veteran writes:

> There was a hole in the ground, covered with a mat and steps going vertically down into a cave. It was built by the Royal Engineers [usually from the north] and there were bunks for sleeping in, food and a loo, and as soon as the enemy arrived, we were supposed to disappear at night and go in there.[8]

Two miles from where these words are being written still stands a bungalow where FANY drivers with the Auxiliary Units were stationed.

An attempt to amalgamate Section D and MI(R) was not likely to be a success and it was clear that a fresh start should be made with the objective, now that North-West Europe was occupied, to carry the war into the enemy camp by other than military means. On 27 May, 1940, the War Cabinet endorsed a Chiefs of Staff recommendation that 'a special organization would be required and the plans to put these subversive operations into effect, together with the necessary preparations and training, should be proceeded with, as a matter of urgency'. Neville Chamberlain had resigned as Prime Minister on 10 May; Winston Churchill took office as head of a coalition government, but it was the former who, on 22 June, as Lord President of the Council, initialled as approved the War Cabinet Minute of 19 July, 1940, creating 'A Special Operations Executive to coordinate sabotage, subversion and secret propaganda against the enemy overseas'. The new organization was placed under the aegis of the Minister of Economic Warfare, Dr Hugh Dalton, a left-wing economist. On asking him to accept this assignment, Winston Churchill exhorted, 'And now, set Europe ablaze'.

Sir Frank Nelson, a former British Consul in Berne and former Member of

Parliament, was appointed head of SOE, with the code title CD (which passed to his successors). Sir Charles Hambro became his deputy. Few former colleagues of MI(R) made the transfer; a notable exception being Vera Long (later to come to Italy as a FANY) who thereby became one of the founder members of SOE and a valuable one.

Colin Gubbins, having put the Auxiliary Units on their feet, was clearly due for a new posting by November, 1940. Hugh Dalton needed to appoint a Director of Training for SOE and recalled dining at the Polish Embassy on 18 November, 1938. He wrote:

> I sat beside a most intelligent British soldier. He knew eastern
> Europe well and was both pro-Polish and pro-Czech. This most
> intelligent British soldier was Colin Gubbins. Next year when I
> was Minister of Economic Warfare and looking for a good soldier
> to help me plan and train personnel for special operations in
> Europe somebody mentioned Gubbins. At once I remembered
> this Polish dinner party and, after much battling with other
> claimants for this body, I got him and he rendered splendid service
> in a field increasingly important for our war effort.[9]

On 18 November, 1940, Brigadier Colin Gubbins began his career in SOE, first, starting up a programme of training for which his experience had so well prepared him and, secondly, providing stations and schools where training for agents of many nations was to take place; also 'holding houses' for men and women who were waiting for missions. Eventually, the planning of operations entered his field, as he had been promised it would. By mid-1944 the organization, at its peak, numbered nearly ten thousand men and three thousand women; most of the women were FANYs.

The origins of the FANY Corps were dictated by the needs of the age in which it was created. During Kitchener's Sudan campaign of the eighteen-nineties, a certain Sergeant-Major Baker was wounded in action. He became only too aware that no means existed by which men in his position could be given emergency medical treatment and then transported to a place of safety and succour. He conceived a scheme whereby a troop of expert horsewomen, trained in first aid, would ride (side-saddle, of course) on to the battlefield after a skirmish, tend to the wounded and remove them as fast as possible by horse ambulance.

It was not until 1907 that the idea became a reality. The First Aid Nursing Yeomanry in that year became the first of the women's services. Girls who had been brought up with horses, and probably possessed their own, began to join. During the years before the First World War a constitution was drawn up and a headquarters established. During that war itself around 400

FANYs drove ambulances and other vehicles in England, France and Belgium.

Between the wars this experience led to a change in name. It was considered that women could provide the greatest use in the event of hostilities purely as drivers, thereby releasing men for the fighting forces. The title *Women's Transport Service FANY* was adopted, but was never popular and the old name, simply FANY, stuck and the Corps was generally referred to as such. On the establishment of the ATS, the Auxiliary Territorial Service, in 1938, girls who had joined the FANY as drivers were given an undertaking that on the outbreak of hostilities they would be permitted to maintain their own identity and headquarters, within membership of the parent organization. In 1939 this promise was revoked; FANY drivers were absorbed completely into the ATS. FANY headquarters agreed to recruit ten Motor Companies ATS, of 150 girls each; independent existence was then required to disappear and the staff at FANY headquarters lost their ATS pay.

This dissolution did not, however, become a reality. Certain FANY officers, veterans of the First World War, took matters into their own hands. Marion Gamwell and her sister Hope, who had been members of the Dover convoys for the transportation of wounded from France, were summoned from their farm in (then) Northern Rhodesia. Between them, this group of women formed the 'free' FANY. Under Commandant Marion Gamwell's imaginative leadership, a policy of freedom of movement and of duties, so long as they fulfilled her stringent principles, was developed in relation to the deployment of FANYs. All were addressed, throughout the Corps, by their surnames only, without mention of rank, from Gamwell downwards. This was an invariable rule – no Ma'ams.

The FANY became the ideal service for the purposes of SOE. There were no military restrictions on the use of arms (as in the other women's services), or how many bathrooms were needed for a certain number of servicewomen. Within Gamwell's remit, FANYs could be sent almost anywhere and undertake almost anything. Bingham was acting as Gamwell's secretary when she received Colin Gubbins' first call for FANY help with packing explosives for the Auxiliary Units. When he moved to SOE, the contact developed to such an extent that she became, until 1944 when she had worked herself into ill health, the officer in charge of recruiting FANYs for SOE; in the early days, the unit was known as 'Bingham's'. She interviewed all applicants at FANY headquarters in the former vicarage of St Paul's church in Wilton Place, Knightsbridge, and expected them all to be able to turn their hands to anything expected of them. She is reported to have said, 'I want girls who have been taught to do as they are told'.

Certainly the requirements of Colin Gubbins' organization were exacting. Within months he had set up an extensive network of training stations throughout England and Scotland for agents of many nations, to prepare them for resistance and sabotage work in the field – Norwegians, Danes, Dutchmen, French, Poles, Czechs and so on. The agents needed to be kept separate according to nationality, and often of political allegiance. They would often be shaken by their experiences of escape from their native lands and apprehensive as to their dangerous future.

These stations and special training schools eventually numbered seventy-seven. They all needed administrative, teaching and domestic staff. FANY personnel were to fill these needs to a considerable extent. Problems at the outset were many: first came security; all was highly secret. No word of the existence of a unit, its function or its inhabitants, was to be divulged to anyone. FANYs were not permitted to tell their parents of their exact where-abouts, or, in many cases, especially in the case of wireless operators, their function; any connection with long-range communication was very secret. All FANY mail was required to be sent to Room 98, Horse Guards, SW1. Often FANYs did not leave the perimeter of a station for several months, on account of operational security. Secondly, much of the work involved, cooking and orderly duties, was menial and not at that time the province of educated women. It would be boring and repetitive; promotion was rare. Yet on the whole FANYs undertook these roles of domestic administration with dedication and even enthusiasm. They recognized the even greater demands being made of the agents in their care. Thirdly, relationships with the often volatile men in training could be difficult to handle; support and under-standing, rather than romantic attachment, were the order of the day. Some FANYs who had served in SOE establishments in England came on to the Mediterranean.

FANYs also served in various capacities at SOE's London headquarters in Baker Street and the surrounding neighbourhood. The 'cover' for the office to the outside world was ISRB which stood for a meaningless term, the Inter-Services Research Bureau, to provide a spurious explanation for the fact that men and women of various nationalities and uniforms went in and out of its doors. On outstations and abroad, the London office was invariably referred to as 'Baker Street'. Douglas Dodds-Parker claims the credit for first intro-ducing FANYs to the headquarters office. A few girls eventually had staff jobs, but most were secretaries, recruited in the main from the well-known London secretarial colleges. Some of the FANY secretaries who went to Algiers, Cairo and Italy, had been employed as civilians in Baker Street and became FANYs; others joined SOE through the Corps. The former civilians were required, as other FANY recruits, to attend basic training.

By 1943 this took place at Overthorpe Hall, a former stately home near Banbury, and was of around fifteen days' duration. Girls urgently needed abroad, such as Prudence Willoughby (Hannay) who had worked in Baker

Street as a civilian and was badly needed in Bari, was only there for five days. Drill, Corps history, First Aid and chores were the programme. For some reason, perhaps it was to disabuse girls of the idea that they were in for a soft war, some of the chores were very basic indeed. Pauline Ratsey (de Haan and later Moore) on her way to Italy, remembers cleaning rows of taps and lavatories, while Ann Bonsor, one of the North African group, was told to black lead a grate, which found her somewhat at a loss. Uniform was acquired during basic training; service dress and greatcoats were made to measure; the rest, apart from the leather belt, was kit issued to the ATS scale. There were two types of hat – a peaked cap, with leather strap over the crown, and the characteristic FANY 'bonnet' (so-called as in certain Scottish regiments), a beret, with maroon flash and FANY badge.

During the end of 1941 Bingham was requested by SOE to train FANYs as wireless operators; she had already agreed to train coders to encypher and decypher signals traffic. Missions in occupied countries were growing in number. More personnel than the Royal Corps of Signals could supply were required at the home base stations to receive their communications and send replies. Over one hundred FANY coders and wireless operators were trained and then posted to the Mediterranean between 1942 and 1944.

As for which department of signals a recruit was to be trained, this was determined largely by the operational needs of SOE at a given moment, also, to some extent, by the presumed aptitude of a recruit. Gamwell and Bingham between them appear to have made the initial decisions, though these could be altered later. Marjorie Lewis (Clark), later in North Africa and Italy, who accompanied another pupil from Cheltenham Ladies College to London and FANY headquarters simply as an act of friendship, found herself enrolled also. Gamwell had commented that, as she was Welsh, wireless operating was her milieu, and so it became. The inference was that musical girls would have an advantage. Diana Thatcher (Trollope), also to go to North Africa, was selected for the wireless operators' training on the grounds that she had been a student for a year at the beginning of the war at the Royal Academy of Music.

The training of future coders usually took place at Thame Park, Station 52, over a period of a few weeks. They were made familiar with various codes and cyphers then in use, both in communications with the field, and main-line stations, such as Cairo. In the early days a code called Playfair was taught. It involved putting messages into rectangular 'boxes' on squared paper according to a numbered order of letters determined by the line of a poem (of which some were original and some borrowed) or sentence from a book. The message was encoded by selecting letters from the opposite corners of the rectangle. This code was superseded by a more secure one, named double transposition. Again, it was worked in 'boxes' on squared paper; it placed the letters of a message horizontally under a 'key' word or words which were put in numerical sequence; a fresh selection was made by transposing them vertically, again in numerical order; the final version was read horizontally. The field operator and base coder would be in possession of the identical poem or novel from which the 'key' word or words would be drawn; the page and line would be indicated in figures at the beginning of the message.

Both these codes became largely obsolete when One-Time-Pads were used almost exclusively for field traffic, and were considered nearly unbreakable, as the letters of the original message were not used at all, merely replacements which appeared on a list used only once, of which both field and base coders had an identical copy. 'Main line' traffic between base stations, such as London, Cairo and Algiers, was encyphered with what was called the 'War Office Book', all numbers. A FANY coder recalls that it was red in colour and that 0359 was the number to be encoded for 'and'.

Great care needed to be taken to include two types of 'checks' in every message, a 'bluff' check, to confuse the enemy, and one 'true' check which it was hoped would not be discovered. Many field operators in the heat of the moment left out their checks when encoding messages. At the base, two possibilities occurred to the coder: was this a genuine lapse or had the set been seized by the enemy and was being worked back by them, as happened on several occasions. Peter Wilkinson records[10] that Alfgar Hesketh-Pritchard,[11] operating with him from the Austrian border under extremely difficult circumstances, appeared to forget to put his checks into three successive messages. They received some strange requests from base as to the name of Wilkinson's aunt's dog in order to establish his *bona fides* and that the set was not being operated by the Germans.

The training given to FANY wireless operators was much longer and a great deal more arduous. It took place for the most part at Fawley Court near Henley (Station 54 A) and also at Thame Park. Some men and women failed to grasp the hang of it at all and the fall-out rate was high. Some of those who found it not within their particular capacity became coders, others became registry clerks, or responsible for the copying and distribution of signals. Teleprinter or switchboard operating were other options, all vital parts of the communications process. The wireless operators' course was at least four months in length; one significant fact was that operators had to reach a high speed in words per minute, at least twenty. This was much higher than peacetime requirements of the services or post office. It was vital not to keep a field operator working his or her set for more than a quarter of an hour, because of the efficient 'direction-finding' equipment employed by the enemy. Transmission could be traced by special travelling vans, patrolling where it was considered sets might be.

The early part of the wireless operators' training involved mastery of the morse code, with which those who had been Girl Guides were already familiar. This knowledge needed to be transferred to operating a special key which represented the dots and dashes in terms of short and long sounds. When proficiency was attained, the mock practice key became part of a B 2 radio set which relayed the sounds into the atmosphere and could be captured at a distance on a specified wavelength, previously determined. Joan Ogilvy-Dalgleish (Hole), later in Algiers, records her training at Fawley Court early in 1943. She was part of a group of twelve girls who sat at a series of wooden tables, practising their morse on a dummy key day after day. As it became possible to speed up, one moved up to the next table, with an instructor sitting at the end. Most trainees would stick at one letter and not be able to overcome the resultant pause for a short period. There was a test once a week, when the atmosphere was extremely tense. Ann Bonsor remembers going to a cinema and quite involuntarily turning the sign EXIT beside the screen into morse. Probably on this account, wireless operators, like coders, became obsessional; many FANYs have never lost the skill, only some of the speed, fifty years later.

For the last part of their training wireless operators were often posted to Scotland to take part in a scheme called SPARTAN, at Dunbar. FANYs would be based in a mobile signal station, to which agents in training, dispersed throughout the countryside, would work back their sets. Before proceeding overseas, most coders and wireless operators received some experience on an operational station, dealing with live traffic from the field. This would be at Station 53 A, Grendon Underwood, or Station 53 B, at Poundon. Messages came in from Holland, France, Denmark, Norway and so on. During their earlier training wireless operators would have become familiar with the Q code and the sending and receiving procedures based on this international method of communication; no other means were allowed, *never* plain language, though some agents in distress, anger or jubilation, might sometimes resort to it.

A FANY wireless operator on duty at her set would be allocated to what was known as a 'sked' (terminology for an expected message at a previously defined time from an agent), with the appropriate frequency, code name and call sign, by the signal master, or other authorized person. She would listen for the three-letter particular call sign of the out-station which should be calling at intervals of one minute, and then listening for one minute. If contact were established, the home operator would send the call sign, followed by QRK *How are you receiving me*, plus IMI *Question mark*. The field would answer QSA *Your signal readability is*, followed by a number from one to five. If it were over three, and therefore fairly audible, the home operator would wait for the field to send QTC *I have a message for you*. Field messages were always sent first. With numbers less than three, each group of five letters (the invariable number in which signals were sent) would be repeated. The base operator then took down the message in pencil in block capitals on special forms, and then wait until QRU appeared *I have nothing more*. If the base operator had messages, the procedure would be reversed. To ask for repeated groups, or QRS *send slower*, was not well regarded, unless interference was particularly bad, since it would expose the field operator to danger. At the end of a transmission, the base would send VA *close down*. In the event of sudden enemy attack, the field could send QUG *I am forced to stop transmitting owing to immediate danger*, whereupon a FANY operator would report this at once to her senior officer. In the event of gross inaudibility, it was possible to ask for help from a second base operator, but this was an exceptional measure in particular circumstances. 'Listening watches' were set up when a field mission failed to respond at its allotted time according to its signal plan.

A specialized training was given to become a signal planner. A small group of FANYs learnt to provide a signal plan for every mission which went into the field. It included a call sign by which to be recognized by the base station, an allocated frequency, obtained by the supply of the appropriate crystals (two slices of quartz cut to a precise wavelength which determined frequency, about the size of a postage stamp) and specific times on a regular basis at which attempts to transmit to the base station were to be made. Trained signal planners who undertook this skilled technical work were given the rank of Lieutenant.

Another technique in which FANYs were instructed later in the war was that of 'finger printing', ie the recognition of morse-sending methods. All who learnt to send morse developed their own individual style. If an agent in occupied territory were captured, attempts would often be made to work the radio back to base in England. A FANY operator who could detect a change in field operator would prevent unwise future communications, drops, or reinforcements to that mission.

Most FANYs in SOE were young. This was true of those who were posted to the Mediterranean. All who went volunteered to do so and needed the permission of their parents if they were under twenty-one years of age. Most of us were between the ages of eighteen and twenty-two. There were a few seventeen-year-olds and a handful of FANYs who had already been up at Oxford: Evelyn Green (Mackay), Daphne Park, Elizabeth Mercer, Prudence Willoughby and Margaret Marshall (Gauld). The reasons why it was found necessary to send such young women abroad were several. Older girls were often the mothers of little children and needed at home. Secondly, the Conscription Acts then in force directed girls over twenty-one into various forms of war work; it might be into a factory. The services put in their requirements at various stages: one month WRNS recruitment might be closed, or only wanted cooks; similarly with the WAAF and ATS. Eventually SOE put forward its own needs to the Ministry of Labour for FANYs, but this was quite late in the day, when many young girls had already been posted abroad.

All FANY trainees in signals began with the rank of volunteer. Before leaving for the Mediterranean some girls received letters from Gamwell to announce they had been promoted to corporal or sergeant. There was some ill-feeling associated with this process, since it appeared arbitrary and not necessarily associated with operating skill. Promotion in the FANY Corps, in spite of responsibilities, and the fact that some girls were held against vacancies for male officers in a unit's War Establishment, was slow in comparison with the members of other forces, at times non-existent. FANYs needed to look for alternative rewards and compensations for their hard work and dedicated service.

Another problem area was that of lack of trust. Wireless operators were not informed as to reasons for their training in their skills and the fact that they were to work to sets in enemy-occupied territory until they were posted to an operational station. A report issued after the war regarded this as having been an error of judgment on the part of those in command:

> During the first period of training, FANYs were kept in total ignorance of the purpose for which they were learning wireless. This was a gross fundamental blunder on the part of the training authorities. There would have been no lapse of security had the FANYs in training been told in the right way about the job for which they were intended to be used. A fillip would have been given them, a sense of purpose, a sense of privilege. They could have visualized the reason for the daily monotony of the morse table. They would have been given something to look forward to and an incentive to become accomplished. Young girls who have just left school must be given such an incentive.[12]

Experience showed, the report continued, that FANY operators were capable of a higher grade of perseverance than their male counterparts, provided they were trained in the right way and not turned against W/T at the outset.

Similarly coders had problems with the methods by which they were told of the purpose of their work. Some were badly affected by stories of what would occur if they breathed a word to a soul. Eleanor Hodder, trained as a coder for posting to North Africa, was made a 'bundle of nerves' when it was explained to her in considerable detail what might happen to a field operator if she did not get messages to him accurately and fast enough. FANYs were often given their security briefing in a manner that was almost terrifying. Christine Dury (Parker) and Daphne Dawes (Iles) were so frightened by this on their way to Italy, that they dared not look out of the window of the plane. Intimidation would seem to have been a sure way of inviting girls to make mistakes in their work. Examples of how well FANYs reacted in stations where they were trusted and relied upon, tell their own story. In this regard both Major-General Gubbins, Douglas Dodds-Parker and Gerry Holdsworth led the field.

After the war, the FANY authorities felt obliged to defend their policy of allowing young girls to go abroad as members of the Corps.[13]

> It should be placed on record to the credit of this young generation that they did their responsible work exceptionally well and beyond the hopes of their military officers. Their security was good and they seldom got into trouble.
>
> Had the country's peril not been so great, the Corps would have hesitated at sending such young girls overseas to difficult climates.

Chapter Two

"WE TOOK UP OUR POSITIONS"

NORTH AFRICA

Algiers in North Africa was, at the end of 1942, the first destination for FANYs who were to serve in the Mediterranean. No longer the *mare nostrum* as conceived by the Roman Empire, Mussolini's Italian Empire had for the past few years occupied a fair portion of its shores: its own seaboard in Italy; Cyrenaica and Tripolitania, conquered in 1912, making the Italian colony of Libya, Albania, invaded on Good Friday, 1939, Greece in 1940 and Jugoslavia in 1941. These territories had been joined in several areas by its Axis partner, Hitler's Germany, notably in Tripolitania, in January, 1941, with the despatch of units which later became the celebrated *Afrika Korps*. Thereafter the war in the Western Desert was waged with varying success on both sides until the final outcome of a victory for the Allies in the spring of 1943.

TORCH, an Anglo-American landing in North Africa, took place on 8 November, 1942. Lieutenant-General Dwight Eisenhower was Commander-in-Chief of a force of 65,000 men and 650 warships. Control of the region, the French colonies of Algeria and French Morocco, had been in the hands of the Vichy government of metropolitan France. The landings took place on three sites, Casablanca in French Morocco, Oran and Algiers in Algeria. Not all three areas were seized without loss of life and, although a ceasefire was achieved within a matter of a few days, there were political problems for months to come. Richard Hoggart, with his customary respect for language, gives a graphic account of the landing in his book *A Sort of Clowning*.[1] Just before the assault the radio began to crackle as a message was beamed to the coast. President Roosevelt had recorded an announcement which began '*Nous sommes arrivés parmi vous*' in an accent which Hoggart considered made

Churchill's French sound Parisian. Word came quickly that, in a quite literal sense, the coast was clear, and they took to the boats.

Eisenhower's brief was to secure his position in the North African territories so that he would be able to advance towards Libya and attack the Axis forces from the west. Moreover, Frenchmen and French territory could be recovered for the Allied war effort. Thereafter Allied Force Headquarters set up its position in Algiers under General Eisenhower until he left in the spring of 1944 to direct the invasion of North-West Europe. AFHQ left for Caserta, east of Naples, in July of that year.

The SOE contingent with TORCH, codename MASSINGHAM, assumed that its activities in North Africa would be in support of a military operation. But to General Gubbins it made sense that a more permanent Anglo-American unit in the vicinity of Algiers would provide a base for future special operations into Europe, especially southern France. A restructured MASSINGHAM, with its other code name, to put people off the scent, Inter-Services Signals Unit 6 (or ISSU 6), was thus born.

A group of FANYs who called themselves the First XI, five personal assistants and five coders, all Ensigns, plus their CO, Captain Curry, left London on 22 December, 1942, for North Africa. Mary McVean,[2] a cousin of General Gubbins, described her inclusion in this highly selected band. She had been recruited for what had come to be called 'Bingham's unit' at the end of 1941 and sent to Station XVII at Brickendonbury Manor between Hertford and Hoddesdon, which dealt with sabotage techniques. FANY duties were as driver/orderlies. After three weeks five of the FANYs, including McVean, left to open Station XVIII at Walton-at-Stone, Hertfordshire, the first purely Polish holding station for men trained to go into the field. The girls' duties were arduous: cooking, waiting at table and housework, as well as driving, in a team that operated well together for almost a year. Their reward was the creation of a hospitable atmosphere for the Polish officers, many of whom had endured perils in their escape from their own country. Walking over the Carpathian mountains in the snow with frostbite was one experience; evading capture by taking refuge for some months in the Warsaw sewers was another. What awaited them on their return to Poland was even more alarming.

Bingham's invitation for Mary McVean to train as a coder and go to North Africa took her by surprise. She was already thirty years of age but need was felt for some stability in the group. The training at Fawley Court, Station 54A, she found difficult, after months of nothing but housework. A dinner arranged by Bingham at the Hyde Park Hotel on the night before the departure of the eleven was attended by Gamwell who gave each girl a pith helmet in FANY colours, to add to their already large pile of luggage: camp beds, gas masks, tin hats, waterbottles and food for the first part of the journey. It was pouring with rain at the army railway station at Addison Road, Olympia, as they waited for the troop train to Greenock. There they went aboard the P and O liner *Strathaird*, converted into a troopship. After lying at anchor in the Clyde for a few days while the convoy and accompanying warships assembled, they sailed on Boxing Day, going right out into the Atlantic.

There was only one emergency, when a German U-boat was spotted, but chased off by the escorting naval vessels. Twenty-two physiotherapists were the only other women on board, with 5,000 men. A previously published account that the group had travelled on an earlier convoy on the *Scythia* which was torpedoed off Oran in mid-December is not accurate; that ship limped into harbour with a party of Queen Alexandra's Military Nurses on board, who lost most of their possessions.

The First XI landed safely at Algiers and made their way by truck on 3 January, 1943, to their new living quarters at Cap Matifou, on the coast a few miles east of the town. A further party of around ten FANY Ensigns travelled to Algiers by sea in the spring and arrived on 23 April, 1943. They were all well-trained personal assistants with more than a school certificate knowledge of the French language. During that summer the first group of FANY wireless operators, accompanied by some more coders, twenty-five in all, left England on the *Orion* on 19 July.

A long journey from London to Greenock on a train without a corridor, with a Guards brigade, provided no food and no loos. There was a stop at a station where the WVS (Women's Voluntary Service) provided tea and sandwiches and another in the country where FANYs and Guardsmen left the train on opposite sides for the bushes. On arrival at Greenock next morning, FANYs were teased that, as the ship was lying beyond the quay, climbing on board would be by rope ladder. However, their fears were not realized. Since it was a cold dawn, a rum ration was provided when a tender had deposited them on the ship.

Single cabins were adapted to take three; the ship was very full and, in order to offset the cramped conditions, some of the FANYs joined in the exercises devised on deck for officers and men: leapfrog, human pyramids and other energetic forms of physical training. There were bruises next day and one or two black eyes, but a commendation for sportsmanship for the FANYs from the OC Troops was included in the following day's Standing Orders. Battledress was required to be worn during the night as well as the day, which was a wise precaution; there was an attack on the convoy. Orders were given to proceed to a lower deck when the noise of depth charges and gunfire lasted for what seemed a long time. No news was given as to the outcome. Ann Bonsor, one of the wireless operators, remembers the exact length of the journey; she was able to read *War and Peace* from cover to cover.

No one was aware of the ultimate destination, but those who thought that the harbour in which the *Orion* had tied up was Algiers had made an accurate guess. Betty Hannah (Norton) was happy to realize that she had come to a country where she could make use of her knowledge of the French language. She had earlier made her escape from unoccupied France, where she had been living with her French stepmother, by crossing into Spain over the Pyrenees and then to England. There was a long wait for transport to the camp, which was a new location. MASSINGHAM had moved, since the first FANYs had arrived, to the *Club des Pins*, fifteen miles west of Algiers, a resort of villas on the beach. In the July sun everyone had become very thirsty. Lunch of army ration spam was set out on trestle tables in the FANY mess, with bottles of *vin ordinaire* and warnings that the local water was not fit to drink. FANYs filled their enamel mugs with copious draughts of the wine. Putting up their camp beds in their sleeping quarters afterwards became a matter of some hilarity.

On 23 September, 1943, London SOE cabled MASSINGHAM that eight further FANY wireless operators, four registry clerks, four switchboard operators and two clerks would be arriving on the next convoy. This they did, having travelled half way to America to elude the U-boats. Margaret Marshall, a switchboard operator, had just left Oxford with a degree in French. She later achieved commissioned rank, but this group, like its predecessor, were FANY sergeants, corporals and volunteers. Their consequent inability to meet socially with their relations and friends from home would have placed considerable restraints on their time off, let alone where they could spend it. As a remedy, all future FANYs going abroad were regarded as Cadet Ensigns and given officer status, though their own rank, for the purposes of pay and seniority, remained. They wore one pip on their shoulders, plus a maroon cloth bar, to differentiate them from FANYs who had been properly commissioned and carried the appropriate responsibility.

The flow of FANY personnel to Algiers from the United Kingdom continued throughout 1944, though on a lesser scale, when it was overtaken by postings direct to units in Italy. But, in the meantime, there had been journeys to Egypt and fresh SOE personnel for the unit in Cairo.

CAIRO

The reason behind the arrival of many thousands of British and Commonwealth troops in Egypt and the creation of a theatre of war in that area can be explained, in its most simple and telling form, in three words – the Suez Canal. It was imperative in time of war for Britain to maintain command of the unfettered use of the Canal for the movement of supplies, oil and troops from Australia, New Zealand, South Africa, India and so on. Although the British occupation of Egypt had been brought to an end in 1882 and the Protectorate which followed had ceased in 1922, the Anglo-Egyptian Treaty of 1936 left Britain with the right to defend the Suez Canal. An article in the Treaty which could be invoked in time of war, and was so, laid on the Egyptian King the requirement to provide ports, aerodromes and means of communication to this end.

On 21 June, 1939 Lieutenant-General Sir Henry Maitland Wilson arrived in Cairo as General Officer Commanding British Troops in Egypt, or BTE, one of the many initials current in wartime Egypt. His headquarters were in the large old-fashioned Semiramis hotel on the banks of the Nile that one passed on the way to Grey Pillars in the Garden City, headquarters of the Commander-in-Chief, Middle East. General Sir Archibald Wavell, who had arrived in Egypt on 2 August, 1939, held this post from February, 1940, until he was sent to India and replaced by General Auchinleck in July, 1941. General Sir Harold Alexander took his place in August, 1943.

The situation facing the two generals was grave from the start. The Italians had very large forces to the south in Ethiopia and Eritrea which they had invaded in October, 1935, and which had become Italian East Africa. In addition, on Egypt's border was the Italian colony of Cyrenaica, which housed a quarter of a million Italian troops. On 10 June, 1940, Mussolini declared war on Britain and the desert war began. With the Canal secured, thousands of British and Commonwealth troops began to enter Egypt. The German army, as already stated, came to Italy's assistance in January, 1941, thereby building up the size of the confrontation.

SOE's involvement in this theatre became consequent upon the next moves of the Axis powers into the Balkans. Its beginnings lay in a Section D office in Belgrade in the early 1940s. Its head was known as Caesar, not particularly original, since his first name was Julius. He was surrounded by men who would later take their place on missions back into the area from Cairo, the subject of a later chapter. The pro-Allied coup by Colonel Simovic which replaced the Regent, Prince Paul of Jugoslavia, by his nephew, the young King Peter, at the end of March, 1941, was only marginally helped on by SOE, who had little time to reap the benefit. German troops entered Jugoslavia by way of Bulgaria in large numbers on 6 April. Meanwhile Italian forces had invaded Greece in October, 1940, through Albania, already in their hands; they were joined by the *Wehrmacht* in November.

A contingent of the British army, with some Australian and New Zealand troops, made an attempt to come to the help of Greece the following April, in a campaign which was a costly failure. It did, however, involve a certain number of German divisions which would otherwise have augmented Hitler's forces with which he invaded Russia in June, 1941. Opinions differ as to whether the number was sufficiently large to have had a significant effect on slowing up the rate of advance into Russia, a matter of consequence.

The Belgrade SOE office retreated to Cairo where it had a close view of a series of British reverses in the Western Desert during the early summer of 1942. The German General, Erwin Rommel, and his forces broke through the Eighth Army Gazala Line west of Tobruk; (my future husband was taken prisoner in this battle). German troops pressed east to Mersa Matruh, only sixty miles from Cairo, which set up consternation in that city and was known as 'the flap'. Files were burnt and women and children evacuated to South Africa and Palestine. But the line held and the victory of British arms at el Alamein in October, 1942, heralded a change of fortunes in the desert war. Meanwhile SOE's Cairo office had expanded its scope and activity, so much so that by the autumn of 1943 it was seriously short of staff.

I joined SOE in September, 1943, with potential usefulness as a German speaker – at least, that was my father's supposition. He was a civil servant, knew some of the SOE bosses and the function of what was referred to by its members as 'the firm'. At my first interview at Baker Street I was told, 'I hear you've volunteered for Cairo as a coder'; it was the first I had heard of it, but duly acquiesced. With nine other girls, I shortly found myself in the FANY Cipher School in the converted stables opposite FANY headquarters in the vicarage of St Paul's Wilton Place. It was intended that we should attend a fortnight's course on coding. There were also various formalities of a medical kind – examinations and injections (one sharp one against yellow fever at the School of Tropical Medicine had a profound effect on the manner of my journey to Cairo). We received a very reasonable talk on security at Baker Street, when we heard that SOE was a clandestine organization working to support resistance movements in occupied countries. From Cairo, to which we were being sent, we should be in contact with missions to the Cetniks in Jugoslavia. The use of this term was an abiding memory. There was no question of our being enrolled as FANYs, which was the case of girls travelling to Algiers. The ATS authorities had raised objections to any other women's army service in Cairo, unless it was absorbed. Joining the FANY Corps was to come later.

The first week of the coding course passed off fairly smoothly. I made two friends, Eleanor Burgess (who subsequently married Basil Irwin who dropped into Jugoslavia and later northern Italy) and Anne Burrill, the wife of a Gunner Major stationed in India. We were still friends fifty years later when they both sadly died in 1996. At the beginning of the second week came news that we should be leaving England on the following Saturday. Five of us had priority passages on a Liberator from Lyneham via Gibraltar and Maison Blanche in Algiers; the other five, also with priorities, were to travel by flying boat from Poole harbour via Ireland, Lisbon and West Africa. The need for coders by SOE in Cairo had been represented as extremely urgent. Eleanor, Anne and I were to travel to Cairo on the Liberator.

My farewell to my parents and my sister was rather a wrench and took place at Charing Cross station. Making my own way to Paddington, my choice, I found the remainder of the group plus a Baker Street courier with two items of news. The first was that no one was to leave that afternoon – both planes were delayed until the following day. The second piece of information revealed that one of the girls detailed for the flying boat had failed to visit the School of Tropical Medicine for the injection against yellow fever, so I was to take her place and she mine. Not wanting to repeat my family farewells, that night was spent in Anne Burrill's mother's home at Gerrard's Cross.

Next day five of us boarded the British Overseas Airways Sunderland flying boat in Poole harbour, to find that the windows had been covered with netting and of the outside world we could see nothing. The seating was extremely uncomfortable with tin seats facing inwards, as in a tram. Around twelve passengers thus accommodated, (with most of the available space occupied by crates of cargo) were the five SOE coders, a man of some presence who was travelling to Lagos by the name of Smith, clearly a *nom de guerre*, Charles Empson (later British Ambassador in Santiago), making his way to the British Embassy in Cairo, and a few other men, one of whom was accompanied by his wife, the only other woman, who looked extremely tense until our arrival in Lisbon. Everyone was, of course, in civilian clothes, since we were passing through two neutral countries.

The flying boat landed on the River Shannon in Ireland. Passengers were taken off by lighter and driven by coach to the Glentworth Hotel in Limerick. That evening a walk after dinner in streets ablaze with light was a contrast to the black-out in the dimmed towns of England. More surprises were in store at breakfast next morning, when a waitress asked 'One or two eggs?' Looking back on food in England during the war, scrambled eggs created from a dried powdered mixture was one of the nastier restrictions.

In the evening we drove back to the Shannon where the river was running very high; the flying boat was bucketing about at anchor and the waves smacked against the fuselage as the pilot attempted to take off along the surface of the open sea. The tense lady sitting opposite to me looked tenser than ever and sat with her eyes closed. The captain came down from the cockpit to ask how the passengers were faring and, after a few more attempts at lift-off, decided to call it a day and try again the following evening. Flights to Lisbon, for this was our next destination, always took place during hours of darkness. There were Messerschmitts, which had been what was described as 'unpleasantly active', stationed along the French coast, in proximity to the Bay of Biscay. They had accounted for several British losses, including one carrying Leslie Howard, the celebrated British actor.

The Glentworth Hotel in Limerick was unable to take the whole party, and I found myself in a servant's bedroom in the attic of the Dunraven Arms at

Adare. There were more eggs at breakfast, and a brilliant sunny day with a long walk in the lush Irish countryside. Two children with bare feet caked in mud, walking along the road, came begging; they had black shawls over their heads and shoulders, as was the custom with Scottish fisherwomen. The scenery reminded me of the view of Ireland given by one of the first coloured films to be made in England, *Wings of the Morning*, with singing by John McCormack, the celebrated Irish tenor. My resolve to return to Ireland in peacetime was not carried out for another twenty years, when there was a rather wet holiday with my husband and children.

Lisbon was an even greater culture shock early the following day. The flying boat moored in the River Tagus and we passengers were taken to the Avenida Palace Hotel in the centre of the city. I woke late because sleep had been well nigh impossible on the flying boat. At a writing desk in a drawing room, trying to give my family a description of what was permitted to be told, there was conversation in German going on behind my back. Peter Lee, the Chief Security Officer at MASSINGHAM, who had also stopped at Lisbon, later spoke of the thrill of 'real' black coffee at the Avenida Palace Hotel; such were our highlights during the war. Bickham Sweet-Escott,[3] in his memoirs, writes of his week in Lisbon waiting for a passage to England with four false starts. He thought the city a sort of western Istanbul, full of agents, double-agents, *agents provocateurs* and secret organizations of all the combatants. Oblivious of these distractions, the SOE party allowed ourselves to be transported to Estoril, a smart seaside resort, for the afternoon, until it was time to board the flying boat for a long sleepless night to the Gambia. Blankets were provided, as the night was cold, and also boxes of food which included delicious fruit which had not been seen in England since the war.

A very humid atmosphere was our first impression on landing at Bathurst. During a temporary pause in a rest house on the shore, Europeans with yellow faces and shaky hands lit the inevitable cigarettes. We had also been advised to take anti-malarial tablets, but in our case only for a short period. The next two days were spent in a series of huts some miles down the coast, a transit camp for passengers and crews. It was possible to bathe amid great Atlantic rollers, but on account of the great humidity, my hair was not dry for days. There was a strange spidery creature in my hut to which I gave a wide berth and removed with a shovel.

The flight on to Sierra Leone became much more interesting, since the netting on the windows had been removed and, being now beyond the range of the German fighters, the flying boat flew lower and it was possible to see the details of the West African coastline. Freetown had a splendid natural harbour, but at the time poor housing for the greater part of the population and open sewers down the middle of streets. We five girls slept in a curtained-off portion of a men's dormitory, in iron bedsteads covered with mosquito netting. It was a relief to leave for Abidjan, in what was then the French Ivory Coast, for refuelling, and then on to Lagos.

That comfortable BOAC transit camp was completely wired over, like a cage for raspberries, with electric fans and warm water with which to wash off several days' dirt. Dinner was at the home of the SOE representative in West Africa. Next day there was a change to a land plane in which to fly across Nigeria and French territory round Lake Chad, to the Sudan and Khartoum. The passenger compartment of the plane had been completely stripped of seats and largely filled with machine tools in boxes, with little space left for people for whom there were mattresses. The first stop for refuelling was Kano, a large walled town in northern Nigeria, and the next Maiduguri where, there being no sleeping accommodation for women, the SOE party was placed with various officials of the Colonial Office. Two of us were guests of Rex Niven,[4] in charge of an area the size of Ireland and a million inhabitants. He was a charming host and kept us endlessly interested in his conversation.

The lights failed at supper and the acetylene lamps which hissed continuously on the table encouraged every kind of insect to buzz round the light. The walls were covered with a host of little brown lizards who battled for space with the praying mantis with their razor-sharp antennae. The ceiling was home to a myriad of moths who dropped to the table cloth (and us) at regular intervals. On the floor small armour-plated insects went on walk-about. All these creatures were harmless enough, unlike the tsetse fly against whom Rex Niven gave us pillow cases in which to place our legs underneath the table. Snakes came inside sometimes, he said, to eat the toads. That night I put my underclothes inside my mosquito net, so that they were not inhabited in the morning.

As we flew over the Chad region on our way to Khartoum, the pilot invited me into the cockpit, to see giraffes, zebra, buffalo and various kinds of deer scampering across open country, disturbed by the sound of aircraft engines flying low. It was a thrilling sight. Fuelling strops at el Geneina and el Fasher in the Sudan were the last before Khartoum, where we spent a hot night, followed by an even hotter stop at Wadi Halfa next day, sitting in a tent, covered in sand flies. At last we reached Cairo on 6 October, ten days after leaving England. The temperature was a good deal higher than the city had known for many years.

Commandant Marion Gamwell flew to Cairo by the short route in October 1943, in order to persuade the ATS authorities to relax their ban on members of the FANY Corps coming to Egypt, as an operational necessity for SOE. She was a forceful personality and emerged victorious. She went on to travel overland to India to establish a role for FANYs in that sub-continent.

The first contingent of twenty FANYs for Cairo left London on 10 November, 1943. Evelyn Green, daughter of a Leicestershire vicar, had come

24

down from Oxford university earlier that year. She wrote a diary during her journey from Greenock on SS *Highland Princess* in which she provided much graphic detail. The *Highland Princess* was an old meat ship of the Nelson line, which formerly operated on the South American run. It had been converted to a troopship to take as many men and women as possible. It was a 'dry' ship which meant that there was no alcohol on board, but most people smoked, and after dark when the 'black-out' procedure had to be observed on deck, the overcrowding and smoke below made the atmosphere fairly unbearable. The FANYs were placed in fives in a former two-berth cabin, but, as Evelyn observed, if this was considered a squash, the sight of the soldiers below deck made her think of the slave trade. Being in a convoy made everyone feel safer than had their ship sailed alone. The ship's barrage balloon, which had been named 'Blossom', was regarded as quite a personality, as it floated proud and plump at the stern.

The first few days were bitterly cold, with icy rain and sleet blowing on to the deck, but as the ship sailed further south the weather became so warm that many men and women sat about on the boat deck in their short sleeves; the sea was sometimes calm enough for them to dance in the afternoons. Constant messages came over the loud speakers: reminders about having life-jackets close at hand at all times, boat drill, the black-out and when rubbish could be tossed overboard. Two days were chosen by the enemy for aerial attacks on the convoy. One of the accompanying vessels went down with some casualties. The first bomb dropped before the alarm bells rang and the troops crowded on the deck. Then came the instructions to go below and sit in cabins in tin hats and struggle with life-jackets and water bottles, while the ship's guns made earsplitting, though comforting, noise. Some FANYs were later asked to help cut sandwiches. The deck was covered with empty shell cases.

During the earlier part of the war, losses at sea had been so considerable that it had led to an embargo on women travelling to or through the Mediterranean at all. Most of the British desert army had been transported to Egypt via South Africa, round the Cape. Casualties at sea among service-women throughout the war amounted to 126, of which nine were FANYs. The worst disaster was that of the SS *Khedive Ismail*[5] which was sailing to Ceylon from Mombasa with 1,511 people on board, on 12 February, 1944. She was attacked by a Japanese submarine, broke in half and sank in one minute and forty seconds. Of a group of nine East African FANYs from Kenya, only one was saved. Gloria West was sitting on deck with a friend when a torpedo struck. Her friend told her to jump into the water, far below, which she did, and was eventually picked up by a naval vessel. Her friend was drowned. Fifty-one nursing sisters and seventeen WRNS also lost their lives on that occasion, as did another FANY in a ship sunk by a U-boat in 1939.

Irene Morson, who later went to MASSINGHAM as a FANY, had a lucky escape while still a civilian when a group of German planes dive-bombed a ship on which she was a passenger, lying one and a half miles outside the harbour of Alexandria in August, 1941. She was taken into a lifeboat and then to another vessel for nine hours. When she reached shore in Alexandria, still in her pink satin pyjamas, she had been counted among the dead.

The *Highland Princess* reached Suez on 3 December, 1943, after nineteen days at sea. The FANYs arrived at Cairo railway station by train just after seven o'clock in the evening. In the midst of much clamour and bustle and unloading of luggage, they observed an Egyptian put down his prayer mat on the platform to say his prayers. The scene was bathed in a strange bluish light which was Cairo's attempt at a black-out. Though brighter than anything experienced in England, it made everyone look bilious. A waiting truck, with another for luggage, transported the FANYs along the seven miles north-east of the city to their new home in the mess at Heliopolis.

A further draft of twelve FANY coders arrived on the first day of 1944, followed by a small group of five in the charge of Lieutenant Gwen Johnson who was the first signal planning officer to be posted to Cairo. The final draft to Egypt of coders and secretaries came at the beginning of March on SS *Stratheden*, later sunk. Letters home described the journey as 'brilliantly exciting'. Life in England, after three and a half years of war, held many restrictions, so the provision of fresh fruit, butter, sugar, chocolate and even boiled sweets on board appeared unbelievably luxurious; troopships victualled in countries without rationing. And then there was the company of a captive audience of attentive escorts. Home-sickness did not seem an issue. For many girls, so recently having left school, the companionship with one another was just an extension of life on the playing field and dormitory. To be young in 1944 was to be young indeed, in ways not comprehensible today. Although there were alerts in mid-Atlantic and depth-charges against a submarine off the Island of Crete, no one seemed unduly anxious. It was not until news of casualties became known that the full impact of war made itself felt.

The Cairo FANY mess grew to include around fifty-six members by the spring of 1944, but in wartime nothing was static, and by April there were moves afoot for some, who went off to take up their positions in Italy.

Chapter Three

NORTH AFRICA

Few of the FANY who were posted to MASSINGHAM knew of their destination until their arrival in Algiers. Some girls, getting wind of the word, tried fruitlessly to look it up in an atlas. Elizabeth Fooks (Way), who was already working as a secretary at Baker Street, had been attracted by the country essays of the writer H.J. Massingham and thought this an indication that she should volunteer to go to a place with his name. FANYs who were told to paint the address ISSU 6 on their kitbags were equally in the dark. It was to be a highly unusual unit, one of the most unusual of the entire war, on a number of counts: its personnel came from four nations, British, American, French and Spanish. Unlike SOE stations in the United Kingdom, it was both a training as well as an operational unit. There were considerable political overtones which hampered the smooth planning and running of the missions launched into occupied territory. The extensive signals department, which gained for itself a reputation for efficiency and dedication, was largely operated by young women whose ages ranged from eighteen to twenty-three years of age. Conditions of living on the camp were for the most part harsh and the climate subject to extremes of heat and cold. Impetigo, dysentery and plagues of locusts were unwelcome visitors. Yet, few of those who served at MASSINGHAM talk of it now except in terms of an exceptional experience. It was a self-contained community, set apart fifteen miles outside Algiers, bound by a common purpose. It can best be described in terms of the relation of its component parts to the FANYs.

BRITISH

General Gubbins was the dominant personality behind the setting-up of MASSINGHAM, although, in view of his other responsibilities, he paid only fleeting visits from his base in London. It was he who had made many of the significant appointments in the shape of the men he knew well and trusted, and laid down the pattern for the future working of the unit. After his visits in January and the autumn of 1943, there were changes and fresh motivation. As he had shown on their arrival within SOE, he encouraged the deployment of FANYs and in his report,[1] following his autumn visit to North Africa, he made special reference to them: 'A debt was owed for their high class of work' and having saved SOE from 'a very acute man-power crisis'. They were 'working excellently and their discipline was good and they were well-regarded by the other services'.

Lieutenant-Colonel J.W. Munn RA, a regular soldier and former head of SOE's training section, was initially placed in charge. His Baker Street secretary, Ann Tod (Delves), was turned into a FANY and, after her time at Overthorpe, became one of the First XI who went to North Africa in December, 1942. This practice of enrolling civilian staff who were already familiar with the workings of the organization was followed in a number of subsequent cases. As second-in-command General Gubbins chose Lieutenant-Colonel Douglas Dodds-Parker, formerly a member of the Sudan Political Service, who had come into SOE in 1940. Warned by Peter Wilkinson, largely as a joke at the time of a possible invasion of England, that it had taken the Greeks six hundred years to be free of the Turks, he had accepted a posting to the Middle East. His appointment on his return in May, 1941, involved him in employing FANY, while he was responsible for the running of the Operations Room at Baker Street and for air and sea transport in and out of western Europe for SOE personnel. Following General Gubbins' visit to MASSINGHAM in January, 1943, he appointed Douglas Dodds-Parker as head of the unit, which he carried on with considerable skill. His régime has been compared with that of a bracing Oxford Preparatory School. The continued benevolent paternalism towards his FANY charges, many themselves so recently out of school, created an atmosphere of hard work, but free of tension. The former merchant bankers, David Keswick and Francis Glyn, who had proved themselves elsewhere in SOE, were appointed to the political intelligence side.

Major Peter Murray Lee, formerly head security officer at Baker Street, found himself transferred to MASSINGHAM by orders of the General, with a large staff of Field Security sergeants. His personal assistant, Ensign Ruth Hermon-Smith, another recent Baker Street FANY, wrote an account of her experiences of the new assignment in North Africa:

> My main impression of those months was just work, work and more work. Our official working hours were eight to one and five to eight, but apart from meals and a couple of hours at midday,

when it was impossible to work because of the heat, we went on from eight in the morning till ten or eleven at night. We just never stopped and there were no fixed days off. Whenever you touched a piece of paper, it stuck to you.

Peter Lee recorded his initial awareness of the vulnerability of MASSINGHAM, with its exposed position on the beach. An enemy submarine attack was all too possible and the large signal station could have been destroyed and overrun. SOE had no artillery at MASSINGHAM. Lee was apprehensive, but relied on the shortcomings of German intelligence. All officers carried revolvers during the opening months of MASSINGHAM's life and the FANY First XI were issued with coshes on a spring, tipped by a malevolent steel knob. 'I still have mine', writes its owner.

As the months went by, all sections of MASSINGHAM developed in size and scope. From a handful of officers, other ranks and FANY in the spring of 1943, the unit trebled by the autumn with a greatly expanded operational programme and administrative machinery to match. It provided opportunity for the recruitment of more FANYs, whose numbers rose to over one hundred by the summer of 1944.

AMERICANS

The Anglo-American flavour was a reflexion of the nature of the allied force which had taken part in the TORCH landings. It was to operate again in the HUSKY attack on Sicily, the OVERLORD invasion of north-western Europe on 4 June, 1944, and the smaller assault, though closer to hand for those in North Africa, that of ANVIL, later renamed DRAGOON, on the coast of the south of France on 15 August of that year. Officers and men of the United States Air Force operated with Squadron 138 of the Royal Air Force from the airfield at Blida, a short distance from the MASSINGHAM campus. FANYs flew often with United States pilots, who were invariably hospitable in giving them lifts. Douglas Fairbanks junior, the film star, was among them and 'was very kind, and took us out to meals and gave us signed photographs'.

The parachute school was a United States responsibility, with FANYs among the parachute packers. Patricia Wilson (Selbourne), a wireless operator, writes:

The Americans at ISSU6 were involved with parachute dropping and training. There was a *Dakota* aircraft on 'detached duty' and it would pick up trainee agents at Blida and they would drop into the dunes around the camp.

She and Patricia Dunn (Ansell), another wireless operator, with some other girls, practised safe landings by jumping from various specially set-up pieces of equipment – a wrecked fuselage of a plane in the woods to the east of the camp, towers and high wire pulley contraptions. In the event, neither they nor any other FANY were permitted to parachute from aircraft at MASSINGHAM, on orders from London, although a few did so in Italy. One FANY made a quick jump from the jeep of some Free French soldiers who were giving her a lift from Algiers but did not intend to stop at the camp gates!

FANYs enjoyed invitations to the parachute school mess where there was '*real* coffee, real butter, waffles, fresh fruit, fried chicken, bacon and maple syrup. They liked our meals (tinned m and v [meat and vegetables] and spam) because they were different. American sergeants gave our mess fresh oranges and vegetables; we went on picnics with them in the mountains'. Those Americans with an operational and training role were members of the OSS, Office of Strategic Studies, the United States' version of SOE, created in June, 1942. With SOE, it had played an intelligence and communications role in North Africa before the TORCH landing. Co-operation between SOE and OSS at MASSINGHAM had been laid down earlier in Washington and was to be perpetuated. OSS had its own operational programme of drops into southern France and therefore its own training units in the neighbourhood of Algiers. Gradually joint British-American missions were devised in which eventually Frenchmen also took part, but this lay in the future. By August, 1944, Sheila Cook (Prag) recalls going to work as a coder, not in the large British signals office on the campus, but by truck to an OSS establishment on the edge of Algiers.

Where 'official' America differed from 'official' Britain was in the attitude of its leaders towards the leaders of France. After the French armistice, the United States, unlike Britain, did not sever all its diplomatic relations with the Vichy government set up by the aged Marshal Pétain, nor had it withdrawn its consuls in North Africa. On 17 April, 1942, the French four-star General Henri Giraud, familiarly referred to as 'King-pin', was secretly rescued from imprisonment in Koenigstein and smuggled through France, to arrive in Algiers by submarine. The Americans hoped he would rally French forces in North Africa round him and recreate a French army with him as commander-in-Chief. Meanwhile the British government was pinning its hopes upon Charles de Gaulle for this role, who as a Brigadier-General was sensitive about his lower rank and seniority (and on other grounds also).

From 14–24 January, 1943, Winston Churchill, British Prime Minister, and Franklin D. Roosevelt, President of the United States, came to North Africa and met with the combined Chiefs of Staff in conference at Casablanca in French Morocco. Roosevelt showed himself antipathetic to de Gaulle, who arrived at the conference on 22 January in a recalcitrant mood.

The British tried to persuade him to co-operate with Giraud, but it was not until June that the long-awaited French Committee of National Liberation, FCNL, was finally formed to direct the French war effort in all its forms and locations with de Gaulle and Giraud as joint Presidents. De Gaulle had left London with his staff for Algiers on 29 May, 1943. Hereafter, he was locally known as *Ramrod*, for reasons that become obvious. He proved himself a more adroit politician than Giraud, who on 7 June, 1943, virtually handed over most of his powers to de Gaulle. The possibility of a serious and lasting split in free French loyalties, and the permanent creation of rival factions, had been averted.

FRENCH ELEMENTS AT MASSINGHAM

The TORCH invasion of North Africa had caused German forces to feel so threatened that they took over the whole of the formerly unoccupied zone of southern France. The number of French people attempting to escape across the Mediterranean increased considerably, particularly among young Frenchmen who were trying to avoid being deported to work in German factories. The French Section of MASSINGHAM employed a number of FANY secretaries and a few FANY staff officers, all of whom would have been aware of the political and operational situation. The French Section was at first run by thirty-four-year-old Jacques de Guélis, son of a French father and English mother. He had been a liaison officer with the British Expeditionary Force, had been taken prisoner after Dunkirk, and managed to escape to England. On joining SOE, he had parachuted into France on a mission, and thereafter come to MASSINGHAM. As a member of Baker Street 'F' Section under Lieutenant-Colonel Maurice Buckmaster, and since he was recruiting agents in North Africa, still under French sovereignity, he became *persona non grata* with General de Gaulle. De Guélis was replaced as Section head on orders from Baker Street by Lieutenant Commander (now Sir) Brooks Richards RNVR,[2] who had been engaged on SOE naval operations between Gibraltar and Corsica. His two FANY assistants, Ensigns Barley Alison and Valerie Gibson, worked on a shift system, so brisk was business, with Lieutenant Jackie Porter FANY as a key staff officer of the Section.

Many other FANYs had strong French connections: Marie-Louise Newman and Desirée Kennard (Vivier) had mothers who were French. Betty Hannah had a French step-mother. Several girls – Aline Elwes (McDonnell) was one – had been to school in France and others for various reasons spoke the language well. Some had French friends who had made their way to North Africa. Through their work and the training programme, girls met agents of French nationality who were preparing to re-enter their own country.

Sympathy for the plight of France under foreign occupation, and especially for the members of SOE who had already been infiltrated into their dangerous situations, ran high. This was particularly so in the case of the FANY wireless operators who communicated daily with them over the air waves.

Incidents occurred when transmission suddenly ceased in mid-flow, which caused anxiety and stress. Ann Bonsor tells of receiving an unexpected and highly forbidden example of morse in plain language, in the midst of a message in code from an operator in France – BOCHE, BOCHE, and then silence. Audrey Swithinbank (Rothwell) was aware of a sudden continuous buzzing sound, instead of a morse message, coming from the field. It was reported later that the sender had been killed while transmitting and fallen on his key.

In their time off some FANYs rode with the crack French-colonial Spahi regiment, with their red cloaks and splendid arab horses. Some would visit the holding unit at Sidi Ferruch for French agents awaiting missions, with the code name LULU, in the charge of Captain John Goldsmith, who had spent many years in France running racing stables. He made several wartime return visits. A set of small bungalows on stilts over the sea accommodated the men and there were facilities for swimming and other sports. Wine was donated by the French owner of a vineyard in the neighbourhood. Dances were attended by FANYs, and often girls and Frenchmen would sing together. Patriotic songs included *Le Chant des Partisans*, music written by Diana Thatcher and words by Ann Bonsor, which related to the activities of the *Maquis* (see p. 50).

SPANIARDS

After the TORCH landings the allies discovered camps of Spanish Communists who had been imprisoned under the French régime. *Tiny Hands* was their nickname among the British, since their salute was a clenched fist. Fifty of them were employed on the camp at MASSINGHAM for a variety of jobs: these included packing containers of supplies to be dropped into the field, maintaining vehicles, and a role in which they often encountered FANYs, guarding the beaches during the hours of darkness. Wireless operators and coders coming off duty during the night in hot weather would run the gauntlet of the Spanish guards when they plunged into the sea, casting off their clothes.

After the armistice with Italy, some aspiring Italian agents came to MASSINGHAM to be trained.

The early days of the unit for the First XI were spent, as has been stated, at Cap Matifou, and the little fishing village of La Perousse in a house by the name of *La Maison Blanche*, with the signals office on wooden supports above the sea a short distance away. As the FANYs sat on duty at night their chairs shook and swayed as the house was often rocked by bombs falling in the distance. One night most of the girls were at a party on a corvette in Algiers harbour when a raid began. On their return, they related how they had helped to fire the guns on board. In February, 1943, the whole unit moved to the west of Algiers to a location of former holiday homes on the beach. Here a vast camp was erected with the many villas, which were scattered among the sand dunes, turned into offices, messes, accommodation for men and girls, and all the requirements of a military unit: Q stores, cobbler, sick bay, motor transport lines and ration depot. At a greater distance beyond the perimeter fence were the facilities for training agents in sabotage and demolition, use of weapons and so on.

The villas occupied by the FANYs differed in size and distinction: all had stone floors, no heating, neither baths nor hot water and were built for summer rather than winter occupation. The girls who arrived in the warmer weather were more enthusiastic than a group of five who came in November and shared a former garage attached to a house. 'After each inspection, we were promised a move into a villa, but it never happened because they said we kept the garage so well.' Rooms had no furniture and girls slept on camp beds with three grey army blankets. Sheets were obtainable from the Quartermaster's stores. There seems to have been a shortage of pillows; letters home requested pillows and dressing gowns, which were not part of standard issue. In order to improvise, FANYs stuffed underclothes into their khaki pillow cases. Kitbags remained the only receptacles for clothes and possessions, together with bedside tables created from orange boxes and decked with parachute material. Rooms reflected the individuality of their occupants, with flowers and many photographs of parents, brothers, sisters, friends and dogs pinned upon the walls. In the summer FANYs wore khaki drill skirts and shirts and sometimes bush jackets: service dress was restricted to ceremonial occasions, as for the visits of dignitaries, 'when we nearly died of the heat in ties and stockings for some general'. In winter, many girls lived in their flannel striped army pyjamas, which they never took off, topped by men's battledress 'blouses', and thick khaki trousers, army boots and often greatcoats as well. Washing underclothes and shirts was a problem without hot water. Visits were made to a neighbouring village where Arab women did laundering if they were provided with soap (part of everyone's allocation).

The first XI, who, with the second contingent, were all officers, had their meals in FANY Mess I. The arrival of the large group of wireless operators and coders in July of 1943 gave rise to a second mess for those who were not commissioned, in the shape of FANY Mess II where life was less formal, (although officer status was given to all). FANY Mess II had no cooking facilities and the cook, who was a private in the Army Catering Corps, coped, stripped to the waist, in an outside trench, while the FANYs in summer ate outside, sitting on benches at trestle tables. His streaming torso made them unenthusiastic about the doughnuts which he sometimes made for them by pouring petrol on the sand. Later the Americans provided a cooking stove and a covered hut for meals in the winter.

The FANY wireless operators had a less than encouraging welcome on their arrival. One of their number writes:

> The first morning we reported at the signals office to be greeted by the officer in charge of signals, a huge, imposing man, not pleased to see us. He told us that wireless telegraphy was no job for women; that we were probably here with the hope of 'lotus-eating' (we were too naïve to know what that meant); that the splendid signalmen [a group of whom had been receiving and sending all the traffic until that time] would resent and dislike us and that it was his intention to get us all sent back to the United Kingdom on the first possible convoy. Until then he was obliged to employ us. Mixed shifts were unthinkable, so there were to be two all-female shifts and that he had the facility to monitor our work from his office. Indeed he did, and one could hear the morse echoing round the dunes on several occasions. It all sounds rather depressing, but we were young and enthusiastic; we had a wonderfully friendly relationship with one another and the place was beautiful. Far from resenting us, or hating us, the signalmen became our friends. Convoys left, but there was no word of our going on one. As the war progressed, male operators were posted to other places and one day the officer in charge of signals called a meeting and told us that we could no longer have single-sex shifts because all his best operators were women. In fact, he was really the kindest of men and would do all he could for his personnel. We got a nice rest hut with means to brew up and even a few comfortable chairs.

In the signals office, the coding room led out of the space allotted to the wireless operators. Lieutenant Dorothy Temple (Wakely) was responsible for signals intelligence in her office on the first floor and was regarded with awe for her quick brain. It was she who devised the signal plans for agents, telling them their call signs, frequencies and the times and days on which to contact base, occasions which were named 'skeds'. She would visit AFHQ for the frequencies she needed, also members of the RAF who controlled the aerials, so that they would be pointing in the right direction. She would sit on a bench in the sand, if it were good weather, and explain the intricacies of his signal plan to young operators going into southern France.

In England Dorothy Temple had been taught to put lists of missions with their code names and call signs, frequencies and times they would come on the air, up on the walls of the signals office for the benefit of wireless operators. At MASSINGHAM, directly she had done so, she was instructed to take them all down again. The crew of an enemy submarine on landing could learn the names and frequencies of all missions in southern France. She complied, whereupon a visiting official rebuked her for having neglected her duties in not providing such visible lists. Normally a shift's 'skeds' would be written on a blackboard and FANYs or signalmen allotted to the time when a field operator (who were nicknamed 'pianists' and their sets 'music-boxes') was due to come up with his call sign. It was exacting work. The reception could be extremely poor, with atmospheric interference, possible jamming and faint and sometimes inexpert sending. German direction-finding being so efficient, it was dangerous to ask for repeats and, for the same reason, messages needed to be sent as fast as possible. Girls were sensitive and alive to these problems and, in the same way, FANY coders were considered conscientious in their efforts to unravel 'indecypherable' messages.

Some girls found the shift system trying, particularly long shifts at night. It could be hard to keep awake, especially when the signal traffic was between main-line stations ie such as Algiers, London and Cairo and eventually Tunis. The codes were taken from a cipher book, all in figures, which meant five sounds in morse for every figure; nearly everyone faltered at some time, but it was, in these cases, possible to ask for repeats. Sleeping in the daytime was a problem for some. 'I have had six hours sleep in the last three days', wrote one FANY, but there were long days off after a spell of night duties.

The most spectacular feat carried out by the MASSINGHAM signals FANYs, both wireless operators and coders, was their handling of the communications which negotiated the armistice between the Allies and Italy in the late summer of 1943. That this should have happened was consequent upon a series of factors which conspired to come together. First, during the Casablanca Conference in January, it had been agreed that Sicily should be invaded as soon as possible: the last of the Axis forces, German and Italian, were driven out of North Africa on 13 May. To put Italy out of the war was the next objective. Operation HUSKY, the invasion of Sicily, began on 10 July. SOE personnel followed closely in the wake of regular forces. As described in a following chapter, they formed the prelude to the setting up of a SOE unit in Italy, where FANYs were soon to move in.

No doubt as the result of the invasion of Italian territory came the resignation of Benito Mussolini. The King of Italy, Victor Emmanuel III, who was seventy-four years of age and had reigned since 1900, appointed in his stead

Marshal Pietro Badoglio, aged seventy-two, as Prime Minister. As a stimulus to action, General Eisenhower made a broadcast to the Italian people on 29 July, suggesting that 'unconditional surrender' did not mean the imposition of dishonourable terms. At this point Harold Macmillan,[3] Resident Minister in Algiers on the British side, was called to London, when 'short terms' which General Eisenhower could use in negotiations with the Italians were drawn up with Anthony Eden, the Foreign Secretary. On 17 August General Eisenhower sent for Harold Macmillan and showed him the text of telegrams which Sir Samuel Hoare, British Ambassador in Madrid, had sent to the Foreign Office. The Italian General Castellano, Chief-of-Staff to General Ambrosio, and Signor Montanari of the Italian Foreign Office, had called to see him. Their pretext was as members of an Italian delegation travelling to Lisbon to effect an exchange of Italian/Chilean diplomats, consequent upon the cessation of Italian/Chilean relations.

General Castellano had a letter of introduction from the British Minister at the Holy See (incarcerated in the Vatican), stating that the General was authorized to speak for Marshal Badoglio. Instructions were then issued on the allied side to send two senior officers to Lisbon in civilian clothes, without alerting the suspicions of German intelligence, which was energetic in that city. A civilian aircraft and passports were hurriedly provided. They returned from Lisbon on 20 August with the information that General Castellano was prepared to accept unconditional surrender on behalf of the Italian government. He was handed terms of a military armistice. It was not possible for him to return to Rome without the Italians from Chile, who were providing his cover story, so midnight of 30–31 August was given as the final date by which an answer as to acceptance of the armistice was to be made.

A short time earlier at MASSINGHAM, a young Englishman, Richard Mallaby, was being prepared for a mission in Italy. He had spent his boyhood near Siena on a series of farms owned by his English father; his stepmother was Italian. The family had made its way to England at the beginning of the war when Dick, as he was known, joined the Devonshire Regiment and later transferred to No 8 Commando in the Middle East, where he joined SOE and received his parachute and wireless operator's training. He was posted to MASSINGHAM where parachute drops into water had been practised and where he was pronounced suitable for a mission to Lake Como.

Dressed as a frogman, with a radio, collapsible dinghy and lifebelt, he left Algiers on the night of 13/14 August, 1943. His instructions were to establish contact with certain named Italians. His signal plan code name was MARASCHINO and a second plan MUSCAT was designed by Dorothy Temple for the Italians he was to meet. He dropped into the lake near some fishing boats and began to row himself ashore when he was spotted. Shots were fired and he told his assailants he was an Italian pilot who had baled out of his plane. He was put in manacles and placed in a cell with other prisoners; his equipment and radio set were confiscated. As he did not come up on his assigned frequency according to his signal plan, a listening watch was established at MASSINGHAM. News of his capture was soon received.

By 25 August the Italian government, obviously alarmed because there was no sign in Rome of General Castellano's return, sent a second pair of representatives by air to Lisbon in the shape of General Zanussi, assistant to General Roatta, Chief of the Italian General Staff, and a Signor Lansa di Trabia. They were accompanied, as a guarantee of their good faith, by the British General Adrian Carton de Wiart,[4] who had been removed a few days earlier to Rome from an Italian prisoner of war camp at Vincigliati; he had been incarcerated in various camps since April, 1941. Zanussi took him to General Roatta and they spoke French. The Italians wanted an armistice. One dove had been despatched, but it had not returned.

J'ai envoyé une colombe, mais comme elle n'est pas retournée, je vais envoyer une seconde.

The two generals went to Rome airport, which was swarming with Germans, with their companion, for the flight to Lisbon.

Meanwhile, Dick Mallaby, in his prison at Como, suddenly underwent a change of circumstances. He was taken to Rome and, after an interview with General Castellano, newly returned to Rome, Mallaby agreed to operate his set back to MASSINGHAM if he were permitted to add messages of his own. Clean clothes and good food were provided. Lieutenant-Colonel Roseberry, head of the Italian Section of SOE in London, travelled to Lisbon to meet the second Italian delegation. He issued a signal plan which had been drawn up with the code name MONKEY, by which communication between Rome and MASSINGHAM would be transmitted on an SOE radio set (by Mallaby), together with a novel *L'omnibus del Corso* by Sanminiatelli, the basis of a code in double transposition. The second copy was sent to MASSINGHAM, where four FANY coders were selected for the work of immense secrecy about to begin: Leo Railton, Sue Rowley, Barbara Tims and Paddy Sproule were considered to have the necessary intelligence, speed and competence.

Stringent security arrangements were made. They worked in pairs, on eight-hour shifts, locked into a type of washroom on the camp, where no one was allowed to enter except the FANY officer in charge, Lieutenant Peg Todd, Douglas Dodds-Parker and Peter Lee. The key to the code (the novel) only arrived from Lisbon via London by courier hours before it was needed. FANY wireless operators maintained a listening watch in the signal office at

MASSINGHAM on the MONKEY frequency, but were unaware of the fact that there was anything special about that particular set. Contact with Mallaby from Rome was first made on 30 August, 1943, who also later sent some signals of a personal kind on his own signal plan MARASCHINO. FANY coders began to work flat out in their washroom.

A longer and more comprehensive instrument of surrender than that given to General Castellano was handed to General Zanussi in Lisbon. He suggested that the Italian government might find it more difficult to accept this, rather than the shorter one. The date by which answer was required was put back.

Meanwhile news of German troop movements flowing steadily into Italy were being received. This was confirmed by General Zanussi, who left Lisbon for Gibraltar with his colleague, and on to MASSINGHAM where they were placed under the care of Peter Lee, chief security officer. Signor Lansa di Trabia, who spoke excellent English, said as they talked about opera that he was worried that Americans would bomb his record collection in his villa south of Rome. A letter to General Ambrosio in that city, to the effect that the short terms of surrender would be acceptable, was taken to Italy by Signor di Trabia. It also stated that General Castellano should make his way to Sicily to sign an armistice.

At the headquarters of General Alexander in Sicily, Castellano and Zanussi were reunited and there was discussion that an American airborne division should land near Rome as an encouragement to Italian forces in the neighbourhood. After several more hitches, at 4 pm on 3 September a communication came from Rome over an SOE network; General Castellano was authorized by the Italian government to sign acceptance of the armistice conditions. At 4.30 pm the military armistice was signed at Alexander's headquarters at Casabile. Earlier on the same day allied troops had landed on the mainland of Italy across the Straits of Messina.

It was decided that the simultaneous announcement of the armistice by both sides should coincide with the airborne landing near Rome. On the night of 7 September the American General Commanding the airborne division managed to make his way by corvette to Italy and, bravely under cover, on to Rome to discuss the details of the enterprise. The result was a signal via the MONKEY set to MASSINGHAM on 8 September from Marshal Badoglio. Announcement of the armistice was not possible. The proposed airborne operation could not be carried out: German forces had become too strong. When this message was relayed to General Eisenhower, he replied with the demand that broadcast of the armistice on the Italian side must go ahead, as it would on the Anglo-American, a promise he carried out later the same day.

Douglas Dodds-Parker, in his book[5] written after the war, describes the tension among the small informed circle at MASSINGHAM. Although almost continuous communication had until now been maintained, MONKEY had been off the air since 6 pm. To general relief, at 7.45 a message was received that Badoglio had made his broadcast to the Italian people. In addition to the traffic on MONKEY, Dick Mallaby had on 4 September sent encoded messages on MARASCHINO to Teddy de Haan: 'Will carry out your instructions . . . Wish I were with you. My regards'. He sent his love to various FANYs. On 9 September the MONKEY plan operated from Pescara; the King of Italy and Badoglio had left for the south and Dick Mallaby also. Soon they established themselves at Brindisi, where the saga is continued in Chapter 5.

Altogether, the number of signals sent to Rome via MONKEY are considered to have been around fifty-one, and sixteen or so received, up to 8 September. Considering the short operating time, this reflects credit upon the coders and wireless operators concerned. Thereafter, this traffic continued to be heavy, with Dick Mallaby assisted by Italian naval wireless operators at his end, until 20 September, when the communications between MASSINGHAM and Brindisi were placed on a more permanent basis.

The next excitement was the seizure, by the Allies, of the French island of Corsica, which had been occupied by Italian troops since November, 1942. After the surrender of Italy, German forces had begun to move in from Sardinia. The local Corsican *maquis* seized the opportunity to give trouble and the Germans had already taken the decision to evacuate when French troops and a few agents, both trained by SOE, landed at Ajaccio on 15 September, 1943. After some loss of life on the Italian side, the island was cleared of Germans by 4 October. The Royal Navy established a base there and it became a useful launching point for the infiltration of agents into Italy on the north-west coast, and into France on the south, under the leadership of Lieutenant-Colonel Andrew Croft (one of General Gubbins' original colleagues with the Auxiliary Units), with the code name BALACLAVA. His book *A Talent for Adventure* describes his exploits. A solitary FANY, Alice Pitt, was stationed on Corsica for eight or nine months as secretary to Lieutenant Paddy Davies RNVR, the intelligence officer on the island. It became a favourite place for FANYs to visit, on the somewhat flimsy excuse of taking supplies to Alice. Andrew Croft's book and log give the names of some of those who did so.

On one occasion two FANY wireless operators and a coder made the flight out to Corsica for a few days after a spell of night duty and were unable to return before their next shift. They feared they might be sent back to England. Captain Betty Sale, the Australian FANY Commanding Officer who had taken over from Captain Curry, was a fair-minded woman; these were skilled operators who had worked hard, so she overlooked the misdemeanour.

Taking off by air became a regular way of spending free time after long spells at night. Patricia Wilson had a friend in the United States Air Force who flew her to Rome in July, 1944. She wrote to her parents:

> It wasn't actual leave, but just a few days off between changes of shifts. People were very sceptical about our going at first because they didn't think we would get back in time. You see, we left after duty on Sunday and were due back for duty on Tuesday night at eight. We flew over the Anzio beaches and beach-heads – it was ghastly; for about at least fifty miles there wasn't a house left whole, or even with a roof – all the fields were pock-marked with shell-holes etc – all the bridges were broken – everything was blackened and burnt – it was miserable. It must have been a *terrific* battle.

In his book,[6] Air Chief Marshal (as he became) Sir John Slessor writes of his occasional meetings with his FANY daughter, Judy, who was a coder stationed at MASSINGHAM. 'She visited me later in Caserta, having thumbed a quite unauthorized ride in the tail turret of a Liberator being delivered for 105 Group.'

Girls wrote with gratitude to their parents for allowing them the opportunity of being at MASSINGHAM. 'I am lucky to be here,' wrote one. 'Thank you for letting me have this experience, I shall never regret it.' Discounting the fact that no one would want to worry their parents by sounding unhappy, and that the nature of their work could not be revealed, letters that have been preserved are enthusiastic and high-spirited, and appreciative of those features of their lives that could be described: friendships, time off, the sea, the scenery, the mountains, the flowers. Some girls were obviously more sensitive to their surroundings than others.

A FANY secretary wrote of the vases of flowers in her office: roses, sweet peas, lilies, orange blossom, cornflowers, geraniums and asters, and of the bright colours of the villas perched on the beach; also of the concerts and operas which she enjoyed in the nearest large town (not disclosed, which was, of course, Algiers), when she was not on duty and had friends with transport. Parties were a considerable subject of correspondence and the friends who took FANYs as their partners.

> I went to a marvellous dance the other night; 30 miles away. We danced on the roof of a club where there were chinese lanterns, palms and other decorations.

There were some scruples about the possible effects of so much attention; 'Parties nearly every night at present. I am becoming very spoilt. I have been plied with invitations every night next week . . . Girls are very scarce out here, but it's difficult to make excuses sometimes and refuse.' 'It is really lovely out here with the heat and swimming. I wish you could see the flowers; each day we put some to arrange round the rooms, my bedroom is filled with all different varieties.'

Several letters explained that it was not easy to keep clean with nothing but cold water. The cook would provide a jug of hot water for hair washing. Requests for parcels from home included 'anything pertaining to cleanliness would be welcome – a flannel, for instance'. The stock at the NAAFI was limited. A Scottish doctor made his appearance, whose influence resulted in showers for the FANYs, but the water was seldom hot. Some girls played tennis in their free time: 'A charming French family known to one of the FANYs have a tennis court, my French is improving.' Others went sailing. The Naval element of SOE MASSINGHAM had a flotilla of small craft which was deployed delivering and picking up agents and putting weapons, explosives and supplies into occupied territory. Some of these were sailing ships which could operate silently on a coastline with a vigilant enemy. Chief among the Naval men was Commander Gerard Holdsworth RNVR whose legendary exploits in Scandanavia and off the western coast of France preceded his arrival in the Mediterranean. He later became the colourful head of No. 1 Special Force, code name MARYLAND, at Monopoli, a successor to MASSINGHAM, on the east coast of Italy. A description has survived of a group of FANYs swimming 'like mermaids' out to one of his ships anchored alongside the beach.

An entertainment at Christmas, 1943, directed by a member of the Tennant theatrical family, included numerous FANYs. Yuletide Follies was a variation on Cinderella, written mainly by a member of the unit, with a large number of local references. Joan Tapp (Taylor), a wireless operator, was in the title role. She writes:

> All the costumes were made of parachute silk and various impro-
> visations and the dress I wore for the finale was hired in Algiers.
> The scenery was made in the camp. The Americans lent us
> materials and the RAF dealt with the electrical side of things.

Musical girls, of whom there were several, formed a choir which sang Stainer's *Crucifixion* in April, 1944, at the English Church of All Saints' at el Biar in Algiers. The Padre from a convalescent depot and his patients also sang. Unfortunately the main tenor was declared fit and returned to his unit a week before the performance and had to be replaced at the last moment.

As the weather became hotter in the spring of 1944, so did the pace of work heat up and become all-absorbing. Harold Macmillan in his *War Diaries*[7] showed himself a veritable weatherman in relation to the temperature: '7 May insufferably hot; 16 May a cold *mistral*; came on to rain in the night'. A FANY wrote home, 'The sirocco, a hot wind from the desert, suddenly swept down on us today – it is stifling, just like an oven – we had to be content with all the windows shut in the office.' In its wake came clouds of locusts, apparently the first in the neighbourhood for twenty years. They hung about for several days and demolished everything green in sight. Mounds of dead locusts littered the beach. Mosquitoes also became more troublesome and 'were raging fast and furious . . . We are bitten all over,' although everyone slept under nets. Mepacrin, yellow tablets against malaria, had been issued to all ranks in the early days of MASSINGHAM, but were discontinued because it was decided that 'these were the wrong kind of mosquitoes'.

Preparations for the invasion of north-western France in 1944, codenamed OVERLORD, involved those in the Mediterranean in widespread plans for diversionary tactics – keeping German forces tied down in the south of France and to prevent their swift movement north when the time came. Administrative changes at MASSINGHAM were made to deal with operational necessity, and training was accelerated. A new department named SPOC, Special Projects Operations Centre, was set up on an international basis, run by British, American and later also French officers, to plan future activities. Leadership was held jointly by Lieutenant-Colonel John Anstey, who had been second-in-command to Douglas Dodds-Parker (and who had assumed the latter's position also, to allow him to pursue a greater liaison role with AFHQ), and the American Lieutenant-Colonel William R. Davis. New facilities were provided outside the *Club des Pins* campus, in the shape of over twenty-five tents, nine Nissen huts and a wooden mess hut, near the Villa Magnol on the outskirts of Algiers. The new premises opened on 23 May, 1944.

There was an increase of staff at this juncture, including a fresh batch of FANYs from England in May, 1944. June Mecredy and Ishbel McKenzie, who had worked at Station XII in Hertfordshire as well-trained secretaries, were posted to SPOC when they reached MASSINGHAM and found themselves, not within the campus, but under canvas at el Biar, slightly south-east of Algiers. Their arrival had been remarkable, for in the draft on the ship from Liverpool was Judy Slessor. At Oran, when they disembarked, they were met by her father in his own plane; all flew to Algiers, where her astonished companions enjoyed lunch at Air House before being delivered at MASSINGHAM. Later SPOC FANYs moved to the twelfth floor of a block of flats in Algiers, where the lift often failed. They went to work by truck and sometimes did not return until ten or eleven o'clock at night, after a long day. Ishbel was required to make SITREPS (situation reports) to be sent to London on signals from the field. Some of June's work was in French and she used her French shorthand. Elvera Burbeck also arrived in May, 1944; she had completed an intelligence course in England to teach her how to plot road and rail targets for destruction. Margaret Graydon (Connor) was secretary to Major Desmond Bailey, who was in charge of operational stores; a seeming tube of French toothpaste was, in reality, an abrasive material which frosted over when applied to windscreens, making driving virtually impossible. Packets of French cigarettes disguised incendiaries; milk churns and shabby suitcases concealed wireless sets, and bales of material of French origin, would be made into clothes for agents.

Some FANYs took part in training programmes: they learnt to handle various weapons, including sten-guns, and also unarmed combat. A sergeant, who was a member of the same course, thinking to catch one of the girls unawares, tackled her suddenly from behind. She recalls her astonishment (and no doubt his) when she put what she had been taught into action, and threw him to the ground. Sabotage training and demolition took place in the hills and on some occasions FANYs who were wireless operators took part in training schemes with radio sets to simulate sending and receiving messages over a distance in the field. Patricia Wilson describes one such in the Atlas Mountains, which was particularly energetic:

> We went on a sort of scheme, frightfully strenuous and we felt very important. About ten of us and some men went for about a two-hour drive in jeeps and trailers and open lorries etc, then climbed up about 2,000 feet on an almost vertical mountain in the hottest part of the day. I just can't describe it, we were sweating blood. About three-quarters of the way up, we came to a fountain and trough and we all sat in it, fully clothed, because of mixed company. We had to stop twice and rig everything up and do a bit of work. The scenery there is just wonderful . . .
>
> We eventually reached the top and had our late lunch, but we were all in such a state, we could hardly eat, but it was worth it, the view was stupendous and it was marvellously cool. We did more work there and managed to hear the news. Coming down was almost as bad – frightfully steep, our knees were all wobbly. There were two majors in charge of us . . . We had to wade across a river at the bottom, it was going at a terrific rate, but luckily wasn't too deep.

Ann Bonsor, on a similar exercise as a wireless operator to the beautiful village of Chrea, nearly 5,000 feet above sea level, was so struck by the surroundings that she wrote a poem of which the first verse captures the scene:

The quiet of the hills seeps around us
With rich scent of the pines in the breeze.
We are far from the war and its backwash,
Life is secure in the depth of the trees.

Aline Elwes, who was a fluent French speaker, was part of a team who helped to train prospective agents in groups of ten or twelve. The curriculum included basic news from contemporary France and conditions which might be expected, ie the days the metro would not be working, police methods, and so on. She would teach them simple disguises, forging, house-breaking and how to remember the identity of strangers, writing letters with hidden messages, etc.

A scheme to teach agents in training how to locate a contact in a town involved several FANYs. They would put on civilian clothes, be given a password and travel into Algiers to mingle in the traffic and then reach a specific destination at a specified time. Ann Bonsor remembers her password, when accosted at *La Grande Poste*, with '*Parlez-vous Français?*' she was to reply, '*Oui, mais plutôt comme une vache Espagnole*'.

Douglas Dodds-Parker was proud of the achievements and atmosphere of MASSINGHAM and of his FANYs, and invited inspection by senior officers from Allied Force Headquarters, even from General Eisenhower himself. Harold Macmillan came often to bathe on the beach, also the Duff Coopers after their arrival in Algiers. King George VI made a visit in June, 1944. Joan Tapp writes:

> I certainly recall the flap when VIPs were around and, as regards
> de Gaulle, we were in Algiers itself when there was a huge parade
> for him. Friendly gendarmes gave us a place on the edge of the
> pavement. Most impressive were the French troops in full
> regalia, the Goums and the Spahis; the resurrection of France
> beginning.

Whether or not there should be an allied landing in the south of France, after that of OVERLORD in the north, was a matter which preoccupied Allied leaders in the early summer of 1944. Differences of opinion between British and American leaders delayed a decision. It would appear that Churchill favoured a landing near the Istrian peninsula, given the code name, by reason of the geographical configuration of the site, ARMPIT; whereas the Americans favoured landing on the south coast of France, the code name for which operation was ANVIL. On 1 July, 1944, Harold Macmillan visited General Alexander at his headquarters at Viterbo in Italy; the latter was reconciling himself to the fact that, if ANVIL took place, he would be required to relinquish three American and four French divisions, together with some air power. He was himself in favour of ARMPIT as the better option. On the following day came a telegram from London: ARMPIT was off, ANVIL on. Alexander was summoned to the Prime Minister. The landings took place on 15 August, with the new code name DRAGOON. In the end the argument that French forces must be allowed to free France was a powerful one. On hearing that the liberation of southern France had finally begun, FANYs who were working in the signal office at MASSINGHAM recall that, with a sudden rush of sentimental enthusiasm, they all sang the *Marseillaise*.

The weeks leading up to the invasion were times of considerable activity. Shift work became the norm for more FANYs, not only for those employed as wireless operators and coders, who had always worked round the clock. Secretaries also went on during the night and many were required to change jobs at a moment's notice in order to do whatever was necessary. 'I am having to be a switchboard operator for a week or two', wrote one, 'and some of my friends are doing the same, or else they are on the teleprinters. I am working flat out at the moment.' Wireless operators sat at their sets 'until I ached all over'. Gwen Gurnat, a coder, writes, 'On occasions we worked till we dropped and our eyes hurt. I had to sit in a dark room'. FANYs were also required to help prepare clothes for agents to wear in the field and sew in French tailors' labels. One FANY officer, as part of her role in issuing equipment to agents, was responsible for offering them the 'L pill' or lethal tablet, which would kill them instantly if they were captured. Few accepted it.

A special SOE unit, the members of which, at the suggestion of General Gubbins, who had strong Scottish connections, were called Jedburghs, had been highly trained for six months at a former stately home, Milton Hall, near Peterborough. Selection was careful and screening strict, for Jedburghs were to be members of small teams in dangerous and exposed positions in territory occupied by the enemy. Personnel were British, American and French, in cases of operations in France. Arthur Brown,[8] one of their number, writes of their role:

> In so far as there was a standard operation, it was the drop of a team to a dropping zone (organized by an SOE agent), rallying the local maquis, arming and training it and holding it back until orders came from the army command to destroy this target, attack that or harry the other. Equipped with a radio which gave direct access to the allied quartermaster's stores, persuasion was not difficult. What was, was damping down local rivalries and the political in-fighting which made for many a sleepless night. But for the most part, an offer of arms and explosives in return for cooperation and the acceptance of minimum direction was usually

too good to be passed up by men who, until then, had been fighting the enemy on their own and now had the chance of an allied HQ on their doorstep, staffed by officers in full uniform – in some cases in highly illegal uniforms, since the Scots among the Jeds insisted on going on operations in the kilt.

Twenty Jedburgh teams were allotted to drop into southern France from MASSINGHAM. General Gubbins selected Daphne Park[9] who had been a FANY coding instructor in England, to be their briefing and dispatching officer. Born and brought up in Africa, she had completed a degree in French at Somerville College, Oxford, less than twelve months before. She was twenty-two years of age. Sent to Gamwell to be commissioned as an Ensign, Daphne Park set off by air in May, 1944, from Lyneham to Gibraltar, and on to Algiers on a high priority passage. She was the only woman on the aircraft, with senior officers who objected to the quantity of what they considered unnecessary personal baggage – heavy kitbags of briefing equipment which she was required to keep near her. Little did they know the value of the francs therein contained.

One of Daphne Park's duties was to attend meetings when the allocation of passages on flights which would take men over France to be dropped by parachute would be made. Claims for priority were strenuously argued and she was required to make a case for her own people. At one such meeting she was so tired by the exertions of her job that she dozed off. General Stawell, who was in the chair, rapped on the table to secure attention, whereupon Daphne Park woke up and said, 'Come in'. Years later, she recalls, she met General Stawell in St James's Park when she was a senior civil servant. He recognized her and reminded her of the incident.

The Jedburgh teams, the norm being a British, an American and a French officer, together with a British sergeant wireless operator, were stationed at a site known as Camp W, a château near el Riath in an orchard of nectarines. They dropped as arranged during July and August, 1944. Some of the code names of their operations were of a strange medical flavour: CHLOROFORM, VEGANIN, EPHEDRINE, NOVOCAINE. There were some casualties, but all the Jedburgh teams in southern France evaded capture. The awards that followed revealed their bravery. Failure of communication took an amusing turn. The leader of one team who sustained a compound fracture of his leg as the result of his drop was believed to be saying, '*Doucement, doucement*' to the Frenchmen who were carrying him. In fact, he was calling for the wireless operator, Sergeant Loosmore.

Having dispatched her sixty charges, Daphne Park accepted an invitation from some officers to go to a restaurant for lunch in the mountains near Blida. They set off in a jeep which they left outside during the meal. Later they found it had gone. 'We were in deep trouble.' The local policeman said he could not help, as there were prisoners in his gaol. So Daphne Park was left in charge of them, with a sten gun, while the policeman and the remainder of the party managed to retrieve the vehicle.

Some dramatic situations took place within southern France immediately before the landing. One was the tragedy on the Vercors plateau where the *Maquis* rose prematurely and could not hold their position. What was badly needed was artillery and none was forthcoming; the loss of life on the French side was agonizingly heavy. Commander Brooks Richards' French Section was known by the initials AMF, as compared with 'F' Section under Colonel Buckmaster and the Gaullist 'RF' Section, both in London. AMF's only woman agent was the Polish Christine Granville[10] who dropped from Algiers into southern France on the night of 7/8 July, 1944, as PAULINE, to the JOCKEY mission under the leadership of Francis Cammaerts, who was known as ROGER. She was to act as his courier. Paddy Sproule had taught her coding. I had known her slightly in Cairo, where I had lent her my spare set of FANY buttons for the purposes of having her photograph taken for her official pass. Christine's considerable acts of bravery in the field have passed into legend; there have been many accounts, some of them contradictory, and the sequence is not always easy to determine. What is clear is that Christine landed in the Vercors and made contact with Cammaerts. They managed to leave the Plateau before the main German attack on 17 July and, with the help of a *maquis* car, and taking back roads and trails, made for Seyne in the Basses Alpes. This became his headquarters, in association with a French SOE agent, Commandant Sorenson, code name CHASUBLE. On 11 August they were joined by Major Alexander (always known as Xan) Fielding, who had been brought up in southern France and had already undertaken SOE missions in Crete. His code name was CATHÉDRALE and that of his companion, a South African, Captain Julian Lezzard, was ÉGLISE. (Lezzard, who was partly Jewish, suggested that SYNAGOGUE would have been appropriate, but this was disregarded.) They made two earlier attempts to land by parachute, but on neither occasion was the pilot able to locate the required lights on the dropping zone. On the third the American despatcher told Fielding, 'Quit worrying, Buddy. This crew always dumps its load'. Lezzard was seriously injured in the drop.

Part of Christine's mission was to try and reach a number of Polish nationals who had been forcibly enrolled in the German army and encourage them to desert. She managed to contact some who ran a clandestine organization centred at Mont-Dauphin. A more difficult assignment was to make her way to a fort in the *Col de Larche* on the Italian border south of Meyronnes, where 150 Poles were manning the garrison. A French patriot took her by motorcycle to the house of a guide, who led her up the

47

1,994 feet of precipitous mountain, mainly through woods of larches. She achieved a meeting with her contacts and many Poles defected as a result, with their arms. Before doing so, fifty of them removed the breech-blocks from the heavy guns and brought with them mortars and machine guns to join the *maquis*.

While Christine was away from Seyne, on 13 August Cammaerts, Fielding and Sorenson were arrested at a roadblock and taken to a prison at Digne. Their driver, Claude Renoir, son of the painter, was allowed to proceed and took the bad news back to Seyne, where Christine joined him later in the day. She then bicycled the twenty-five miles to Digne and succeeded in entering the prison, on the pretence of being ROGER's wife. The prison was in the charge of the *Milice Française*, a Vichy police force which collaborated with the Germans. She realized that she must act quickly before the Gestapo became aware of his true identity. She sent a message, via CHASUBLE's 'pianist' Auguste, to MASSINGHAM for over a million francs to be dropped immediately; this was done on 16 August. Christine, with her forceful personality, after long argument, threatened two of the guards with what would be the consequences to them personally when the Allies entered the town if they had been the cause of the prisoners having been shot. She promised safe conducts and a huge bribe. Cammaerts and his colleagues were led out of the prison on 17 August; Christine was waiting for them. A *message personelle* on the BBC later included the words *Roger est libre; félicitations à Pauline*; felicitations indeed. Christine was awarded the George Medal and Order of the British Empire for her courageous and resourceful actions.

As the result of the Vercors tragedy and two other operations which did not go well, Brooks Richards records that morale was low in the field at the end of July, 1944, and there were fears that the landing would be fiercely resisted. News which came from certain quarters in France, however, indicated that the Germans were on the defensive and only moved when in considerable strength. The prognosis was that, once through the coastal defences, it would not be difficult to get quickly through to Grenoble. In the event, the 15 August landing was not seriously opposed and this is exactly what happened. Within a fortnight French Section FANYs from MASSINGHAM were on their way by air to Aix-en-Provence:

> We taxied along a runway remarkable for the number of bomb craters on either side of it. It was night-time before we packed into jeeps to move to our destination, which turned out to be Avignon. All along the route we were constantly stopped by excited groups of Resistance workers, most of them armed with a motley selection of guns and all of them prepared to fire if the answers were not in order. It was a hair-raising progress.

Betty Hannah made a flying visit to her French stepmother near Aix, whom she had not seen since 1942, before her adventurous journey over the Pyrenees. Sympathetic pilots gave her lifts. Captain Betty Sale, in granting her leave, remarked, 'Mind you come back'.

Avignon became an international headquarters, British, American and French. SOE's task was a debriefing one: agents were asked to give account of their missions, and whether their training and equipment had been of use. After around six weeks some FANYs went on to Paris, where the debriefing role continued. Interviews were held with agents who had been in concentration camps and who found seeing the trappings of civilization again profoundly moving.

MASSINGHAM's existence had served its purpose and, by October, 1944, the remainder of its members left for other theatres, mainly for Italy, for which campaign MASSINGHAM had already begun to prepare, and was its legacy. Douglas Dodds-Parker had already left, with the move of AFHQ to Caserta near Naples in July. He set up a small unit by the name of HQ Special Operations (Mediterranean) Liaison, code name SPEEDWELL, taking with him as coder/secretaries FANY Ensigns Vera Aungiers and Leo Railton and a small staff of soldiers. They occupied the Villa Ciombrone overlooking the Bay of Naples which had been requisitioned by Malcolm Munthe during the early days of the Italian campaign.

599 agents had been dropped from MASSINGHAM and 1,916 operations had taken place, carrying 2,000 tons of stores into southern France. Dorothy Temple's notebook of signal plans (now in the Imperial War Museum) for sets operating into MASSINGHAM total 196, though not all will have become active. They will have been worked by approximately thirty-seven FANY wireless operators, and their male counterparts, and thirty-six coders. Staff officers, secretaries, translators, clerks, drivers and others accounted for approximately forty-one. Just over 115 FANYs were stationed at MASSINGHAM, though not all simultaneously. There had been times of strain, some illness, mainly various forms of dysentery and skin problems, desert sores and impetigo. A few FANYs had been repatriated on account of sickness, but most had stood up well to the conditions. Survivors speak of the richness of the experience; memories and friendships endure.

Betty Sale was made a Member of the Order of the British Empire for her sensible care; Peggy Thynne, a senior wireless operator who had served in the Post Office before the war, and two coders who worked on MONKEY, Leo Railton and Sue Rowley, were mentioned in despatches. An unexpected tribute came from Leo Valiani, a democratic socialist who had spent many years in prison during the Mussolini years. He was at MASSINGHAM preparing to return to Italy, where he was to play a prominent part in the organization of resistance:

This is the base from which the wireless operators, English girls, tall refined and beautiful as I've never seen such in England; enchanting as if they had come out of a novel of Walter Scott, send messages to their friends who fight behind the enemies' lines in France, Jugoslavia and Greece, and they receive answers of the same kind, 'Come and land here quickly'.[11]

CHANT DES PARTISANS

C'est nous qui brisons les barreaux des prisons pour nos frè-res

Chapter Four

CAIRO

MO 4, LATER FORCE 133

Leopold Ranke's adage that history has to show 'what it [the past] was really like' has been quoted many times and I do so again. In Ranke's case, he was writing the *History of the Popes* through the medium of countless documents; in mine, I am recalling Cairo in wartime and the role and life of FANYs stationed there during the years 1943–44. My claim to be able to describe history is based upon the fact that *I was there*. 'What it was really like' is bound to have a degree of subjectivity.

Conditions could not have been more different from those at MASS-INGHAM, given in the previous chapter, but one factor remains constant. It is the common purpose of the two units: to foster resistance in the countries occupied by the enemy, by various means of support, both human and supplies; to build up indigenous forces and, where considered appropriate, perform acts of sabotage to hinder the movement of enemy troops. But even here were variations. Whereas the main thrust of MASSINGHAM's efforts was directed towards one primary target, namely France (and latterly Italy), SOE Cairo's concern was clandestine activity in most of the countries of the Balkans, whose governments and past and recent histories were, to put it mildly, volatile.

Political factors were constantly to affect military objectives and, most serious of all, many of the forces of resistance to the enemy had their own long-term political agendas, whereas SOE was in the much simpler ball game of trying to vanquish that enemy as expeditiously as possible. These two conflicting principles bedevilled SOE activities based on Cairo. Moreover, parties other than local SOE and resistance forces had an interest in the Balkans, such as the Foreign Office, SOE London, the governments in exile of the occupied territories and their monarchs, and GHQ, Middle East. All had viewpoints of infinite variety. Since all the foregoing factors so dominated what went on in Cairo, they must be kept in mind as a backcloth to the lives of all of us who happened to find ourselves in this most extraordinary of scenes.

My own arrival at the beginning of October, 1943, happened to coincide with a crucial series of events, both within the SOE office, which was known at that time as MO 4, and within what was commonly referred to as 'the field' in the Balkan countries. Inability to find suitable staff on a permanent basis was a continuing problem in the office. Originally, its members tended to be civilians who had lived in the countries of Eastern Europe in one capacity or another. It might be mining, journalism, folk-lore or botany; they were apt to be knowledgeable, yet independent. Lieutenant-Colonel S.W. Bailey and Captain (later Lieutenant-Colonel) D.T. Hudson had been employed in the British-owned Trepca mines as mining engineers; Hugh Seton-Watson was an expert in Balkan languages; Mrs Fanny Hasluck had spent over twenty years in Albania. Major Basil Davidson was a former journalist in Hungary. Gradually they were joined by members of the services and civilian secretaries and coders from London.

The staffing crisis began at the top; frequent changes of leadership had taken place. One prospective commanding officer was shot down over the Bay of Biscay by German fighters and spent the rest of the war in a prison camp. More often, the changes were the result of an annual autumnal 'purge', as a consequence of inspections from London. Lord Glenconner, who was *en poste* on my arrival, was the sixth man to run SOE Cairo in just over two years. His second-in-command was a regular soldier, Brigadier C.M. (known as Bolo) Keble, who, although a man of considerable energy and fixity of purpose, specialized in making enemies. Between them they managed greatly to increase the number of missions in the Balkans, but without the forward planning which would take into account the infrastructure of support which was needed at base. For example, signal traffic from the field began to escalate to such an extent that it exceeded the capacity of the coders in Cairo to decypher it. Although the crisis has been exaggerated in the telling over the past fifty years (serious technical difficulties responsible also were comprehensible only to signals officers), problems undoubtedly existed. In addition, criticism was often levelled at MO 4 as to their reading of events on the ground, sometimes unfairly, as field staff had a clearer vision and more realistic grasp of conditions than the armchair critics.

Within a few days of his being made head of SOE, General Gubbins left for the Middle East. His first stop was Cairo, where he landed on 15 October, nine days after my own arrival. (He later went on to MASSINGHAM). News presently percolated that Lord Glenconner had resigned and would be returning to England and that Brigadier Keble had been posted elsewhere. Our new boss was to be Brigadier William Stawell MC, a Sapper who had been Deputy Director of Military Intelligence at the War Office in 1940 and had served in the Balkans in World War I. He was to be promoted to Major-General (I was to see him on an almost daily basis on my move to his headquarters in Italy). As Stawell was General Maitland Wilson's choice, General Gubbins had seen fit to acquiesce that a soldier be placed to head SOE Cairo with effect from 20 November, 1943. The name of the unit was changed from MO 4 to Force 133.

It was agreed that General Stawell should move his office to Italy as soon as possible, and that overall direction of activity in the Balkans should pass from GHQ Middle East to AFHQ (then in Algiers, later to move to Caserta). Also agreed was that political decisions should still continue to be made in SOE London, but that some degree of local autonomy should remain with SOE Cairo.

Activity in the field in the Balkans, in the way of infiltration of agents after the retreat of June, 1941, began in September of that year. The following is a cursory and greatly simplified account of events as they stood at the time of my own entry on the Cairo scene. It provides a background to the work which we were all called upon to do. At the end of August, 1941, British clandestine radios based in Malta and at the naval station in the estuary of the Severn picked up messages from the mainland of Jugoslavia, south of Belgrade. A Serb officer of the royal Jugoslav Army, Colonel Draza Mihailovic, was trying to make contact. It was the beginning of a relationship which was to cause not ripples, but great waves of controversy, during the next fifty years or so, breaking out afresh as the documents of the case and the experiences of the officers concerned were examined once again. In the belief that here was an attempt to offer organized resistance to the German/Italian occupation, SOE Cairo put ashore from a British submarine on the coast of Jugoslavia on 20 September, 1941, Captain Duane (usually known as 'Bill') Hudson with two Jugoslav officers, Major Ostojic and Major Lalalovic, together with a Jugoslav wireless operator. The code name of the mission was BULLSEYE. The party took two radio sets which did not last long: one could not be carried easily and required mains electricity; the other burned itself out. Hudson was out of contact with Cairo for some months during bad weather conditions.

Before making contact with Mihailovic and his followers, who were known as Cetniks, Hudson came across an unexpected source of resistance to the enemy in the shape of Josef Broz, nicknamed Tito, and his Partisans, of whom he was previously unaware. On reaching Mihailovic, Hudson tried to effect a united front between the two, and was nearby when they met, but without success. By the spring of 1942 Mihailovic's profile and reputation had strengthened: he became a popular hero, had been promoted General and appointed Minister for War by the Jugoslav government-in-exile. SOE, anxious for more information as to the situation, sent in some additional agents, whose missions did not succeed.

Eventually, in December 1942, Lieutenant-Colonel S.W. Bailey, another fluent Serbo-Croat speaker, was parachuted into Serbia on Christmas Day with the code name RAPIER. His brief was to report on the military value of the Cetnik movement. He was followed by additional missions, several of which were manned by Canadians of Jugoslav origin, until there were ten in the country by the spring of 1943; supplies were dropped to them. Finally, a decision was made to send a Military Mission to Mihailovic, code name SERBONIAN, led by a senior officer, Brigadier Charles Armstrong. In September, 1943, he arrived with a team of saboteurs who carried out the destruction of several strategic targets. At the same time disturbing news was being received of collaboration on the part of Mihailovic and his troops with German and Italian forces, and with the puppet government, led by Milovan Nedic and under enemy control. This was not all. Other reports implied that Cetniks, rather than fighting Germans, were fighting Partisans.

In Cairo, through the medium of a previous posting, Brigadier Keble was in receipt of decrypts of intercepted German signals traffic from the Balkans, which appeared to him to confirm the truth of these suspicions. It also seemed to suggest that the Partisans were a good deal stronger, better organized and more effective in the harassing of the enemy than had been previously supposed. A mission to Tito was mounted in May, 1943, with the name TYPICAL, led by Major (later Lieutenant-Colonel) William Deakin, a former Oxford don, who had assisted Winston Churchill with historical research, and a member of the staff of SOE Cairo. Partly on account of his reports and of the intercepts, a Military Mission was sent to Tito, as the result of high-level discussions in London. Its leader, Lieutenant-Colonel (to become Brigadier) Fitzroy Maclean, a member of SAS and a Member of Parliament, was the appointment of Winston Churchill himself.[1]

On Maclean's arrival in Cairo he and a greatly incensed Brigadier Keble had a stormy meeting in Rustum Buildings, the seat of SOE Cairo, which caused lasting damage to Maclean's overall opinion of SOE. On 8 September, 1943, Bill Deakin, in Bosnia, received a telegram from Cairo to warn him to expect Maclean; he arrived by parachute on 17 September and was taken by truck to the town of Jajce, where Tito had his headquarters. The two men began their long association with a discussion on how the forces they represented could help each other.

A similar situation as in Jugoslavia, in regard to organized resistance, developed in Albania, except that it divided itself not only on political but also on racial and geographical lines. The two main racial groups were Ghegs to the north and Tosks to the south. By the end of 1941 an Albanian Communist

Party had been formed among the Tosks under the leadership of the Comintern-trained Enver Hoxha, who in September, 1942, formed a partisan movement under political direction, Levisiya Nacional Clirimtara or LNC. The first SOE mission entered Albania, via Greece, in April, 1943. It was led by Lieutenant-Colonel 'Billy' Maclean, with Major David Smiley, and code-named CONCENSUS. Contact was made with the LNC. They also later encountered rival organizations of more conservative elements which had established themselves in the northern Gheg territory, the Bali Kombetar (BK) and Zogists under the leadership of Abas Kupi. He had unsuccessfully attempted to persuade the movements to work together.

British missions were later despatched to both north and south, though conditions remained difficult and there were some serious losses of life. Late in 1943 a British Military Mission was infiltrated, led by Brigadier E.F. (usually known as 'Trotsky') Davies, with Lieutenant-Colonel Arthur Nicholls as second-in-command. They were over-run by the enemy, with Albanian collaborators; Nicholls died of exposure after winning the George Cross; Davies became a prisoner-of-war.

Ill-fortune also followed early attempts to penetrate Romania, Bulgaria and Hungary. Major David Russell, with the code name RANJI, was killed on the first mission to Romania in June, 1943, possibly because he was known to be carrying a large number of sovereigns. Major Basil Davidson failed to enter Hungary in September, 1943, but lived to undertake further operations.

Special operations in Greece, in so far as sabotage was concerned, began with considerable success, under political conditions of great complexity. A radio set had been left with a Greek agent in Athens on the departure of the British in 1941. Through this means a reception could be arranged on 1 October, 1942 when a team of nine British officers and three sergeants under Brigadier E.C.W. Myers RE, with Lieutenant-Colonel C.M. Wood-house as second-in-command, dropped into the Delphi area of Greece. The operation, code name HARLING, had as its objective the destruction of a bridge and viaduct over the Gorgopotamos River which carried the railway which connected Salonika (and therefore ultimately Germany) to Athens and the port of Piraeus. Supplies were carried by this means from the fatherland to German troops fighting in the desert war. On 25 November, 1942, the heavily guarded bridge was put out of action for some weeks by a combined sabotage operation led by the SOE party, with the co-operation of two separate Greek resistance movements. One was a group from ELAS, a fighting force, controlled by a communist organization EAM, which had been established in September, 1941. The second group was EDES, the national republican Greek league, which was right-wing, led by Colonel Napoleon Zervas. It looked from a political point of view to General Plastiras (in exile) as its titular head. More will be heard of him in 1944. The event at the

Gorgopotamos bridge was the first and last occasion on which the two politically dissimilar organizations were to combine together. Less successful were the arrangements made to evacuate the British party. The submarine which was to relieve them was required for other purposes and Brigadier Myers was forced to remain in Greece till the following August, 1943. During this time he became increasingly aware of local conditions.

The second successful operation was a deception to try and persuade the enemy that the HUSKY invasion of Sicily in July, 1943, was, in fact, to be a landing in the Balkans. Communications were sabotaged over a wide area, under the code name ANIMALS, to give the impression that an invasion was imminent. A demolition, carried out by the SOE group, without Greek assistance, closed the Salonika-Athens railway line as it crossed the Asopos River for four months. The deception proved effective, also in that certain German divisions which might otherwise have been moved to Italy stayed put.

An RAF pick-up operation to fly out Brigadier Myers at long last included, not only Major David Wallace, a former member of the Foreign Office, who had joined him, but six Greek resistance leaders. At the last moment the ELAS representation was increased from one to four, under the leadership of Andhreas Tzimas; the other two Greeks were non-Communists, including one member of EDES. Their reception in Cairo by the Greek King George II (who had fled there into exile) and his government was icy, particularly when arguments followed that these men be included in that government. They also pleaded that the King should not return to Greece until a plebiscite agreeing to his re-instatement should have taken place, an expedient to which he was forced to accede in 1944.

Heads rolled as the result of this episode. The Greeks were swiftly returned to their native land, with Brigadier Myers forbidden to enter Greece again. The departure of Lord Glenconner and Brigadier Keble stemmed partly from this same cause. SOE was held responsible for the débâcle which was regarded as 'meddling in politics'. The return of the Greek King to his throne was part of Foreign Office policy, despite the fact that his previous connection with the right-wing dictator Metaxas had made him so unpopular that his presence in Greece was opposed. Myers had become more aware than London of conditions within Greece and the possibilities open to the waging of war in that country. It was a dilemma to be repeated in areas in which special operations were required to take part, and the same difficulties will be seen again in Italy.

A strange sequence to this event took place many years later when, in the 1970s, I had reason to visit the Cistercian Monastery of Mount St Bernard in Leicestershire. A talk with the Prior, Father Luke, revealed that he had been in the Royal Air Force in the Balkans in 1943. As Wing Commander Duncan Harris, he had been the pilot of the aircraft which had flown Brigadier Myers and his ill-fated party of Greeks out from Thessaly. Now a Trappist monk, he described the circumstances. He realized at the time the possible repercussions of the journey. At a safe distance from the event, he and I laughed at the troubles he had unwittingly unleashed.

Only one area remains to be accounted for as background to SOE Cairo and its activities. SOE missions made their way to Crete from October, 1941, and throughout 1942 and were able to remain, due to the courage and resilience of the Cretan people.

My own first impression of Cairo was of the sweltering heat. Although already October, the temperature was unusually high. On 7 October it was 118° in the shade. The hot dusty streets were crammed with humanity which seemed to represent the culture of several centuries. Donkeys, mules, carts transporting all manner of goods, handled by peasant Egyptians, poorly dressed in long white robes, formed one stratum. Their black-clad wives, often veiled, followed at a respectful distance. Other women, with sickly babies, their eyelids thick with flies, begged on the pavement. The trams that rattled their way down the main thoroughfares had scores of men clinging perilously on the outside on the narrow foot-plates, as well as crammed to suffocation within. By contrast, smart limousines with uniformed drivers bore suited businessmen and officials, with claret-coloured tarbooshes on their heads, to their places of work. Sometimes elegant women would be accompanying them, but seldom. They were not often seen in public places. Banks were like palaces, with marble floors and pillars.

The armies of several nations were well represented by officers and men in khaki-drill uniforms in various stages of wear and laundering. Soldiers wore long baggy shorts, open-necked shirts, thick woollen socks and army boots. Their headgear provided variety and distinguished British from Australians, New Zealanders and Poles. Senior officers from GHQ, who had access to batmen and dhobis, and who wore shoes, were smarter, but some of those on leave from the desert army looked strangest of all. They presented an appearance which left no doubt whatever as to whence they had come. This was doubtless the idea. A newspaper published daily for the forces (the *Union Jack*) included cartoons focused on current events and personalities. One set portrayed a couple of officers, veterans of the desert, who were named 'The Two Types': with their coloured scarves in lieu of ties, corduroy trousers and suede boots, they were drawn in various situations, sometimes in conflict with the Provost-Marshal's department. Another cartoon showed 'Jane', a nubile young woman, whose adventures involved her, all too often, losing her clothes.

A feature of the Cairo streets, at certain hours of the day and evening, was the GHQ 'bus'. Fleets of them were adapted three-ton trucks, with a row of benches fixed down each side of the back and one bench down the middle. From 7.30 until 8 am, these 'buses' would ply their way round various routes.

Men and women who worked at GHQ and MO 4 were required to get on at various specific collecting points, nearest to where they lived. Work began at 8.15. At 1.15 buses returned and the process would start again at 4.30. Evening office hours were 5 until 8 pm when the bus ran the last trip of the day.

On our arrival in Cairo, our party of five was taken to a pension on the Sharia Malika Farida (Queen Farida Street), where we found the five others who had preceded us in the Liberator from London, including my friends Eleanor Burgess and Anne Burrill, also some new arrivals from South Africa. Next day we five newcomers were shown the drill as to the nearest stopping place of the GHQ bus and bowled along a street called Kasr el Aini, parallel to the Nile. It passed an area known as the Garden City, where many officers lived in flats. At a huge building, flanked by sentries, called Grey Pillars, the GHQ contingent got off and MO 4 people remained for a few more blocks, until we reached Rustum Buildings and the home of SOE Cairo.

Various formalities and interviews followed, at the end of which I found myself, not among the coders on the fourth floor, but in a series of rooms, which also housed an emergency wireless station, built on the flat roof of the building, accessible by means of an iron ladder. Here Lieutenant-Colonel R.A. Meers, Royal Corps of Signals, recently appointed, had his office with his staff. I was to work in his department. Although I had come all this way to be a coder, it was not difficult soon to be swept into the very busy circle which revolved round the dynamic personality of the Chief Signals Officer.

More than just two heads had rolled in the autumn of 1943. The crisis caused in the summer by the delay in the decoding of telegrams had wide repercussions: members of other departments, even quite senior officers and secretaries, had been required to carry out stints of decoding to reduce the back-log. Jill Luttman-Johnson, personal assistant to Colonel Phil Macpherson, head of personnel and finance (by whom I was also interviewed) made a tour of certain towns in South Africa to recruit volunteers. Twenty-four coders had also been borrowed from GHQ. But this had not been the full extent of the Signals problem; solutions were needed to a host of technicalities. A decision was made to replace the Chief Signals Officer.

It was clear from the purposeful way in which he strode into the office each morning that Colonel Meers was a new broom, intending to sweep exceedingly clean; as a result things hummed in his vicinity and my work was reasonably interesting. I saw a number of telegrams from the field and typed outgoing ones. Most paperwork naturally concerned signals matters: provision and replacement of sets, crystals, spares, generators; but as communications were such a vital part of the missions, I knew something of what was going on, and especially on the training, the selection of wireless operators and their progress in the field. I shared one of the roof offices with Captain 'Pat' Riley, who was kind in putting me in the picture. I recall one incident where a wireless operator in Jugoslavia had reacted in such a way to his dangerous circumstances that he had come to the conclusion that he was St Paul.

Leaving the office at 1.15 meant walking into the blazing white light on the roof, with the distant shimmering view of the Citadel to the south, crowned by the vast dome of the alabaster Mohammed Ali Mosque, and its twin minarets.

The pension where we were housed left a good deal to be desired: there were eight double bedrooms for the ten of us recently arrived from England and the first members of the group from South Africa. Some of them had been employed on naval cyphers in Cape Town and were no longer required there, as fewer convoys were using that route. Everyone commented on their good looks; we English girls were envious of their clothes, in comparison with our own experience of clothing coupons which severely restricted what we could buy. SOE had taken over the whole pension which was run by a Hungarian woman with red hair by the name of Stephanie. Her ranting and raging at the Sudanese suffragis we found unattractive and prevented our hearing conversations on the telephone. Food was badly prepared and we had problems over washing and ironing our clothes; the suffragis only cleaned. Eleanor and I hung pants out on our balcony with string and safety pins. Worst of all were the insects; the floors of the bathroom at night were thick with various kinds of beetles, cockroaches and flying objects; it was impossible not to tread on them. My first-ever encounter with bedbugs was also daunting and the bites worse. A rumour was rife that the old Kasr el Nil barracks on the riverside had bugs that were the descendants of those which bit the troops of General Gordon on his way to Khartoum in the nineteenth century; they were invincible.

Most horrific of all was the death of Cynthia, one of my companions on the journey out by air. She became ill after less than a fortnight in Cairo. I recall seeing her propped up in bed in her room, a picture of misery. After a few days in hospital she died. We were never given a clear diagnosis. We had all been inoculated against several tropical diseases, including yellow fever, which she could have contracted in West Africa. (Lord Moran,[2] doctor to Winston Churchill, struggled to prevent his patient travelling to Ghana, because he considered the yellow fever injection dangerous.) My parents were not told of this sad happening in my letters home.

Shortly before the end of October news came that we were to leave the pension for fresh surroundings. One of Thomas Cook's houseboats, a paddle steamer which in peacetime took tourists up the Nile and was now moored off the far side of the island of Gezira, had been requisitioned for female personnel of MO 4. We were to be joined by others, still on their way from England, or South Africa.

Gezira, in the Nile, was a real solace to life in Cairo. About two miles long and half a mile wide, it was in 1943 a really attractive place. There were large villas with gardens, tree-lined roads and, above all, the Gezira Sporting Club, which most of us decided to join. In the daytime one could play golf, squash, tennis, cricket and polo, swim in the pool or, when there were race meetings, enjoy the horses. A restaurant provided meals at lunchtime, and in the evening dinner and dancing to a band on a cool outdoor terrace, with lights among the trees. What was so remarkable about Gezira was that, unlike the rest of Cairo, it was so *green*. Lawns, the golf course and cricket pitch were watered every morning. From the houseboat one could walk over the golf course to play tennis on a day off (once a week) in the very early morning when it was still cool. A slight worry was a warning we had received that we must *not* fall into the Nile; the water was seriously polluted and the worst contamination was caused by bilharzia, a liver-fluke which could enter one's system; the treatment was unpleasant. As we made our way over the soggy golf course in our sandals, we would imagine the liver-flukes having a field day.

The houseboat had around eighty cabins on three decks. On the top deck were wicker chairs and tables to sit out, a quiet room for writing and a dining room for meals. I was fortunate enough to have a cabin on the promenade deck, one down, and facing the river. Eleanor Burgess and I shared a bathroom which led out of our individual cabins. They were small, but had the furniture we needed – a bunk bed, wardrobe, chair and dressing table – but we were to discover that in the winter months it was very cold, for there was no heating. The only way to keep warm was to go to bed immediately after dinner. This opportunity did not come often, because we all went out in the evenings a great deal; making friends who invited us was easy. Within a few days I was being asked to dine and dance at Gezira, or other places; the *Auberge des Pyramides* was particularly attractive, or the Turf Club, the Continental Hotel, the Officers' and Sisters' Club at Heliopolis. The celebrated Shepheard's, with its exotic decor, was another favourite, but the army closed it down for a time because there had been complaints about insanitary conditions in the kitchen.

Lili Marlene was a song which was played often by bands in Cairo, adopted by the British desert army from the German *Afrika Korps*, whose favourite it was. If ever I hear it now, its sultry tune is powerfully evocative and carries me back immediately to Cairo evenings and the extraordinary life we had there – special operations during the day and dancing half the night.

Breakfast was at seven and by half-past seven we were on our way to the nearest stop of the GHQ bus, now through pleasanter surroundings than the Sharia Malika Farida, and by the Gezira route. The mooring of the houseboat was a grassy bank with palm trees; a gangway led aboard. On the opposite side of the road was a large mansion flying a Greek flag; it was the residence of the Greek King George II and offices of his government-in-exile, where the fateful meetings of the *Andartes* (guerrillas) had taken place. During the afternoons we would sleep on our bunks in the really hot weather, before going back to the office for the evening stint, or we would have lunch at Gezira. Two tea shops, by the name of Groppi, sold extraordinarily delicious cakes in an attractive setting: a real 'tea garden' outdoors under trees where it was relatively cool. Invitations to join other tables could become oppressive, because girls were so thin on the ground. Two FANYs were once walking back to Cairo for exercise from the leafy suburb of Maadi where they had spent the afternoon. Sixteen cars stopped to offer them lifts.

I enjoyed a visit to the *Mussky*, the Cairo bazaar area in an old part of the city. Here narrow covered streets, dark and mysterious, some paved, others of beaten earth, led through a maze of shops with open fronts. Men sat working, either cross-legged or on stools, at the entrances, beating copper and silver vessels, and sewing. Although some shops appeared small, they often revealed themselves as large premises, with wooden galleries and inlaid ceilings further within. Intricate silver work and elaborately embroidered brocades were displayed in glass cases. Other shops sent forth exotic smells of various kinds. I bought a few presents which were within my price range for my family.

The caller at the office one day was a friend of my parents, Wing Commander Redding, who had come to Cairo with General Gubbins, on his tour of inspection. His first words were, 'Goodness, you're like your father'. He took me to lunch and a swim at Gezira. Many years later I saw the General's report[3] on the visit, which, among other comments, expressed his admiration for the way in which Colonel Meers had reorganized the signals of MO 4: 'Meers still has a large task on hand'. The pace in his office certainly confirmed this. Another of my father's friends, Charles North of the Air Ministry, who lived in a large flat overlooking the Nile, was also kind and acted as a go-between for parcels to and from my family. He had lunch parties on Sundays where there were always a number of agreeable people. His ancestor lost Britain her American colonies, but my host told me that he had made up for it by marrying an American.

A fellow passenger on the flight out from England, had been Charles Empson, who joined the British Embassy staff; when his wife Monica came out to Cairo, I was their guest on a number of occasions. We met again years later when we all lived in Kent.

Towards the end of October Lieutenant-Colonel Tamplin died suddenly at his desk. Sudden deaths were not unknown in the field, but hardly expected on the first floor of Rustum Buildings. He had been in overall charge of the

Country Sections; each also had their own departmental head, and staff of assistants, Greece, Crete, Jugoslavia, Romania and so on, and dealt with operations in that area. Following the Italian Armistice of September, 1943, and the advance of the allied armies on the east coast of Italy, steps were taken to establish a forward base there, for the Jugoslav and Albanian country sections, from which planes could fly men and materials to the Balkans rather than continuing to use Derna in Cyrenaica, which involved a very long flight. Such a base was established in Bari in that same month (to be described in a future chapter), and the first group of girls as secretaries and coders left for Italy shortly afterwards. It included Annette Crean (Street) who had been secretary to Brigadier Keble, and Nina Tamplin, widow of Guy.

I wrote home on 9 November, just a month after my arrival, and mentioned that I had been ill for a few days. Cairo proved to be an unhealthy place, with a good deal of sickness among Europeans; probably among the population at large also, of which we were unaware. The main reason was without doubt the absence of sanitation among the poorer inhabitants. The air we breathed was heavily polluted and what we ate and drank loaded with a deposit of bacteria; and then there were the omnipresent armies of flies. The slightest scratch or bite was septic within twenty-four hours. The charming, elderly English Dr Pochin, who had spent a lifetime in Egypt, suggested sending me, with a high temperature, to hospital, but I pleaded to stay on the houseboat; luckily the hospital did not have a spare bed. The next features were large and painful sores on one foot and hands which had to be dressed each day at the Anglo-American Hospital on Gezira and covered in bandages. Lots of nice visitors cheered me up, mainly officers from GHQ in their afternoon spare time. It became necessary to be admitted to the hospital in the end, when, under a general anaesthetic, the sores on my hands and feet were opened up by an army surgeon. The next fourteen afternoons were spent lying in a wickerwork *chaise longue* on the terrace of the hospital, as I wrote to my parents 'having flirtations with the other patients similarly ensconced, and all male'. My faithful friends continued to come and see me, but I was longing to feel better and back on my feet. A bacteriologist took a blood sample, with the result that it was decided that I was to have fourteen days' convalescent leave before going back to the office. Dear old Dr Pochin, at least he seemed old to me, took me out to dinner one evening from the hospital in his car. We swapped life-stories and on hearing of my birth in Germany, told me that he had studied in Heidelburg and Frankfurt as part of his medical training. In the midst of a khaki-filled restaurant, we began to cap each other's singing of the enemy's songs, *Die Lorelei* and *Alle Vögel sind schon da*, which were among my favourites as a child.

On 2 December I finally left hospital and next day made for Alexandria. An ATS officer at GHQ, a colleague of one of my friends, had fixed up for me to stay with a family who had offered hospitality to convalescent service-women. I rushed to the office for my railway warrant and into an antiquated taxi which became rammed from behind by the fender of another in a traffic jam; the two became inseparable. Swearing in Arabic followed, and a crowd gathered, which, with gigantic heaves, managed to disentangle the two vehicles. I was set upon by Egyptian porters at the station and just caught the train to Alex.

My hosts were a French-speaking Jewish family, long established in Alexandria; a hospital and a road were called by their name, Menasce. Robert Menasce held a commission in the British Army in the Intelligence Corps; his wife Lilliane was much given to good works and ran clubs and canteens for servicemen; a young son was at boarding school. Lilliane's father and mother shared the large mansion, and in many ways, her mother, Linda, was the most remarkable member of the family; dark and striking, she spoke five languages, had visited much of Europe and possessed a large collection of classical gramophone records which she played to servicemen on Fridays, when she also lent them novels, especially those of Proust. She and her daughter ran a free soup kitchen for poor Jewish people.

The Menasce family's circle was wide and varied. It was a fascinating fortnight that I spent among their cosmopolitan friends and shared their charitable and cultural interests. Most remarkable was that they did not move solely among Jewish families, but spread their net towards people of other religions and races. They spoke English for my benefit, but French also when they realized that I had a knowledge of the language; their kindness to a complete stranger was infinite, and they took a great deal of trouble to see that I enjoyed myself. Most of the mornings were spent sleeping until lunchtime, while during the afternoons, I accompanied Lilliane to her clubs and hospitals. In a tented hospital out at Mersa Matruh we distributed sweets and cakes to men in bed. We took an RAF pilot with badly burnt hands for a ride round Alex and I served hundreds of pieces of toast in a servicemen's club from a machine which toasted eight pieces of bread and my face in one action, before placing the toast under baked beans. A friend of Lilliane ran a clinic for poor Egyptian women in a run-down district, far from the Corniche and smart parts of Alex. Here I observed her trying to effect cures from a variety of ills that afflicted women covered from head to foot in black clothes. They were unwilling to remove any garments, and merely pointed to the source of a medical problem.

During my visit came the news that the Queen, Farida, wife of King Farouk, had given birth to her third daughter. Everyone was agreed that her days as a consort were thereby numbered.

Most enjoyable of all, during my time in Alex, was crewing for various members of the Yacht Club in dinghy races round the various naval vessels in the harbour. One of them asked me rather nervously before setting off whether I could swim. On my last afternoon, crewing for a naval officer, which was rather a cheat, we came in first in our race. Evenings were spent at concerts, a play, a cinema and many dinner parties. Much recovered and refreshed, but also longing to be back at my job, I returned to Cairo and the office on Sunday 18 December, after sick leave of six weeks and three days. I was expecting recriminations from my colleagues, but there was a warm welcome from the Colonel downwards, which made me realize how ill I had been. (I had no time off for medical reasons for the remainder of my two years' abroad.) There was masses of work, which was welcome. What I had missed most while away was my mail from friends and family; it was wonderful to find nineteen letters waiting for me on my return from Alex.

During my weeks on sick leave two events had taken place in Cairo of which I was unaware. The first was the conference at Mena House, near the Pyramids, of President Roosevelt, Winston Churchill and their large staffs, together with the Chinese General Chiang Kai-shek, with the code name SEXTANT. It took place from 22 to 26 November, when many of those present flew on to Teheran to be joined by Josef Stalin at a second conference with the code name EUREKA from 28 November to 1 December. Among the subjects discussed was the second front in western Europe, OVERLORD; also the landing in southern France, ANVIL (later called DRAGOON). At the latter conference, the decision was taken to support Tito's Partisans. Churchill and President Roosevelt returned to Cairo when SEXTANT resumed on 3 to 7 December and Churchill took the opportunity, while in the Middle East, to discuss Jugoslavia with several members of SOE out of the field.

Fitzroy Maclean flew from Jugoslavia to Cairo to meet Churchill and brought Bill Deakin out with him. General Gubbins was also present.[3] The decision to support the Partisans had already been made and that supplies should no longer be sent to Mihailovic, because of the danger (expressed by Colonel Bailey) that he might use them to fight his own countrymen. Mihailovic's concern, it was considered, was more to consolidate his own forces, with a view to the political future when hostilities were over, than to oppose the Germans in the short term. Reprisals, undoubtedly a consequence, would have harmed those upon whom he depended for support. Churchill maintained after the war that, useful though these personal testimonies were, and the reports already sent in by these officers as to the strength and organization of the Partisans, they only confirmed what he had gathered already from the decrypts of enemy signals traffic.[4]

The second event of consequence in the last month of 1943, as the result of the lifting of the ATS embargo, was the arrival of the first group of FANYs on 3 December: twenty young coders under the command of Captain Norah Coggin. She was tall, slim and had style, in her thirties, with long fair hair pinned into what was then called a 'French pleat'. Her dress uniform (which she wore exclusively) was well-cut and elegant; she was determined that her charges should appear the same. The girls' hair was required to be above collar length and there were to be no sling handbags; FANYs might carry leather brief cases. Cream shirts could be made in Cairo, in place of the khaki ones, and silk stockings worn off duty, instead of the issue lisle variety. The result was what she set out to achieve: the FANYs presented a very smart appearance. I recall an occasion after I had myself become a FANY and was living in the mess; she spotted a sartorial flaw in mine. It had to be put right at once.

As living quarters the FANYs had been assigned a large mansion built of white stone and marble in the suburb of Heliopolis, seven miles outside Cairo; two other similar houses, for sleeping only, were later requisitioned, when four more groups of FANYs arrived. Each house was surrounded by wrought-iron railings, and there were wide marble steps leading to a pillared porch and front door. Inside the walls were white and the floors and staircase again marble. Meals were very formal, according to Captain Coggin's wishes. FANYs sat at a long table, with two wings, and were served by tall Sudanese suffragis, dressed in white robes, white turbans and sashes of different colours. Within five days of the arrival of the FANYs, Generals Gubbins and Stawell had been asked to dinner.

The seven-mile drive down to Rustum Buildings was accomplished in a three-ton truck provided with benches, similar to the GHQ bus. Other members of the SOE staff, housed in a nearby mess, used it as well. The FANYs were soon assimilated into the Cairo routine, as we earlier arrivals had been: fairly arduous work, followed by crowds of invitations during free time. As the first group were all coders their working hours were on a shift basis. The signal traffic to be decoded reached the coding office by teleprinter from the transmitters and signal office which were situated beyond Mena House and the Pyramids. There were no FANY wireless operators in Cairo; those who worked out at Mena were all men, members of the Royal Corps of Signals. The contents of messages had a wide range: requests for various supplies and stores, ammunition, clothing for troops; information on the enemy, its movements, disposition and strength; sabotage carried out; the state of resistance forces and their morale; the weather for the assistance of air operations. Telegrams to be encoded came by hand from other departments in Rustum Buildings.

Brigadier Keble had claimed in September, 1943, that he had eighty missions in the Balkans. This is thought to have been somewhat of an exaggeration and may have included main-line stations such as London, Algiers, Tunis, Istanbul, and later, Bari. Certainly, by early 1944, more missions had been established, particularly in Greece, and the traffic, despite the efforts of Colonel Meers to rationalize it, and prevent the sending of long signals, was heavy. For example, the report of Colonel Bailey from the Mihailovic mission of RAPIER in November, 1943, took ninety-two separate signals.

Those from the field, from Greece, Albania and Jugoslavia, were at that time all in double-transposition codes, as taught to the FANYs in England. Coders varied in speed and competence, some, such as Alice Holland (Bridgewater), excelled in decoding so-called 'indecypherables' – signals which came in with a large number of 'corrupt groups' – and she sat in a separate room and enjoyed the challenge. The bad smell at night through the windows of the coding room has been mentioned by several of those who worked there and that it was thought to emanate from the incinerators of a neighbouring hospital. As the weather became warmer, the girls would buy garlands of flowers, such as syringa, and hang them at the windows as a remedy.

When the drastic shortage of coders had become apparent in the summer, the RAF had been asked whether members of the Women's Auxiliary Air Force might be made available. A small group of WAAF cipher officers arrived in Cairo much at the same time as the FANYs and were accommodated on the same houseboat as myself. As they were all commissioned, difficulties presented themselves as the WAAFs took their places beside the FANYs, with no more and no fewer responsibilities; the latter, despite their officer status, were mostly corporals at best. When one of the WAAF officers came up for her automatic promotion, a Lieutenant in the Royal Corps of Signals appealed to Colonel Meers; one of the coders, of whom he was in charge, was of a higher rank than himself. In fairness to the FANYs, it must be said that it was the WAAFs who minded this situation most.

Captain Coggin tried hard to prevent her unit from falling ill and made some rules regarding the consumption of Groppi cakes; the sight of them drove girls wild after years of rationing and she tried to prescribe one only a day for the first three weeks. Certain restaurants were recommended as safer than others. Despite her precautions, many FANYs succumbed; some went to the 15th Scottish General Hospital on the banks of the Nile opposite Gezira, or to a sick bay which was created in the mess; one of the coders was withdrawn to become a medical orderly. Elizabeth Mercer, who came to work as a clerk in Colonel Meers' office, was repatriated with recurrent dysentery.

At Christmas the weather in the daytime was warm and sunny, but quite cold at night. Dancing at Gezira took place indoors. There were lots of invitations and good parties, even some with turkey and plum pudding. The Anglican Cathedral at eight o'clock on Christmas Day was filled with British soldiers, and their voices dominated the sopranos in the singing of hymns. I managed to have Christmas Day as my day off in that week; otherwise it would have been work as usual.

Despite my long absence in November, there was no attempt to prevent my going on leave in February. The seven-day opportunity came up as a matter of course. Anne Burrill and I decided to go to Palestine, as it was then called. We left Cairo in early afternoon of 4 February, 1944, by a train which had *wagon lit* carriages. Anne had been on duty all night in the coding office, so was tired. I was determined to experience crossing the Suez Canal and my first view of Asia, and did so. At Kantara, then the frontier with Palestine, we were all required to disembark for inspection of passes and vaccination certificates, which fortunately we had been warned to take with us. Those who could not produce them were vaccinated by a doctor in an office on the station. The celebrated Palestine Police, in their astrakhan hats, were in charge in force. Our beds had been made up when we re-entered the train and we slept until alighting at Lydda at 5.30 in the morning. It was unexpectedly cold on the platform. We were glad of hot sweet tea with condensed milk in sawn-off beer bottles and buns filled with sausage meat from the station NAAFI. The railway track to Jerusalem at that time (it has long disappeared) ran on a separate gauge from the rest. It wound its way round a series of mountains up to the city at the height of 2,900 feet. Our carriage was filled with Army padres.

Anne and I stayed at the YWCA which had much-needed central heating and such unexpected memories of home as coloured blankets, bedside lamps, and, at meals, flowers on the tables which had patterned table-cloths. We even had breakfast brought to us in bed. We walked a great deal – it was cool enough to do so – and visited Bethlehem, Nazareth, the Lake of Tiberius and various Christian sites in Jerusalem itself. The YMCA had various tours, as Jerusalem was a popular leave-centre for service men and women in the Middle East. In the evenings films and concerts were arranged. One bus journey down to the Dead Sea from the heights of Jerusalem to 1,300 feet below sea level we found extraordinary. At the sea's edge the atmosphere was heavy and oppressive and there was no sound except the occasional lapping of a wave against the shore, no birds, no habitation except for the huts of the extractors of minerals. The Jordan Valley to the north was a surprise, green and lush with palm trees and cultivated fields. With our military passes we were permitted to cross the river on the metal Allenby Bridge, which at that time marked the frontier of Palestine with Transjordan.

The mountainous nature of the countryside attracted us particularly, perhaps on account of our recent experience of Egypt. We revelled in wonderfully fresh air on the top of the Mount of Olives and a hill near Ain Karim where we climbed a rocky path to reach the top. Altogether, it was, I seem to remember, the countryside with its associations, rather than the somewhat tawdry shrines, which we felt entitled Palestine to be called the Holy Land. The journey back to Cairo after six days was made boring on the train by the attentions of a couple of King's Messengers who were short of female company. Some officers on leave to whom we turned for support were not much help either. Unfortunately, the overnight train was several hours late in Cairo and I fled from the station straight to the office, where fortunately not a word was said beyond, 'Had a good trip?'

It was not only the weather that began to heat up that spring. First came a *khamsin*, a type of hot desert wind; the velocity was tremendous – palm trees bent double and the noise was frightening. As for the dust, it was all-pervasive, up in the air like a thick yellow cloud, so that it was dark in the middle of the day, and in our eyes, ears, noses, throats and teeth. A thick layer of grey sediment lay over furniture in my cabin and all my possessions.

It was a Wagnerian prelude to a change in my mode of living. In March word went out that the FANY Commandant, Marian Gamwell, and her sister Hope, had returned to Cairo and were to conduct interviews with those wishing to join the Corps. I should have done so when in England, had this been permitted by Cairo, but now I made my application with four others and everything moved very quickly: a medical examination and an interview with the Gamwells, when they asked me about my schooling and interests. Later the same day I signed on. Next day Captain Coggin took us to the officers' shop in the Kasr el Nil barracks to be measured for our uniforms. Two were to be made, one in barathea and the other in khaki drill, also a greatcoat. Within a few days came the first fitting and within a week the clothes were ready. Coggin insisted on accompanying us to the tailor to see that she approved; she ordered an alteration to the neck of my jacket. Then came a visit to the ATS stores for underclothes, water bottles, tin hat, shirts, khaki drill skirts and bush-jackets and so on. The striped flannel pyjama trousers were rather short in the leg (the big sizes had all gone), but they were indestructible and I was still wearing them in Oxford during the cold winter of 1946–47.

During the short wait for my uniform there was a drama of the first order. One evening at the office all girls and anyone who worked in or with the coding room were told to report to the medical officer in the gloomy basement of Rustum Buildings, where we found a macabre scene. At a table, with a bunsen burner in which to sterilize his instruments, sat an officer of the Royal Army Medical Corps conducting a mass vaccination. Everyone was herded into queues and told to present their bare left arms. A scratch was made on each by the MO with a knife which he then placed in the flame of the bunsen burner. A vaccine was placed upon the mark by a medical orderly standing alongside, plus a piece of sticking plaster. Several soldiers, who worked in association with codes, fainted. We were told that one of the coders on the houseboat was in hospital with smallpox. Those who lived there were told to return immediately and await further instructions. A rumour went round that we should be remaining on the houseboat in quarantine, but by the morning it became clear that we were to go to the office as usual as an operational necessity, but not permitted anywhere else in Cairo in our free time until a clearance certificate that our vaccinations had reacted satisfactorily had been issued. Jan Smith, aged nineteen, who had contracted the disease and occupied a cabin three doors away from mine, tragically died a few days later. No further cases were traced among SOE staff. Ensign Gwen Gurnat, a senior coder from MASSINGHAM who was posted to the Cairo coding room about this time, considered that some measure of disinfecting the premises should have taken place, as she was allocated a place to sit previously occupied by the girl who had died of smallpox.

As with the temperature so also the volume of work in the office increased in March and April, as did my social life. Some of my friends had been posted away, but there were now others. Dinners and dancing, concerts and plays at the Opera House, with London actors, proliferated. Some weeks held almost too many invitations. I enjoyed most of them and was fortunate to meet people with whom it was fun to talk and laugh and try to dance like Fred Astaire and Ginger Rogers. As soon as my uniform was ready I moved up to the FANY mess at Heliopolis. It was sad to leave the houseboat which had been my home for five months, but I came to prefer the new situation on the edge of the desert. At night, on the flat roof under a huge dark canopy of sky and bright stars, I could hear the 'Last Post', as one bugle after another sounded from the various tented camps in the vicinity, and the howling of pariah dogs. A slightly earlier start in the morning was a disadvantage, with a call at 6.30 am; the transport to the office came at seven-fifteen. The girls were friendly and welcoming; I shared a bedroom with two secretaries, Margaret Brown (Kemp) and Hazel Greenwood (Turner), who had come on the last and final convoy of FANYs to Cairo, making about sixty in all. A third house had been requisitioned; coders, who were all on shifts, slept in the 'outhouses' and those on daytime work in the main mess, but, on account of the shift system, the full complement never ate at the same time. Captain Coggin, on her own in command, withdrew Evelyn Green from coding, made her an Ensign and placed her in charge of some of the domestic arrangements: supervising the Sudanese staff and the watchmen who guarded the houses and escorted the shift workers to their quarters as they came and went during the night. A night watchman slept on a mat just inside the locked main gate of the mess. Although we were not officially allowed to go out more than a certain number of times during the week with late passes, this was seldom observed and we would whisper 'Isma' (Listen) loudly from outside to wake the watchman, and he would let us in to creep up the marble stairs to our bedrooms.

The nightwatchmen were called Boabs. Evelyn Green was on good terms with them all and wrote several descriptions of them.[5] One which bears repetition follows:

Boab Talk

As I have lain on my bed in the hot darkness of Egypt
I have listened to the Boabs below having their nightly conversation.
And I wondered what they spoke about,
When the sky was dark and starry and the air still warm.
Was it the high prices of food they discussed or the famine in Upper
    Egypt?
Was it politics, Nahas Pasha and cabinet changes?
Or the bloated Farouk and his lack of male heirs that absorbed them?
And were they joined by the soldiers from over the road
Who had beaten up a man in the guard house that very morning?
Did they discuss the British and their allies
Who swarmed over the country like the eleventh plague of Egypt
And whose womenfolk lived in the houses the Boabs were paid to
    protect?
Or did they speak of their sons and the many blessings of Allah
Who had kept them in health and life in spite of themselves?
As I lay there in the darkness, waiting to be cooler,
I often wished that I understood their language.

FANYs could ask friends to meals, first having introduced them to Captain Coggin, and there were parties every fortnight in the mess, when evening dresses might be worn and there was dancing to a gramophone. She put out an edict later in April that there was to be no exercise in the middle of the day and everyone was to rest, on account of the prevalence of ill-health. She made threats of homeward journeys for those who could not stand the climate. Spending lunch breaks in the garden at Gezira, or at the YWCA, became a practice, rather than face the hot journey backwards and forwards out to Heliopolis in the heat of the day. The YWCA was housed in a lovely palace-like building, with moorish carved screens, galleries, marble floors and Persian rugs. There was a cool garden, places to write, beds to lie on and good food. (I often wonder whether, after the war, sufficient gratitude was offered to the YMCA for the extremely high standard of hospitality they offered to service people.)

The FANY secretaries worked for the most part in the Country Sections in Rustum Buildings – Margaret Brown in the Greek Section with Major Denys Hansom who had been in the field, and Captain Oliver Churchill also, in the Dodecanese islands. They taught her shooting on her day off: 'Four kinds of guns altogether; three revolvers and a sub-machine gun'. She and Hazel had a bad experience on a visit to the Pyramids with a Staff Sergeant with whom Margaret worked in the Greek Section. Climbing up the Great Pyramid was a feat which many felt must be attempted. (It has long since been forbidden.) Both girls had hauled themselves up, reached the top and were on their way down, jumping from one huge stone to the next. Staff-Sergeant Skinner was standing on the stone above Margaret, clutching her hand, when he caught his toe and pitched forward. She let go of his grasp (for which action she later continued to blame herself) and he fell to the bottom and died instantly. She was extremely fortunate not to fall also. The incident did not cease to haunt the girls; it was difficult to know what there was to say in the way of comfort.

FANYs who liked to ride found horses at a Remount Depot at nearby Abbasiya Barracks. Anne Butler wrote to her aunt in England that she would rise at five o'clock in the morning, before it grew too hot, to ride in the desert on her day off.

Gwen Johnson, as a Lieutenant signal planner with Major Grice in the signals department, had a car to take her to the office each day. As one of her duties, she was required to enrol into the FANY and supervise the training of an interesting recruit. (Her later mission from MASSINGHAM has already been described.) In the spring of 1944 a Polish woman Krystina Gizycki (born Skarbek), known by her pseudonym Christine Granville, came frequently to the signals office on the roof of Rustum Buildings for training as a possible wireless operator for work in the field. A series of adventures through the Balkans had brought her from Poland, where she had already undertaken some undercover work, to Cairo. She was not beautiful in the formal sense, but she had qualities of fascination which men found irresistible. When she entered a room every officer looked up; even the austere Colonel Meers became animated. She was to use her unique charm in the courageous operation which she carried out in southern France.

The first FANY coders to go to Italy to the forward base (then called Force 266) left by sea on 4 April, 1944, to join those civilian girls who had been in Bari since the autumn. A decision was made by General Stawell, prompted by various military authorities, that all women in SOE in Italy should become members of the FANY Corps. The next group of civilian girls to go, which included a number of those recruited in South Africa, were interviewed and enrolled as FANYs. It was a similar process to that which had operated in the case of civilians who had worked at Baker Street and then left for MASSINGHAM. The fact that some of the girls already in Bari did not care to become FANYs is part of another chapter.

Work for those who remained was busier than ever. Although only April, the temperature soared; sometimes the usual day off had to be missed. After such a time, a newly-arrived friend, Lieutenant Christine Phillips, a signal planner replacing Gwen Johnson who had gone to Italy, and I decided to make a trip before we ourselves left Egypt. Arranged by a services welfare organization, we joined a day tour to Memphis and Saqqara. Accompanied by three army officers and a British corporal, we set off in a car. We passed the Citadel and the City of the Dead (so-called as a place of tombs abandoned after a plague) and headed ten miles south of Cairo to the ruins of the former Egyptian capital of Memphis. Beyond stood a cluster of smaller pyramids than the ones at Giza, built in a series of steps, diminishing in size. We also entered some tombs which contained remarkable carvings and hieroglyphs; particularly interesting was the burial place of a statesman by the name of Ti, and we promised ourselves another visit. In my case this did not take place for forty-five years.

Advance notice of my own posting to Italy, as part of a large group of FANYs, came up in the middle of May. Lieutenant-Colonel Seddon had been appointed as Chief Signals Officer of General Stawell's new headquarters in Italy, HQ, Special Operations (Mediterranean) at Mola di Bari, fifteen miles from Bari itself. I was to work for him. Jimmy Grice and Pat Riley were to go also from the Cairo signals office. Just at that moment a letter came from my mother with the news that my father, to whom I was devoted, was to fly to Cairo to attend a conference in the very near future.

An application to Colonel Meers for a short postponement of my posting on compassionate grounds followed and was accepted with good grace. On 17 May I managed to gain news that a plane carrying my father would be arriving at an airstrip in the desert that night. I rang the appropriate office at 9 pm and this was confirmed. Anne Butler agreed to come with me to meet him (she was the most stalwart and loyal of friends). We found a taxi driver who pronounced himself willing to follow a metalled road, miles into a barren landscape of sand. At the gates of the airfield I paid off the taxi driver, considering that it would be my father's responsibility to get us home. The sentry was bewildered to see us, but allowed us to pass and, once inside the perimeter, we heard that a plane was due in twenty minutes. To see my father descending the steps of the plane was a tremendous thrill. There was a car to meet him, so the return journey to the FANY mess was achieved without difficulty.

The next five days were full of pleasure as I accompanied my father when we were both free to lunches and dinners. I had a tea party at the mess for him to meet some of my friends and he had one at Mena House for some of his colleagues. 'You are hostess' he said. I was young enough to be pleased. My father bought me a pair of soft leather shoes with crepe soles to replace my army issue ones which squeaked. There was immediate notice of the change and relief at the office. We went together to the chapel of the Royal Artillery Base Depot (in whose parish lay the FANY mess) on Sunday, and had breakfast with the Padre, Tom Adler, the day before my father left. The draft to Italy had gone without me and I settled down to await an air passage. I welcomed the extra time, for I had come to fall in love during the last months in Cairo, my first experience of such strong emotions. J was handsome, with good brains and a short fuse. The relationship lasted longer than it should have done and burnt itself out by the spring of 1946. In the meantime we wrote copious letters and met occasionally during the next year, whenever the war allowed. As he was due to be posted to Palestine, leaving Cairo was not an issue.

No one who experienced Cairo in wartime could ever forget it. Especially to have been part of SOE was so far from the ordinary run of life as to have been particularly memorable. 'It is all such a tremendous adventure,' wrote one FANY back to England; many shared this view. Unhappily, MO 4/Force 133 has continued to draw criticisms, not all of them deserved. That mistakes were made cannot be denied, but the operational role of SOE was not understood by regular forces; the need for secrecy was part of the problem. Communications with the field provided endless technical difficulties and only signals officers really understood the full extent of them; certainly not those who spoke of the suppression of telegrams which the system, however laborious, did not allow.

Those of us who worked in Rustum Buildings recognized the efforts made by the very brave men who served in the Balkans under harsh conditions. They succeeded in hampering the movement of enemy troops by their sabotage. Helped by their encouragement and the supplies that were sent in, the indigenous resistance forces (which were much larger than anyone realized) managed to pin down Axis divisions that would otherwise have been sent to other fronts. The fact that these resisters were also fighting their own battles was no fault of SOE. It was a relief in many ways to go to Italy, but the same problems were to arise there also.

During the day of 3 June I heard that my flight from the airfield of Cairo North would probably leave that night. A truck came to fetch me with my belongings and I flew at midnight, the only girl on a crowded plane. We reached Benghazi early next morning. Breakfast of waffles, bacon and maple syrup (all together) followed, in an American mess where the absence of loos for women was a problem that had to be surmounted. Malta was to be the next stop; the pilot invited me to sit in the cockpit as we flew over the Mediterranean. 'Is that one of ours?' he asked of the observer as we passed a ship far below. A signal was flashed with a lamp and there came a reassuring answer. After lunch in Malta, we flew on to Bari, and my life for the next fourteen months, in Italy.

Chapter Five

SOUTHERN ITALY – I

MONOPOLI: NO. 1 SPECIAL FORCE: MARYLAND

Although the British and American allies had since 1941 continued to bear in mind how the Italians could be detached from their German co-belligerents, a decision to invade Italy was not taken hurriedly. As already written, it was not until the Casablanca Conference of January, 1943, that an invasion of Sicily became certain and not until the second Washington Conference of May later that year that a definite arrangement was made as to the invasion of the Italian mainland. It is hardly surprising. It was a very hazardous campaign; quite how hazardous did not become apparent until it was under way.

SOE activities in Italy before the armistice were handled through Switzerland by the Italian (J) Section of SOE in London under Lieutenant-Colonel C.L. Roseberry. The Allied landing in Sicily of 10 July and on the mainland of Italy on 4 September, in addition to the armistice, considerably increased the potential scope for special operations. The Italian J Section at MASSINGHAM was thereby in need of augmentation. Squadron Leader Harold Crawshaw had been the sole officer and he had to be repatriated on medical grounds. As well as his replacement, Captain (later Major) 'Teddy' de Haan, a number of colourful personalities emerged who had the required experience of the language and landscape of Italy. They were characteristic of a sizeable section of SOE intake: men of cosmopolitan background, yet often British, or partly British origins, and liberal sympathies. One such was Major Malcolm Munthe, of mixed Norwegian and Scottish blood. Having spent much of his childhood on the Island of Capri where his father, Axel Munthe, had written his celebrated *Story of San Michele*, he was a fluent Italian speaker. He had already distinguished himself in the Norwegian campaign and acted as a Military Attaché in Stockholm.

Captain (later Major) Charles Mackintosh was born in Uruguay of New Zealand parentage and had been employed by the Shell Company in Venezuela, when he volunteered to serve in the British army. Shipped to the United Kingdom, a good athlete and swimmer, he was allocated to the SOE paramilitary training unit in Scotland. A posting to Gibraltar as a bilingual Spanish speaker followed; there he was spotted by Gerry Holdsworth and brought to MASSINGHAM as a future operations' officer. To the officers' mess one evening came the news that two potential French agents, on a practice parachute jump into the sea, were in difficulties. Charles Mackintosh and Andrew Croft, casting off all their clothes as they raced along the beach, swam out and were able to rescue them and bring them to safety. It was then they realized that they had had an appreciative audience from the verandah of the FANY mess overlooking the shore.

Another officer with an international background was Captain Dick Cooper, who had been born in Baghdad; his British father was an inspector of a tobacco company, his mother half-Italian, with some Irish blood. Fifteen years of his life had been spent in the French Foreign Legion, where he had earned a Croix de Guerre. Born in 1899, he was already forty-two years of age when he joined SOE. Some days after the allied landing in Sicily Cooper arrived in Syracuse under the name of Arturo Richardo Cavallero. An officer of considerable resource and almost as adept at collecting ships for a private navy as Gerry Holdsworth was Lieutenant Adrian Gallegos RNVR, of British and Greek ancestry. Despite frequent capture by the enemy, and as many escapes, he managed to reappear in Siena at the end of the war, seemingly none the worse for his adventures. FANYs will have had the exploits of these officers often as the focus of their working lives and been the recipients of their messages from the field. At social events in the officers' mess they would have met face to face.

The search also went out for Italian nationals, in exile for one reason or another and willing to return to Italy, there to make contact with those who could be relied upon to offer resistance to the Germans. One of the most distinguished proved to be Massimo Salvadori, son of a prominent Fascist, who had languished in Italian prisons where he was subjected to ill-treatment for his unwillingness to conform. From exile in Mexico he received a commission in the British Army under the pseudonym Max Sylvester. Leo Valiani's admiration for the FANYs at MASSINGHAM implies some degree of association between them and potential agents. Once in the field, their contact, in the case of the wireless operators and coders, would be maintained. Mary McVean records that she taught double transposition codes to a group of Italian wireless operators before they left Algiers. Two of them are identifiable: Sergeant Carlo Denario, real name Leo Donati, had served in the Italian Navy, had become a prisoner-of-war in East Africa and had volunteered to return to Italy in the allied interest. He joined Malcolm Munthe's group near Salerno and was later transferred to the wireless telegraphy school at La Selva in the south.

A second pupil of Mary's was Silvio de Fiori, born in Sicily in 1916. She remembers his 'splendid moustache and liquid brown eyes, and seemed more suited for serenading with a guitar than acting as an agent'. He was one of those infiltrated into Italy by sea from Corsica to work with an Italian resistance group in the Genoa area. Penetrated by the enemy in March, 1944, and its members arrested, Silvio was deported to Germany and did not return.

An SOE advance party accompanied the regular army as it landed in Sicily on an infantry landing craft under cover of darkness. A radio was set up with the code name VIGILANT, to which MASSINGHAM FANYs worked. The object was to try and make contact with anti-Fascists. Somewhat later the celebrated Italian philosopher and patriot Benedetto Croce was rescued by Adrian Gallegos in an Italian motor-torpedo boat from his home in Sorrento, under the noses of the Germans. The vacuum caused by the collapse of Fascism in Italy required that such men of alternative views be freed, or infiltrated, to create a fresh political and social climate. This policy involved Charles Mackintosh in an interesting operation.[1] Two middle-aged Italians of distinguished appearance, one a diplomat, the other a banker, were assigned to him as batman and driver, dressed in the uniform of British private soldiers. Furnished with the requisite passes from Allied Force Headquarters and a high priority movement order, the three appeared at Tunis airfield to fly to Sicily. They caused a lieutenant colonel and two captains with lower priority passages to be evicted from the aircraft. On arrival at Syracuse, Charles Mackintosh discharged his duty as custodian by placing the Italians under the care of Malcolm Munthe. He did not see them again in Italy, but the story does not end there. At a reception at the Italian Embassy in Argentina after the war the incoming Ambassador greeted Charles Mackintosh's father, who was a guest, and told him that he had once been responsible for cleaning his son's boots.

Leo Valiani expressed himself anxious to play his part in the new Italy:

> It is too painful to resign oneself to not being on the spot on the day when the dream of our life is coming true. Then we'll see the uprising of the Italian people and its passing into the democratic field. We eat our hearts [literally liver] out in the exhausting wait.[2]

He disembarked in the dark at Paestum on the mainland of Italy. A code had been worked out for him which he placed in a suitcase with a false bottom.

Malcolm Munthe arranged to drop him a radio set after he had arrived at his destination, which he reached on foot five days later, having walked through the German lines. The heroines of Walter Scott's novels would hear from him again.

The essential requirement for the mounting of special operations in Italy was to secure a new base in that country to shorten the lines of communication. The eastern coast had most to commend it: a series of small ports, some existing airfields and proximity to countries such as Greece, Albania and Jugoslavia, in which SOE was already working. Most important of all, the enemy was concentrating its forces in the north and west and had been driven from the area round Taranto by the activities (operation SLAPSTICK) of a British airborne division which was fortunately standing by on the coast of North Africa awaiting shipment to north-western Europe in preparation for the OVERLORD invasion.

It was not long before the initial contingent of FANYs left MASSINGHAM for the new base, which was to be called No. 1 Special Force, code name MARYLAND, (so-named after the wife of the officer who was to lead the unit, Commander Gerry Holdsworth). But first, the scene for their future involvement must be set.

Earlier groups had begun to converge on MARYLAND from various directions. Dick Mallaby had made his unique way to Brindisi on 10 September from Rome via Pescara, with the MONKEY signal plan and a B 2 set. The next to arrive was a signals party comprising three officers of whom Captain, later Major, Freddy White and Teddy de Haan (as interpreter) were two, plus two MASSINGHAM wireless operators, Sergeant Ken Royle and Sergeant Case, a Jamaican, who had been a post office operator in Kingston before the war. The officers carried side arms, the others not. They flew to Sicily by way of Malta, where they saw Italian warships making their surrender as planned. From Malta a troopship took them to Taranto overnight. On the morning of 10 September they entered the harbour by landing craft, which, with a shallow draft, was safe from mines. Sergeant Royle has left an account of what happened on their arrival. An Italian three-wheeled open truck was requisitioned for him and Sergeant Case, with their code books and a B2 set on a bale of straw, and matches to hand, in order to be able to set fire to them if unfriendly elements still remained in the neighbourhood. The officers rode in a following car. At a road block, manned by Italians, the two vehicles were stopped, but Teddy de Haan explained that for the Italians their war was over and they would soon be home, with British help.

The party drove on to Brindisi where they made contact with Dick Mallaby at Brindisi Castle and handed over the new B 2 set and a fresh signal plan DRIZZLE, devised by Dorothy Temple, recalled after over fifty years by ex-MASSINGHAM FANY wireless operators on account of its evocative name.

This was now to be the new method of communication between the two units and the only signals link for traffic back to North Africa, for the regular army as well as SOE. Radio conditions Sergeant Royle found very bad; he was taken to the Italian Naval barracks to try for better radio contact. The frustration of the FANY operators at MASSINGHAM can be imagined as they tried to listen to the poor quality of the transmissions. Sergeant Royle handed to the naval operators five further signal plans of Dorothy's, which would become future links with MASSINGHAM for operations to be planned by MARYLAND in the future. They all had jewel names: TURQUOISE, RUBY, PEARL, EMERALD and MARCASITE. He also instructed the Italians in the working of a B 2 set.

The immediate requirement was communication with Rome, with a set left there by Dick Mallaby for this purpose. An Italian officer, Captain Vassilli, volunteered to ride to Rome from Brindisi on horseback, through the enemy lines, with a code and instructions in the double transposition method. He carried out his mission satisfactorily. The RUDDER signal plan was activated and formed a clandestine link between Rome and the Italian naval wireless station at Cherito, near Brindisi. All traffic was encoded and de-coded by Dick Mallaby. He also trained around fifteen Italian wireless operators recruited by SIM, a high-grade Italian security service, *Servizio Informazioni Militare.*

Harold Macmillan paid a first visit to the mainland of Italy, which he recorded in his *War Diaries.*[3] He dined at General Eisenhower's headquarters outside Tunis. He heard that, at the Commander-in-Chiefs' conference at Bizerta two days before, it had been decided to form a Mission of some kind which would try and be in touch with Marshal Badoglio and the Italian government. The decision was taken to make it a Military Mission, with Harold Macmillan and his American counterpart as advisers. The pilot of the Flying Fortress at Tunis airfield on Monday 14 September asked this party of two generals and the two civilians where they wanted to go. Taranto or Brindisi was the reply. Were those locations not in Italy? Yes, but believed to be in allied hands. He agreed to take them to Grottaglie, about twenty miles from Taranto. They made a safe landing and caused considerable stir among members of the Italian air force. After a night spent with the Navy in Taranto, the Mission reached Brindisi by road next morning.

At the castle they found the remainder of the Italian government, whom they saw in turn: General Ambrosio, Marshal Badoglio, the King, General Roatta and later General Zanussi, whom they had already met in North Africa and Sicily during the armistice negotiations. Meetings were held on the two succeeding days. On 16 September they spoke with Prince Umberto, Prince of Piedmont, heir to the Italian throne, who spoke good English. The journey back to Tunis was tiring, because the Mitchell bomber was so crowded. Over Sicily the pilot considered he had insufficient fuel to reach Tunis. Only at the second airfield he tried was petrol forthcoming. It was not only the FANYs who made uncomfortable journeys.

Douglas Dodds-Parker was called to AFHQ the day after the announcement of the Italian armistice on 8 September. He was to go to Italy. If SOE wanted airfields and accommodation there, the Bari-Brindisi area was alone available; the terrain towards Foggia to the north was needed for regular forces. General Bedell-Smith, Chief-of-Staff to General Eisenhower, gave him written authority to requisition such facilities as were needed, and this he had copied out one hundred times. With an airlift from the British Sixth Airborne division, accompanied on the plane by his motor-cycle, he landed at Goia del Colle on about 15–16 September and travelled to Brindisi, where Gerry Holdsworth had already arrived by sea.

Dodds-Parker had an interview with King Victor Emmanuel III[4] and congratulated Dick Mallaby on his achievements since last they met. Dick was awarded an MC for his work on MONKEY. He then, on his motor-cycle, placed the requisition notices on as many doors, between Bari and Brindisi, as he supposed would be necessary for the future working of SOE in those areas. Gerry Holdsworth had a particular eye on the facilities in the town of Monopoli, where many buildings were selected. A group of future officers of No. 1 Special Force travelled from Malta to Taranto on the schooner *Gilfredo*, which Andrew Croft had requisitioned in Sardinia: Major Peter Lee, Major (later Lieutenant-Colonel) Richard ('Dick') Hewitt, Captains, later Majors, Alan Clark and Edward Renton, and Charles Mackintosh. They set sail on 26 September and, in spite of the absence of washing or lavatory accommodation, or indeed cabins, a group of around twenty enjoyed the two and a half days without responsibilities sailing on the Mediterranean. The captain threw out a sea anchor from time to time so that passengers could swim. On arrival at Taranto on 29 September they were told by the Naval-Officer-in-charge that they had sailed through two minefields.

On the same day Harold Macmillan flew to Malta, where a conversation on armistice terms was to be held on HMS *Nelson* between General Eisenhower and Marshal Badoglio. The General stressed the paramount importance of the waging of war against Germany; a declaration of hostilities was Marshal Badoglio's duty as soon as possible. Furthermore, the Italian government must assume an anti-Fascist complexion if it was to join with the Allies; their cooperation would depend on this point. The required undertakings were made by the Marshal: the fight would be against Fascism and against Germany; Badoglio, on behalf of Italy, declared war on their erstwhile ally on 13 October. Thus far the omens were good for No. 1 Special Force as it prepared to work and live among Italian people.

For some weeks MARYLAND signals traffic needed to be routed via MASS-INGHAM and worked by FANYs in North Africa. Early in October Captain

Derrick Scott-Job arrived in Brindisi from the Salerno area to take over MARY-
LAND communications; shortly afterwards the first mobile signals unit arrived
from MASSINGHAM. It was the one which had been used by exercise SPARTAN
in Dunbar earlier in the year, well-known as part of their training by many of
the FANYs. Even then, to quote Derrick Scott-Job, the equipment had been
out-of-date and caused endless technical problems. Now in Brindisi, it
was well past its prime; it would give the occasional excited 'chirp' which was
unreadable as morse code.

At a conference presided over by General Gubbins in the middle of October
it was decided that MARYLAND should be given its own charter and maintain
its own communications. Independence from MASSINGHAM may thereby
have been established, but the equipment was poor and it took, in some cases,
a while before a change in field signal plans, to work within Italy, rather than
to North Africa, could be effected. However, a start had been made with
creating radio links with Italian missions: PEARL, with wireless operator Rocco
and code name SEAWEED, had dropped to Bologna on 2 October; MARCA-
SITE with operator Acciarino, was in an area south of Ancona, as was RUBY,
whose operator was unhappily arrested in March; (a listening watch was kept,
as it was thought the set might have ben in enemy hands). SAPPHIRE went to
Sardinia. In addition, there was one radio link, TROUT, with Jugoslavia.

Early in November, 1943, it was decided to move the MARYLAND signals
unit up the coast from Brindisi to Monopoli, where Gerry Holdsworth was
gathering his staff for No. 1 Special Force. Already a training section had been
working there under Major Maurice Bruce. With the development of this unit
on a fairly permanent site and the expansion of independent signals traffic,
the time had come, as a matter of urgency, to ask MASSINGHAM to send some
FANYs. The move to Italy, particularly to Monopoli, on the approach
of winter, was an undoubted disappointment to the seven FANYs who
arrived on 14 November, also for many of those who followed during the next
few months. Only for the FANYs who arrived during the spring and summer
to come, straight from wartime England, was Monopoli not such an anti-
climax as for those who had enjoyed the surroundings and atmosphere at
MASSINGHAM.

The south-eastern seaboard of Italy and the province of Apulia had been a
much-favoured habitat since Greek times. Brindisi had become a Roman city
in the third century BC; here Virgil died in 19 BC. It was the end of the Appian
Way that led to Rome. Barbarians, Byzantines, Lombards, Franks, Saracens,
Normans, Hohenstaufens, Venetians and Spaniards, had landed in Apulian
ports and tried to colonize the interior. Finally, the Kingdom of the Two
Sicilies, with its palace at Caserta, which encompassed the south, gave way in
1861 to the House of Savoy (still the rulers in the 1940s). All these passers-
by left traces of their culture – ruins of castles, cathedrals and churches in

Romanesque, Gothic and Baroque architecture. But in 1943 the im-poverished nature of the region was all-pervading. Past glories had largely departed and left poverty and squalor. Government investment in the south of Italy had been sorely neglected and the population's needs largely ignored. 'Italy begins at Florence' or 'Africa begins at Rome' were current expressions and much of the terrain in the 1940s certainly resembled the then poorer parts of Africa, with inadequately developed land and depressed people. Starvation was a real issue.

Monopoli was in 1943 a small town with a population of 14,000 in-habitants. It was said to be the birthplace of Al Capone, the Chicago gangster – hardly a recommendation. There was a small port, and fishing and farming were the main sources of income. Brindisi, with its much larger harbour, was forty-five miles away and Bari, which provided the only source of leisure activ-ities, was a distance of twenty-six miles. There was in 1943 no public transport. Mussolini had considerably improved the roads in the region during the past twenty years, since they were the gateway to his conquests in Albania and East Africa. Unfortunately, Italian engineering, often so efficient, had failed him here; the camber of the surface was so constructed as to be lethal for vehicles after a short burst of rain. Service people had several, some fatal, accidents.

Gerry Holdsworth had set out to establish a similar pattern of units as existed at MASSINGHAM: a parachute training school near Brindisi airfield; a para-military battle school under Major Denis ('Dumbo') Newman at Castello di Santo Stefano, a few miles south of Monopoli on the coast; 'holding houses' for different types of agents, carefully keeping apart those who should not be aware of each other; a wireless training school at La Selva, a few miles away. Eventually a holding station for British Liaison Officers was established at Castellana, five miles outside Monopoli. In the town itself, the original FANY mess occupied a large four-square building in the centre, Casa Camicia, Via Bixio 192. When numbers increased during 1944, additional accommodation was supplied. The officers' mess was nearby and the oper-ations and country section offices, the Orderly room, sergeants' mess, other ranks' mess, stores, motor transport, and workshop, all within a central complex. Only the signal office was at some half-mile distance, up the coast, at the Villa Grazia.

The first group of FANYs had not experienced an easy journey. They went by road, four hundred miles from Algiers to Bizerta, in an assortment of trucks; then a long wait for onward transportation across the Mediterranean to Taranto on an infantry landing craft. Several days were spent on a turbu-lent sea under primitive conditions. Two personal assistants were included in the party: Ensign Gundred Grogan, who worked for Gerry Holdsworth, and Ruth Hermon-Smith, who continued with Peter Lee in the security branch.

He chose to set up his office in Bari, where a very busy life awaited them both. Many Italians were crossing the lines and had to be cleared as security risks before they could be considered for recruitment into the SOE orbit. Some double agents had entered the Italian security system.

Eleanor Hodder, a former teacher and examiner of dancing, and Ensign Dee Evans were in their thirties, married to serving officers; both were coders, and Dee took charge of the MARYLAND coding office. They were assisted by Doris Duthie and Chris Marks (who later married Dick Mallaby). The seventh FANY was Lieutenant Prudence Macfie who was a training officer, fluent in French and with some Italian; she had been employed in England as a conducting officer for women agents in Colonel Buckmaster's 'F' Section. It was proposed that she should help with the preparation of agents in Italy and the setting up of training schools along the Adriatic coast; to this end she undertook a parachute course. Six FANY wireless operators from MASSINGHAM arrived in January, 1944: Rosemary Dawe (Newman) and Mary de Fonblanque (Duncan) were two with excellent recall. Rosemary remembers the cold; the only heating was a small bowl of lighted charcoal, placed under a table as a foot warmer. There was a bathroom in the mess but heating the water required wood as fuel, which was in short supply. Italian cooks found it difficult to deal with army rations. One dish which remains in the memory was porridge and bacon cooked together. The subject of hectic telegrams to London, Lieutenant Maureen Campbell, a good Italian linguist, had been employed in the Censorship. After being recruited by SOE and the FANY, she arrived by air that winter.

In the signal office the coders worked twelve-hour shifts as there were so few of them. Eleanor Hodder describes how messages tended to pile up. Those that dealt with supply drops were given priority and double-checked. She recalls a remark of Gerry Holdsworth that 'the FANYs were looking wilted'. She took the men in the signal office to task for being unwilling to share sweeping the coding room floor. Two more FANY coders, Pam Faith (Macbeth) and Gillian Grant (de Zoete), came from MASSINGHAM in April, 1944, and the arrival of Ruth Copp (later Lieutenant), who became a signal planning officer, meant that No. 1 Special Force was no longer reliant on MASSINGHAM in this respect. It became possible to change to eight-hour shifts. FANY wireless operators worked alongside some army signallers and the Italian operators from SIM, who were employed until a sufficient number of FANYs arrived from MASSINGHAM, as that unit gradually wound down after the landings in southern France in the autumn of 1944.

Julia Cope (Widgery) also came from North Africa. A trained secretary, she had worked in London for the firm of Jacqmar, the fashion house. A particularly pretty girl, she also acted as a model. When she arrived at MASSINGHAM, the sergeants' mess immediately named her 'Miss ISSU 6'.

1. The author in Cairo, April, 1944.

Ann Bonsor, 'one of the North African group' (p.10).

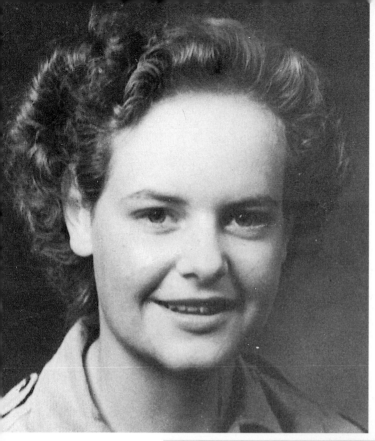

3. Elizabeth Fooks (Way
in Algiers, Septembe
1944 (see p.27).

4. Patricia   Wilson
(Selborne) (see p.29).

5. Margaret Brown (Kemp) in Cairo, 1944 (see p. 69).

Julia Cope (Widgery) 'had worked for Jacqmar, the London fashion house' (p.82).

7. Anne Butler (Younger)
(see p.71).

8. June Stanley (Darton) 'longed for something more exciting.... She was to find it in Italy' (p.98).

Ensign Vera Long was an original member of SOE' (p.98).

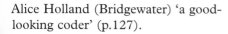

Alice Holland (Bridgewater) 'a good-looking coder' (p.127).

10. Christine Hoon (Kolczynska) from South Africa (see pp105-11).

12. The grave of Dippy Portman (Manning) in Florence. 'You couldn't have found a finer type of Englishwoman anywhere' (p.116).

13. The Signals Office at *MASSINGHAM*, Algiers, 1944.

14. Wireless Operators at *MASSINGHAM*, August, 1944.

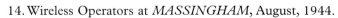

'The eighteenth century Palazzo Albertonza, which had been requisitioned to become HQ Special Operations (Mediterranean)' (p. 123).

Sergeant Jack Ashdown, Ensign Margaret Herbertson (the author) and Captain Ronald Preston (see p. 131) on the balcony of the building above.

17. The author on to
of the *Mangia* towe
Siena (see p. 150).

18. 'Fencing became an interest of mine in Siena' (p. 161). *Left to right*: Margaret
   Herbertson (author), June Stanley, June Wilson, Maestro Barbera, Nora Galbraith,
   Sue Rowley, Jill Johnson, Dick Mallaby.

Julia put down her rapid posting to Monopoli to the FANY CO's fear 'that I spelt trouble'. She became a highly efficient and diligent secretary to Dick Hewitt, as hard-working as she was decorative. When senior Partisan leaders arrived for consultation, Julia would stay until the early hours to type reports. She regretted that she never met the counterfeit expert who was housed in the hills beyond the town. Rumour had it that he had been released from prison and brought to Italy to produce false documents. It appears he was given a pardon after the war, but no decoration. Julia remembers a strong family feeling in the unit; there was coffee at eleven o'clock every day in the officers' mess. If any of the men in the field were in trouble, 'an air of gloom would descend over the whole place'.

La Selva, a unit in a hilly area ten miles to the south of Monopoli, covered with olive groves as the name suggests, trained wireless operators for future missions. Fred Tillson, formerly a warrant officer in the Royal Corps of Signals at No. 1 Special Force, was a cipher instructor at the Wireless Telegraphy Training School, helped by Sergeant Beaumont as interpreter. Since he could speak Italian he was known as *Sergente Tagliatelli*. He remembers working with FANYs and the policy of introducing them to the operators to whom they would be working in the field. In March, 1944, Mary de Fonblanque was one of five girls who undertook a course at La Selva, to listen to the 'keying' of the latest intake of students. If an Italian were captured, and his set worked back to base by the enemy, the change of operator should be recognized. Mary recalls listening to the keying of Lorenzo, who was later dropped to the Veneto on the night of 22/23 April, with the signal plan BIPLANE. After some diffi-culties (his leader was arrested and later escaped), Lorenzo remained more or less in regular contact with MARYLAND until early 1945. If she were on duty, Mary would work his 'sked' and recognize whether he were still in control.

Rosemary Dawe remembers a number of intrepid Italians who came through the German lines to contact the forward unit of No. 1 Special Force, under the command of Malcolm Munthe, along the west coast of Italy. Many who were considered secure and suitable arrived in Monopoli to be trained for the field.

Aided by Commandos and the assistance of Adrian Gallegos as naval intel-ligence officer, an enlarged SOE contingent succeeded in seizing the island of Ischia, which became a sabotage school for the training of Italian agents. The ingenious Dick Cooper numbered hypnotism among the accomplish-ments learnt in the Foreign Legion. At one point on Ischia he placed the two signalmen, Sergeants Hargreaves and Pickering, under a hypnotic trance; when it was time to send an urgent message to awaiting FANY operators at base they needed to be hurriedly revived.

Naples fell to the Allies on 1 October, 1943. The next objective was Rome, though SOE contacts, both men and women, went regularly on foot to the capital through the front line. Following the landings at Salerno in September, 1943, the Allies mounted a second ill-fated assault on the coast at Anzio on 22 January, 1944. Initial success was not maintained and the Germans counter-attacked twice with strong reinforcements. A link-up of Allied forces was not achieved until the spring and only on 25 May were they able to proceed towards Rome. It had been a costly campaign in the matter of casualties, both among the regular forces and in the SOE group.

On Sunday afternoon of 6 February, 1944, Malcolm Munthe and Michael Gubbins (son of the General) were escorting an Italian courier who was trying to reach Rome across an exposed patch of no-man's-land. There was a rattle of machine-gun fire; both leapt into a trench, both were hit. Malcolm was seriously wounded; Michael was dead. (Stretcher bearers from the Irish Guards were also hit, as was a nurse killed by shrapnel, tending Malcolm in a tented hospital.) Sergeant Pickering, their wireless operator, received orders from MARYLAND to liquidate the forward unit. He joined FANYs in the signal office at Monopoli until he went into the field in Northern Italy in February, 1945.

There was a consequence affecting No. 1 Special Force following the Anzio débâcle. Two officers of the Oxford and Bucks Light Infantry were lying side by side in the mud during a lull in one of the Anzio battles. Colin Kraay, who joined the army as an under-graduate at Magdalen College, Oxford, had a considerable interest in ancient coinage. As he dug in the undergrowth he uncovered a Roman coin, whose history he expounded to his companion, Olaf Brann. Some months later both men were recruited to No. 1 Special Force at Monopoli by Dick Hewitt, Colin to the operations' staff and Olaf, who was bilingual in German, as an intelligence officer to the Partisans. Colin later married his FANY secretary, Peggy Prince, and later still became an Oxford don and Keeper of the Heberden Coin Room of the Ashmolean Museum. Olaf Brann's letters to his Swedish fiancée (now his widow), sent via his mother in England, give some idea of the effort expended at Monopoli: 'Working day and night, in spite of the intolerable heat, there is so much to be done'. Staff arriving in Dick Hewitt's office at eight in the morning would find he had worked much of the night.

General Gubbins visited Monopoli after Michael's death and found his kit all laid out as was the custom in the case of a deceased officer. Gerry Holdworth tried to offer comfort, the FANYs likewise. Eleanor Hodder remembers that the General accompanied her to the signal office and helped her decode some messages. For a short time No. 1 Special Force would be without a forward unit, not a state of affairs to the liking of Gerry Holdsworth, who was keen to deal with tactical matters, rather than those, to quote him, 'in the hinterland, which was seeing to strategic ones'. After the fall of Rome in June, 1944, and Florence in August, he was to have his way. A forward unit followed, in which FANYs were included.

One of the problems facing SOE in Italy was similar to that experienced in Greece and Jugoslavia: much of the opposition to the enemy among the Italians, which SOE was, as such, anxious to support and encourage, was based on political lines. It was grounded upon opposition to the Fascist régime and went back to 1926, when Opposition Parties were banned by Mussolini. Some opponents went into exile, others went underground and some paid dearly for their stand. the OVRA, the Fascist police, had a particularly unpleasant reputation. In 1929 a clandestine party, *Giustizia e Libertá*, was founded from which, in 1942, sprang the Action Party, a left-wing organization led in wartime by Ferrucio Parri. Two other left-wing parties were the Communists (Garibaldi), led by Palmiro Togliatti, and the Socialists, with their leader Giuseppe Saragat. The parties of the right and 'moderate' persuasion were the Liberals with their wartime President, Benedetto Croce, and leader Count Alessandro Casati, the Christian Democrats, led by Alcide de Gasperi, and the Labour Democrat Party, led by Ivanoe Bonami and Menuccio Ruini.

There were a few non-political resistance figures with whom No. 1 Special Force had dealings, in particular General Raffaele Cadorna, who later became Supreme Commander of Partisan forces. In the mountains most of the Partisan bands were organized on political lines (although there were some autonomous groups), but as Gerry Holdsworth commented, we 'did not want the Germans to win, and so we accepted any anti-German activity'. Bickham Sweet-Escott[5] had put the matter clearly in an earlier Balkan context: without the political push, resistance could not exist or develop.

On the credit side was the attempt made immediately after the armistice to bring the different political wings offering resistance together in associations, which were named Committees of National Liberation, CLN. The Committee in Milan became the virtual government of northern (occupied) Italy. The German forces treated with particular ferocity members of the Italian army and any who helped escaped British prisoners-of-war. Attempts to send Italians to Germany for forced labour were ill-received. As a result anti-German feeling proliferated and with it the size of paramilitary bands. During the early winter of 1943–1944 over one hundred Italians were being trained as organizers, demolition experts, radio operators and so on, in the installations at Monopoli. Visits were paid there by resistance leaders. Peggy Prince, secretary in the operations and intelligence departments, saw Edgardo Sogno, head of the Franchi group based on Milan, several times in Monopoli. Described in one account as 'a brilliant and fast-moving leader', he appeared at No. 1 Special force on one occasion having crossed the front line on a bicycle. She recalls having recognized him through his various guises by his 'high squeaky voice'.

A congress of Committees of National Liberation was held in Bari from

28–29 January, 1944. Of the ninety representatives, twenty came from Committees beyond the German lines, a triumph of organization and ingenuity. Gerry Holdsworth described bringing Alfredo Pizzoni (also known as Pietro Longhi), one of the main resistance leaders, by sea from Genoa to Taranto so that he could meet and speak with General Alexander. 'I managed to get him back.'

Expansion of No. 1 Special Force's operational plans in the spring of 1944 led to shortage of staff; signals to London produced Pauline Ratsey among the FANYs, as secretary to Teddy de Haan; she later married him. Three coders came from Cairo; a wireless operator from MASSINGHAM, who had the skills, was persuaded to become a secretary. Eleanor Hodder and Dee Evans had carried the administrative side of the FANY unit, which by the end of May, 1944, numbered eighteen, as well as their own jobs in the coding office. This included supervising the messing, the Italian domestic staff, ordering the rations, etc. It was decided to bring in an ex-FANY who had seen service in the First World War, and had reached retirement age in the ATS in Cairo, as an administrative officer. The appointment was not a success and new arrangements needed to be made in September. By the time this had become obvious, Eleanor Hodder had already left for Egypt to take charge of the FANYs in that unit, since Norah Coggin had resigned. The arrival of Evelyn Green at Monopoli provided the opportunity to invest her with the same responsibilities that she had carried in Cairo – to be in charge of the domestic staff and rations. She had empathy with the Italians who worked in the kitchens, and their various idiosyncrasies, and had a certain knowledge of the language. The number of FANYs at Monopoli increased during the summer of 1944 to reach seventy-nine by the end of September. It matched the development of the unit as a whole.

The supervision of FANYs in the Mediterranean was to prove a difficult problem for FANY headquarters in England. With only a few exceptions, as has been mentioned earlier, most of the members were too young and inexperienced to be placed in charge of each other. An expedient was devised by which a request was made to the ATS for the secondment of a group of administrative officers who had initially been members of the Corps and had been drafted into the ATS at the beginning of the war. This worked well and No. 1 Special Force FANYs received, in due course, an administrative officer who was both efficient and sympathetic.

The fall of Rome on 4 June, 1944, was a long-awaited event. Max Salvadori entered the city in a jeep on 5 June with Renato Pierleone, who for eight months, since crossing the lines, had been working with the Rome branch of the Action party. Charles Mackintosh, finding his desk job at Monopoli becoming irksome, received Gerry Holdworth's permission to begin to provide a No. 1 Special Force forward unit. He tried to contact those who had been working in Rome during the German occupation and any allied prisoners-of-war who had been sheltering there, also to set up an efficient radio link to work back to base and to monitor sets in enemy territory. To find a suitable forward headquarters building was another assignment. Gerry Holdsworth resolved to become part of any such forward unit; soon he succeeded in establishing himself in Rome with a small staff, which included his personal assistant Gundred Grogan. Other FANYs were to follow. One of his tasks was to keep General Alexander aware of German troop movements as they came into Italy; also the movement of armaments, when he heard about both through Partisan sources. As bearer of such tidings, he would visit the C-in-C on a regular basis.

Meanwhile, Dick Hewitt, his able second-in-command, assumed the reins at Monopoli with Julia Cope in attendance. Gerry Holdsworth had been a popular figure, since he was proud of the FANYs under his command. Letters survive which register his concern if they were ill or seeming tired. He wrote to Lieutenant-Colonel Peter Ashton, DAA and QMG at HG (SOM) Admin Echelon, on 20 October, 1944, pointing out that he had asked FANY authorities back in February to promote two girls with the lowest rank of volunteer to that of corporal, but nothing had been done. As the two secretaries in question were among those in No. 1 Special Force who had given the longest service, he required that action to be taken. The only reservation that FANYs held against Gerry Holdsworth was that he liked his FANYs to look feminine and held out for a long time against the wearing by them of trousers, even in cold weather.

From now on Rome became the favourite destination for FANY leave. Notwithstanding the difficulties of transport, girls would manage to reach Rome by road or by aircraft, a challenge that was often and willingly taken.

The scope of No. 1 Special Force developed fast during the summer and autumn of 1944. Partisan groups became coordinated into a collective command structure: Voluntary Freedom Corps or CVL, with battalions and divisions, under the command of General Raffaele Cadorna, who was dropped to Lombardy in August. One hundred and fifty Italian volunteers were infiltrated into the area between Rome and Bologna to act as instructors to the Partisans. At the request of the army and General Gubbins, British Liaison Officers, the first in Italy, were dropped into the field during the month of June. The growth and organization of the Partisan movement had reached the stage when it was considered that such assistance would be useful.

Seven British Liaison Officers dropped into various sites in northern Italy between June and July, 1944. Six British and one Italian wireless operator accompanied them. One officer, Major Vivian Johnson, had been on a previous mission to the Dodecanese Islands and took with him the same operator who had been with him on Kos. Fifteen officers were infiltrated in

August. Major H.W. Tilman, a well-known climber and veteran of a mission to Albania, was one. In his memoirs[6] he quotes part of a poem which he found appropriate while poised to drop at the third attempt to find the target:

Nothing to breathe but air,
Quick as a flash, t'is gone.
Nowhere to fall but off,
Nowhere to stand but on.

Captain John Orr-Ewing, now a near neighbour in my village in Kent, was another who went to the mountains of north-east Italy in August, 1944, as did Captain Christopher Woods.[7]

In July two escaped British prisoners-of-war, Major Gordon Lett and Major Oldham, were accepted as British Liaison Officers by No. 1 Special Force; they were able to communicate with base through Italian operators who had already been infiltrated. Several former FANYs have recalled that it was not unknown for Italian operators in the field to send 'loving messages' at the close of signals if they knew that a girl was at the other end. Some would be in plain language, which was strictly forbidden. Derrick Scott-Job, who was in charge of signals at Monopoli, reports that British operators rarely did so, certainly not until after the actual fighting was over. Whether they were less flirtatious, or more disciplined, is an open question. British security was nervous of admitting ex-prisoners-of-war into active SOE operations, because of the risk of spies masquerading as prisoners, but the two officers mentioned were considered genuine.

The most spectacular exploit in August was that of Charles Mackintosh in Florence. The River Arno had become the front line, the Partisans and Germans on the north bank, allied forces to the south. Sniping, machine-gun fire and shelling were constant. Partisans were anxious to make an immediate and suicidal rising on the north side. The Ponte Vecchio was the only bridge not blown by the Germans on their retreat and Charles Mackintosh was able to cross over the river via the top storey of the buildings on the bridge. He laid a telephone line to the Partisans on the far side and established contact with them to prevent precipitate action. Eventually he made his way to Partisan Headquarters, ahead of regular forces, and became, for a short period, the representative of AMG (Allied Military Government) in the city. His radio communication with MARYLAND at Monopoli was poor during the height of the fighting on the south bank (more problems for the FANYs at base), so he searched for an alternative site in more open ground near Gavinana, where reception was improved. He later set up a forward Tactical Headquarters in Florence, where two FANYs came to join his staff.

Meanwhile new FANY arrivals were finding their posting to No. 1 Special

Force more interesting than had been the experience of those who had come the previous autumn. The sun and warmer weather widened spare-time opportunities for bathing and sailing. Above all, the unit had developed its own character and variety with its increase in size and scope of operations. Secretaries and coders were aware of the new burst of activity. A FANY coder writes:

> We took enormous interest in the content of messages . . . The personality of the man in the field always came over, which was not the case with main-line stations [such as Cairo and London] which weren't so interesting to do, rather verbose and consequently rather long.

The excitement of decoding messages from such as Charles Mackintosh, and reading of the gradual capture of Florence, can be imagined. A FANY who, after eighteen months as a wireless operator, began to find the strain too great changed to being a coder; she 'thoroughly enjoyed being able to decypher what was being transmitted'.

Milbrough Walker (Lobanov Rostovsky) writes of the fascination that coding had for her. For most of the summer of 1944 coders were 'inundated with work'. A balcony at the Villa Grazia had been filled in to make an extra coding room. When there was 'a flap' on, additional coders had to be called in, even if off duty.

> You might be at death's door, but you still went back to work when there was a desperate need and on occasions, when there was no room at a table, one would sit on the floor. We were awfully dedicated and once you started work, you didn't notice these things.
>
> One of the most wonderful things at No. 1 Special Force was the fact that we were so completely trusted . . . (In Cairo, we had 'checkers' who checked our work). We were trusted to work well and efficiently and I loved that. Everything depended on getting a message *right*; speed and accuracy were all-important, particularly the latter and you just *never* had to lose your nerve, however fast the clock was ticking towards transmission time. You had to ignore all disturbances; write neatly.

Help and encouragement were given by shift leaders (of whom Milbrough eventually became one) and particularly by Dee Evans, who was in charge of the coding office, who 'never flapped and was a great support'. FANYs recall that some of the men NCOs, who were older than they, were 'kind and fatherly', especially Sergeant Tillson, whom they called 'Tilly'.

There was no communication whatever with the wireless operators who were in a separate part of the building. One minor problem was the way that the Italian wireless operators from SIM wrote their numbers, particularly one and seven, not always immediately recognizable. To this day Milbrough writes the number four in the continental manner.

Social life was also busy. Commando units and the Navy were in the vicinity and to travel by truck to Bari or Brindisi in the evening was not painful as in winter. A favourite respite was Sunday afternoons when the naval contingent would take out a motor torpedo boat, ostensibly for 'engine trials', and there would be tea on board with a group of FANYs and a swim from the boat. As in the case of MASSINGHAM, a certain amount of ill health was endured. The food was fairly poor and the absence of fresh fruit and vegetables probably debilitating. The local population was at such low ebb that they had little to sell. Milbrough suffered from various ills, such as jaundice, from septic mosquito bites and malaria, although southern Italy was not considered to have the appropriate type of mosquito. Her horrified parents received a telegram that she was seriously ill in hospital in Bari with suspected blood poisoning. She believes her life was saved by injections of a new drug, penicillin. A medical orderly told her they were very expensive and costing the army a great deal of money. Convalescence under the auspices of the Red Cross at La Selva made up for the trauma. Partisan sick and wounded, including women, so FANYs reported, appeared to have an aversion to being parted from the grenades they had hanging from their belts.

Jacqueline Dixon (Tucker) was a member of a party of FANY reinforcements from England who came by sea in July. The journey took eighteen days by ship from Greenock to Naples. Trains were beginning to run again in the south of Italy, and thirteen hours were spent sitting on slatted seats to reach Monopoli. The poverty-stricken appearance of so many members of the Italian population was the initial impression made upon the group, as also the primitive conditions of life in the town. Jacqueline developed jaundice on arrival and, while in the 98th General Military Hospital in Bari, her first letter from home announced the devastating news that her father had been killed by a direct hit on their home in an air raid; her mother mercifully had survived. She remembers being surrounded by kindness.

Jacqueline has a clear memory of her life as a coder. Shift arrangements were placed on a board in the FANY mess. To change duties was allowed, with permission. Messages to be encoded or decoded were randomly distributed throughout a shift and those who worked fastest obviously achieved the most. 'We helped each other with difficult signals resulting from poor reception or faulty radios.' Encyphering errors were fewer once One-Time-Pads were used, rather than double transposition codes, as it was a simpler method.

Shift hours, in Jacqueline's time, were 8 am to 4 pm, 4 pm to midnight and midnight to 8 am. At peak times during the day, which was largely for traffic other than from the field, an overlapped shift operated from 10 am to 6 pm. A day off came after finishing at midnight. Often girls would hitch-hike to Bari to meet friends and try and have a bath in one of the officers' hotels, such as the *Imperiale*.

When Jacqueline became a shift leader on 11 January, 1945, her shift consisted of three men and four FANYs. The men were all newcomers and needed over-seeing. She was required to make sure that the shift had a full complement of staffing, to answer the telephone, to allocate and gather up completed transcripts, make tea and sandwiches and organize transport for the girls' return to the mess at night. The cold, once autumn had set in, was extreme at night in the covered-in terrace. Jacqueline recalls gathering wood for a heater and on one occasion breaking up a chair to burn. Christine Dury (Parker) was a newly arrived coder at Monopoli during the summer of 1944. There was nowhere else to rest, during slack periods on night duty, except on the trestle tables themselves. This she recalls having done, with a code book as a pillow. Mary Gammell (Stormonth-Darling) arrived that autumn, having experienced eighteen months in England as an operator on live traffic with agents on the continent. Her father[8] was Chief-of-Staff to General Maitland Wilson at AFHQ at Caserta. Her letters to her mother, which have survived, describe, not her work, very properly, but her leave with her father in the Commander-in-Chief's villa:

> I'm getting acclimatized to this exalted atmosphere, but it's certainly a change from the sergeants' mess . . . I find it most diffi-cult to cope with knives and forks, after having only one for so long.

She made a visit to Capri on the Admiral's Barge which had been the prop-erty of Crown Prince Umberto. In the company of Lady Ranfurly[9] (her parrot had tried to bite Mary the previous day) and Harold Macmillan, by then living at Caserta, they all leapt into the water, looking white and phosphorescent. Trying to help Harold Macmillan back into the boat proved difficult.

> He's rather like a nice walrus and very slippery when wet. By the time we'd pushed and hauled him in, he must have been black and blue.

She also considered the southern Italian population to be in a poor way. The drive back to Monopoli, over the Apennines, involved three punctures, one of which happened in the middle of a town signposted 'Typhoid and smallpox – no stopping'.

It fell to Evelyn Green, with her responsibility for the mess servants, to see more than other FANYs of the Italians who worked for No. 1 Special Force. There would seem to have been thirteen of them: MariaGiuseppe, Donata, Addolorata, Isabella, Caterina, two named Vittoria, Maria, Margherita, Antonietta and Angela, and two men, both named Paolo. Evelyn engaged the mess staff through the local detachment of the Italian army.

> Monopoli il 24 October 44
> Reference to our talk today, I sent you, Sir, these two women for Misses's kitchen. They are two very good and honest and moral women and they can cook good. I hope you will be very content. Many salutes and wishes.
> Yours [signed] Peter Guccione
> Lieut. Italian Army.

Evelyn's relations with them seem to have been as friendly and indulgent as they had been with the Egyptians in the Cairo mess. One of her greatest problems was to protect the FANYs against having their belongings stolen. Realizing that near starvation faced many inhabitants of Monopoli, it was difficult to be harsh, but there were occasions when she felt she must take action. She wrote in her diary of an incident which gives a vivid picture of the surroundings among which the Monopoli FANYs lived:

> Last night a camera was stolen, so I sent to the headquarters of the *carabinieri*. The *Maresciallo* himself, after taking down particulars, buckled on his revolver and set out with an armed soldier to do a house search of the homes of the suspected boys. One felt like a *Gestapo* official looking for someone to beat up. Children fled before us. I saw the electrician and his son emerging from a side alley, but on sighting us they disappeared like rabbits into a hole; two boys of about four years tried to conceal themselves behind each other as we passed. Bolder spirits doffed their caps and said, '*Buon giorno Maresciallo*' in subservient tones.
> When we arrived at the first house in a filthy street near the harbour, the pregnant housewife was gossiping outside. In a strident voice she argued and protested, but we went in relentlessly and began to search. The *Maresciallo* spared nothing. He pulled open drawers, stirred up the contents or tossed them on the floor and even poked his head into a commode, such was his thoroughness. Up and up we went, as there was only one small room on each floor, until we reached an attic where the straw for bedding contained fleas similar to those 'that tease in

the high Pyrenees'; we drew a blank otherwise.

At the next house we visited, children said that their mother was out looking for food, as they were all so hungry, and that the door was locked. 'Ah,' said the *Maresciallo* 'You are hungry, so you have to steal; where is the door?' It was unlocked. Although we found nothing of interest except a baby kicking its heels in a cot, I understood later that this was the home of the boy who stole the camera.

After the search we were overcome by the heat of the day and the stench, so I brought the *Maresciallo* back to the mess to inspect the scene of many thefts and have a drink; his presence shook the servants. Maria could hardly fry a potato for lunch and Margherita protested to me later that I had insulted them by bringing the *Maresciallo* into the kitchen. I told them that honest people should not mind. The carabinieri continued the good work: they arrested four boys who were imprisoned for two days and beaten; they recovered the camera. And the juvenile population was sufficiently impressed by the stir to leave us in peace for some time.

Jane Buckland, a wireless operator, liked to sketch and write poetry in her spare time. She was sketching the harbour from a Jugoslav fishing vessel which was used to transport men to occupied territory across the Adriatic when it put to sea. When her presence became known the ship had to be recalled to port. Her poem on Monopoli follows, but the one she wrote on the boring nature of maintaining a 'listening watch' she is unwilling to have published:

> In a tiny south Italian town
> With houses white and shutters brown,
> Where children run about and play
> Bare-footed in the streets all day,
> Street vendors sell their melons fine
> And greenest grapes fresh from the vine,
> And the Adriatic calm and blue,
> Such fun to watch the ships glide through.
> So far away does England seem
> To me a hazy distant dream.

A listening watch was instituted when an operator in the field failed to respond to his call-sign at the time specified on his signal plan. Base operators continued to listen over a period, in case a mission was in trouble. It was a tedious process, much disliked, as it represented long periods of boredom. Jane on one occasion inadvertently tuned into a news broadcast during a listening watch and received a severe reprimand.

The arrival of Captain Barbara Amos as Commanding Officer of the No. 1 Special Force FANYs on 6 September, 1944, marked a decided improvement in the administration of the unit and morale generally. A former Monopoli FANY writes: 'Barbara Amos was a super CO, very much liked and respected, who really pulled everything together as No. 1 Special Force became so much bigger.' She was a former FANY who had been absorbed into the ATS, one of the group of ATS officers selected for posting to SOE units in Italy. She was warned it would not be an easy assignment. Now in her nineties (1999), she agrees with this forecast. She had no transport of her own and less help than she would have received had she remained in the ATS; merely Evelyn Green as a messing officer and seeing to the Italian staff. A real danger of scurvy among the girls, she saw as a possibility with so little fresh food and only three-quarters of the men's rations, poorly cooked, and often stolen. Jane's 'melons fair and greenest grapes' she saw as a temporary phenomenon. She considered that the FANYs in her charge, over eighty of them eventually, worked hard, behaved excellently and were uncomplaining despite poor conditions and little promotion. A considerable compensation was the friend-ships they made, both inside and outside the unit, and the number of invitations they received to parties and dances from the local groups of Com-mandos, the Navy and members of the Raiding Support Regiment. In summer there was swimming and sailing under perfect conditions. Stephen Hastings, who had been in the field in France and later dropped near Piacenza, wrote disparagingly in his subsequent book[10] of Monopoli, where he found condi-tions bad, 'But there were some good-looking FANYs'.

The friends with whom the girls associated were, however, under constant threat of danger; fatalities occurred which caused much unhappiness. A FANY wrote home: 'Masses of the people I knew in North Africa are casu-alties; it's very dreadful'. Patricia Wilson in a similar letter described a visit she and another girl made to RAF friends in hospital:

> They had been shot down and wounded. They were thrilled to see us. There were six in the ward and they made us talk to them all. One very young boy had lost all his top finger joints by frostbite. He made me write home for him. It was so pathetic. They were all pretty bad, but so cheerful. We are going again on Monday.

On 10 August, 1944, Gerry Holdsworth wrote to the FANY CO at Monopoli. Approval had been given to put a number of FANY personnel serving with No. 1 Special Force into field training. He asked her to call for volunteers. All should have at least two of the skills of wireless operating, coding and shorthand typing, and also possess the necessary physical stamina. The training would involve a parachute course and therefore be rigorous; only the toughest and most illness-free FANYs were to be considered. In a later letter he suggested that he thought Rosemary Dawe a most suitable candidate, with the necessary stamina and technical qualifications.

The reply with the list of volunteers has unfortunately not survived, but it is clear that Mary de Fonblanque was one, for she writes to say that Gerry Holdsworth turned her down on account of her red hair. He maintained that it would draw attention to her in conditions where it might be important to remain inconspicuous. Rosemary Dawe proceeded to parachute training and a course in the use of small arms, but the whole scheme came to an abrupt end when objections were raised at high level and Gerry Holdsworth received instructions from General Stawell, head of HQ SO(M), that no British women were to be despatched into the field.

A locally recruited FANY who underwent parachute training was an Italian, Rosanna Banti, aged nineteen, who, with her fiancé, Giuliano Mattioli, known as Julian Matthews, had been a member of a resistance movement in Rome. There was some question of her going into the field, as her fiancé did, but this never materialized, and she moved into one of the extensions to the FANY mess, next door to a shop in Monopoli, in September, 1944. Mildred Buck (Schutz) arrived shortly afterwards from England, became secretary to Barbara Amos and shared Rosanna's sleeping quarters. They had straw palliasses on their camp beds. Rosanna's fear of being captured by the Germans led to her keeping a revolver under her pillow.

Weather conditions deteriorated severely during the early part of the 1944–5 winter and there was stalemate in the progress of the regular forces' push north, with stiff enemy resistance. Partisan activity was thereby also curtailed, a situation which becomes the subject of a later narrative. Missions from No. 1 Special Force were restricted. Six British Liaison Officers went into the field in September, 1944, and ten, including a new four-man mission in the months of November and December. Lieutenant Robert Clark RNVR, who was engaged to Marjorie Lewis, was one of the latter group. No news from him was the cause of great anxiety, when on one night shift, a wireless operator taking down a coded signal, was aware of a message in plain language at the close: BOB SENDS LOVE TO MARJORIE. It was from Corporal Williamson, wireless operator of the mission COELUM SOUTH. Bob Clark's mission was overrun by an enemy *rastrellamento*, but he had been hidden in a tree for a while by a member of the Partisans, (whom Bob and Marjorie, then married, met after the war). Bob was later captured and taken prisoner by the Germans. His message to Marjorie had been passed to a British operator with the Partisans, in contact with base. 'Imagine the thrill,' she writes, 'to know that he was alive.'

A further twenty-six FANYs arrived at Monopoli later in the autumn of 1944 on the closure of MASSINGHAM. The communications of the

Movements' department were not perfect and some FANYs were to find that they were not expected, and were forced to occupy an empty building. Jacqueline Dixon, coming off night duty, discovered a newcomer in her bed. Patricia Wilson wrote to her parents on 9 October on the subject of her accommodation:

> It really is amazing how comfy and cosy even a garret or cellar can become when we 'campaigners' get settled . . . We have moved our room again. It was decided that it was bad for us to live in the old place, the lice, bugs, drains, windows etc. etc., so about twelve of us were moved out and have come to rather a decent large house . . . Our room is really rather nice; we have two cupboards, a great improvement, and have almost covered the walls with nails, with coats, rain capes, mosquito nets all over them.

She later wrote another instalment in the same vein:

> Last night three of us crept back to the old house and carried off the hall stand because it has a long mirror. It really was funny, we all had hysterics and it was such a light night with huge moon reflected in the mirror. All the inhabitants of the town seemed to come out to see us creep along the street struggling with the huge piece of furniture. It is now safely installed inside our door. We had a hectic time moving because that same day we were asked to go to an extra duty because so many people being ill, or away and so were on duty [as wireless operators] from nine in the morning until twelve at night. We had to move in during the half-hour meal breaks.

On 17 September she had written that she had had her first bath since 29 January. Fresh moves on an individual basis in a northerly direction took place just before and just after Christmas, again the subject of a subsequent chapter. In addition, volunteers were being called for from Baker Street for service in SOE units in the Far East, to which some FANYs from southern Italy responded.

In December, 1944, a decision was finally taken for the headquarters of No. 1 Special Force and its signals unit to move, in its entirety, from Monopoli to Siena as No 5 Army group had vacated suitable premises. A sad event took place shortly beforehand, which story has no known conclusion. Gunner Hunt, a tall and taciturn man, who had served with Charles Mackintosh's mission in Florence with considerable gallantry (he was awarded a Military Medal), returned to Monopoli, where he suffered a psychological breakdown. He climbed on to the roof of one of the offices with a revolver and plenty of ammunition, and began firing at members of the unit below. Eventually he was apprehended and put under guard. The same evening Barbara Amos was aware of a loud noise below her bedroom in the FANY mess. Gunner Hunt had broken down the door of his prison and was at large. Freddy White gave Barbara, who was a good shot, a loaded revolver, armed himself and the two climbed on to the roof to try, from that vantage point, to locate the unfortunate soldier. Presently they saw him and began firing, to encourage him to give himself up. Barbara writes, 'He moved close to the walls of the houses, pausing in doorways . . . He was hidden in a doorway when I fired. After that I never heard of him again. Gunner Hunt disappeared into the landscape.'

Charles Mackintosh concluded the episode in his book[11] with these words:

> Perhaps in some remote Italian countryside a big peasant tills the
> soil speaking to no one who might give him away. I can only hope
> he is happy.

The move of the FANYs of No. 1 Special Force to Siena was conducted with considerable skill by Derrick Scott-Job, ensuring that there should be no dislocation in the signals traffic. Wireless operators and coders were flown to Siena on staggered dates from 25 January to 6 February, 1945, in twelve different aircraft. He writes:

> The challenge which confronted Signals was to maintain constant
> communications throughout the move with the field. The prob-
> lems were (1) the availability of equipment and (2) the existing
> signal plans which would have to work over very much shorter
> distances to Siena and thus require new crystals to operate their
> transmitters at different frequencies . . .
>
> The move was 100% successful. (The only hitch was with the
> first plane load of wireless operators and coders which failed to
> arrive in Siena when expected. Apparently the aeroplane carrying
> them had taken a wrong turning and started heading out to sea.
> The FANYs and other passengers aboard could hear the pilot
> admitting he had no idea where he was. However, he found his
> way back and all was well, apart from his rather white-faced
> passengers.) There were no major breakdowns and the continuity
> of all the circuits was maintained throughout.

He concludes, 'Credit must go to the signal planners and cipher personnel, who had to cope with the detailed planning of the change-over of the sixty to seventy field circuits. A mistake anywhere could have meant a complete break-down of circuits involved'.

The move was universally popular: 'Such beauty after the very dull surroundings in Monopoli,' writes one FANY of her arrival in Siena.

MONOPOLI: FORCE 139: PUNCH

There were two groups of FANYs who lived and worked in Monopoli, but not attached to No. 1 Special Force, which had its responsibility for operations in northern Italy. Force 139, code name PUNCH, was the administrative unit which organized SOE work in Central Europe, in Poland, Czechoslovakia and Hungary. Its head was Lieutenant-Colonel Henry Threlfall who had long been associated with SOE. To him fell the onerous duty of liaison with air force authorities at high level over the provision of planes and crews, in the face of hazardous conditions and loss of men, for operations into enemy territory. The detail of the operations into Poland is set out in a subsequent Chapter.

Henry Threlfall, with Polish Majors Klauber and Thruszkowski, arrived in Italy in the spring of 1944. The airfield at Brindisi, after adaptation, was being used for operational flights, in the place of airfields in North Africa which involved journeys of longer distances.

Two FANYs were posted to his department, housed in the centre of Monopoli. Ensign (later Lieutenant) Vera Long was an original member of SOE, one of the two secretaries to General Gubbins in November, 1940. More recently she had been personal assistant to Lieutenant-Colonel Harold Perkins, head of the Polish section in Baker Street. In civilian life he had owned an engineering works in Poland. Vera's chief memory of her arrival at Monopoli was of having barely survived the journey. She was so severely sea-sick and dehydrated that she became semi-conscious in her bunk. Eventually a resourceful naval Surgeon-Lieutenant put her over his shoulder in a fireman's lift and bore her down several decks of the ship to the sick bay where, after an injection to knock her out and an intravenous drip, she lived to see Naples.

Ensign June Stanley (Darton) had endured several uneventful jobs as a civilian in Baker Street, such as secretary to the head of the Finance Department, and longed for something more exciting. She was to find it during her posting to Italy. On her return from subsequent leave in Florence, she and another FANY were the only passengers in a small Fairchild aircraft (which only carried three passengers). As they came in to land at Ciampino airport, just outside Rome, the American pilot spotted a green light from the control tower. The light was intended to guide in a large

Flying Fortress which roared in on top of them. June caught a fleeting glance of a crowd of American troops who were sitting idly on the ground and suddenly leapt to their feet. The pilot of the Fortress braked hard, burst a tyre and avoided a collision by a few feet. After several hours of investigations, the FANYs were permitted to take off, again in the Fairchild, for Naples.

Conditions in Poland, the loss of many planes and crews and the failure of the Warsaw rising, which began on 1 August, 1944, caused increasingly tragic news to flood into the Monopoli office of Force 139. J.G. Beevor[12] writes of a meeting on 17 August, when he was present with Henry Threlfall in Bari with three senior officers: Air Vice-Marshal Elliot, commander of the Balkan Air Force, ultimately in charge of the Polish sorties, General Ira C. Eaker, and Marshal of the RAF Sir John Slessor, who had flown over that morning from Caserta.

> All the evidence was reviewed . . . Threlfall's vigorous and reasoned pleading of the Polish case was heard. In the end the air chiefs reluctantly came to the conclusion that we had exhausted the resources available.

'To me,' says Beevor, 'and to Threlfall, this was one of the most tragic moments of the war . . . No more flights to Warsaw and its immediate surroundings. Our losses over Warsaw were not made good for over six months and, as a result, we were able to make fewer air sorties to northern Italy.'

Nor had operations to Czechoslovakia a positive outcome. The fierce reprisals which followed the killing of Himmler's deputy, Reinhard Heydrich, in May, 1942, dissuaded further overt activity. The two SOE-trained Czech agents from London who were responsible took their own lives rather than submit to arrest at their last stand. A few missions were put in from Italy, but achieved little beyond the collection of intelligence. A rising in Slovakia, not initiated by SOE, in October, 1944, caused Henry Threlfall to make a short visit from Bari by USAAF Flying Fortress, one of a fleet of six, to an airfield near Zvolen, north-east of Bratislava. He spoke for half-an-hour (with the sound of German guns in the background) with General Golian, in charge of the rising. A number of escaped British and American aircrew were lifted off, otherwise achievement was limited. The enemy overran the area within a few days.

Major John Sehmer of the Tank Corps, who had been on a previous mission to Mihailovic, attempted to reach Hungary via Slovakia, but he and a joint OSS team were surprised by the enemy on 26 December, 1944, and most of them, Sehmer included, sadly failed to return.

Other operations into Hungary were not much more successful. Basil Davidson, parachuted into Jugoslavia in August, 1943, as already stated, had tried to raise resistance in southern Hungary, but without much result. Lieutenant-Colonel Peter Boughey, a former Baker Street officer in the Central European Section, took up residence in the Polish holding unit at Latiano until he was able to persuade the authorities to let him drop near Lake Balaton, in the guise of a sergeant in the Black Watch. He was arrested almost at once and, alone of the other members of his mission, who were all killed, survived to spend time in a series of prisons and camps.

But life in Force 139 was not all gloom. The two resourceful FANYs remained in good heart and joined the remainder of the girls in Siena in the spring of 1945.

MONOPOLI: CLOWDER

The second group of FANYs at Monopoli who were not part of No. 1 Special Force, though they shared its life, was composed of those who were attached to the Mission CLOWDER, whose object was to operate into Austria.

In the autumn of 1943 Peter Wilkinson had written a paper suggesting such a possibility, and that infiltration should take place through Jugoslavia. The idea won the approval of General Gubbins and the SOE Council. It received the code name CLOWDER and was to be controlled directly from Baker Street. Together with a friend of long standing, Major Alfgar Hesketh-Prichard, Wilkinson left for Cairo. In December, 1943, they flew to Bari and arrangements were made with Gerry Holdsworth for CLOWDER's rear link to be established at Monopoli. A few days later, in company with Fitzroy Maclean (who was picking up Bill Deakin) and his signals officer, Captain Hilary King, the two CLOWDER officers, with their wireless operator, Company Sergeant-Major Hughes, flew to Bosnia. They travelled in a DC3 with an escort of six Lightnings of the US 82nd Fighter Group. On arrival in Jugoslavia, Bill Deakin joined Fitzroy on the aircraft and went on to Cairo, while the remainder of the party made their tortuous two-day journey through snow and blizzards to Jajce, the headquarters of the British Military Mission and of Marshal Tito.

On 6 December a long interview with Tito, followed by lunch, had the result for which the Englishmen hoped, approval of the plan to reach the Austrian border and help in the journey north. A signed photograph of Tito, requested by Peter Wilkinson, in order to ingratiate himself with Partisans he might meet on the journey, was also forthcoming. They pressed on, under nightmare conditions, to Slovenia, and then, walking mainly by night over rocky mountainous terrain and in freezing weather, made their way towards the Italian border, much frequented by German troops. They reached Partisan IX Corps in the Julian Alps and on 6 February Peter Wilkinson set off to see how far he could get into Austria and try to discover some courier lines. Despite a fresh set of privations, including frostbite, he was able to record that he had made an excursion into the Third Reich. The first CLOWDER parachute drop arrived on 14 February. On receipt of orders to return to Italy, Peter Wilkinson made the long journey south through Jugoslavia, whilst Alfgar Hesketh-Prichard remained at CLOWDER's advance base at Cerkno. The first attempt at a Lysander pick-up near Udbina in Croatia during the March moon period failed to fly Peter Wilkinson out after four attempts in below-zero temperature. Proceeding on foot to Bosnia resulted in his being picked up by a Soviet DC3 and transported to Bari.

On his arrival at Monopoli Gerry Holdsworth insisted on an immediate visit by Wilkinson to AFHQ at Caserta. During the visit General Alexander asked him to make a presentation of the situation in the Istrian peninsular. The interest seemed to imply that the possibility of an allied landing in that region was in his mind. A signal which demanded an immediate visit by Wilkinson to report in London resulted in interviews with General Ismay at the Cabinet Offices, with General Sir Alan Brooke, the Chief of the Imperial General Staff, and a number of Foreign Office officials, an indication of the importance of the CLOWDER mission. General Gubbins expressed himself in favour of establishing more despatch stations on the southern borders of Austria. An invitation to lunch with the Prime Minister was not received in time to accept. Peter Wilkinson had travelled to Scotland to meet some Austrians who, during internment, had spoken of their willingness to enter Austria as agents and undergo field training. They were to travel to Italy.

Meanwhile, during Peter Wilkinson's absence, Major Charles Villiers had been appointed to lead the CLOWDER base at Monopoli. He was joined from the Austrian Section at Baker Street by Major James Darton, Captain John Wedgwood and a FANY Captain, Betty Harvey (a pseudonym). Their task was to supervise the Austrian agents who were to arrive from various quarters. Two further FANY Ensigns made up the CLOWDER staff: Patricia Jackson (Dean) who worked for two years in Baker Street in a civilian capacity and was sister to General Gubbins' personal assistant, Margaret Jackson, and Alathea Trevor (Woodbridge) who had previously worked for Alfgar Hesketh-Prichard and Peter Wilkinson in the Czech Section.

Betty Harvey, in reality Elizabeth Hodgson MBE, was born in 1893 and was therefore fifty-seven years of age on her arrival in Monopoli. She had worked for many years in Vienna and was in Berne when war broke out, whence she made a rapid exit via France and the Pyrenees, a great deal of it on foot, made possible as she was a fitness fanatic. (She continued rock-climbing in Switzerland into her seventies.) Once in London, she joined

SOE's Austrian Section and, recruited into the FANY, left for CLOWDER in Monopoli. Jimmy Darton records that in view of her age and experience she had been given the FANY rank of Captain, which raised strong objections from Gerry Holdsworth who did not approve of FANYs being given higher ranks, but 'he was won over, as was the case with everyone else on her arrival . . . She continued to be my invaluable and charming assistant until the end of the war'. It appears that her energy knew no bounds. She worked on cover stories and false documents, on preparing men for the field, on the recruitment of Austrians and visiting them in their 'holding houses'. She even ventured into an Austrian and German prisoner-of-war camp, dressed in civilian clothes and wearing a feather boa. One of the prisoners enquired subsequently of 'the nice Viennese lady' who had been to see them.

Peter Wilkinson had planned for Edward Renton, already a member of No. 1 Special Force, to join CLOWDER and drop to Alfgar Hesketh-Prichard at HG Partisan IX Corps, but he became ill. Charles Villiers took his place. In June Squadron Leader Manfred Czernin and an Italian wireless operator dropped to within twenty miles of the Austrian border and dispatched couriers over the frontier. In July two further British officers with four Austrians were dropped near Tramonti. One of the Austrians entered his own country and met Czernin's chief guide there. They were not seen again after January, 1945. To leave Edward Renton in charge of the CLOWDER base and himself return to the field in Slovenia was Peter Wilkinson's next intention, but a signal from General Gubbins prevented his departure. He was to stay in Italy and prepare schemes, with the regular forces at AFHQ at Caserta and HQ Allied Armies in Italy, on what should be CLOWDER's role in the event of a general German collapse. The code name for this operation (which did not eventually materialize) was RANKIN C. In addition he was to earmark stores and equipment which Austrian resistance movements and existing missions might need. (Additional drops to the earlier one had already been made.) Between June and September, 1944, twenty-five tons of stores had been dropped by the RAF to the Partisans. These requirements placed a heavy burden on CLOWDER's limited staff, who, as Peter Wilkinson relates in his book, worked sixteen hours a day during August, 1944.

Ensign Enid Wise arrived in Monopoli on 11 September, 1944, another 'elderly' FANY, born in October, 1891. She wore First World War ribbons, as she had served as a nurse. She was married to Ernst Felix Weiss, an Austrian journalist who was ten years younger than she. They had previously worked in the BBC, he in the Italian, she in the French section. Both were dedicated Roman Catholics. Under the name of Wise, her husband was commissioned in the British Army with the rank of captain and placed, in civilian clothes, in Rome. It was hoped that through sources in the Vatican he might be able to provide a list of 'safe houses' in Austria to which agents might be directed. He also 'screened' anti-Nazi prisoners in a camp near Rome and made contact with the Cardinal Archbishop of Vienna. Evelyn Green, on leave from No. 1 Special Force (in civilian clothes in this instance), visited the couple in Rome, who for some never-explained reason, did not openly reveal that they were married to each other, but that they were a journalist and his secretary. Evelyn wrote in her diary: 'Their conversation is always lively and interesting'.

Charles Villiers was evacuated from Slovenia with ill-health. The weather became increasingly bad in the autumn of 1944, and the RAF found it impossible to make drops north of the Karawanken mountains. Whether or not Alfgar Hesketh-Prichard should be allowed to remain in the field worried CLOWDER's base not a little, as German activity did not lessen. He was obsessed with crossing the River Drau and was permitted to do so. Alathea Trevor writes:

By the time I went to Monopoli, Alfgar was in Jugoslavia trying to infiltrate a band of Partisans into Carinthia, where he hoped to find a potential for an Austrian resistance network. I was to help Betty Harvey with supplies to Alfgar and eventually to the Austrian resisters. I well remember Alfgar's last telegrams imploring supplies which we were unable to send because of bad weather, and the sorrow and frustration we all felt.

Chapter Six

SOUTHERN ITALY – II

THE 'POLISH' FANYS

Of all the nations whose forces operated under the umbrella of SOE, one of the most prominent was Poland. The German attack of 1 September, 1939, with its trumped-up motive, and the twenty-six day struggle which followed, led to occupation, but not total defeat. In spite of great suffering, many Poles were able to fight back. Plans for resistance of a clandestine kind had been laid earlier, partly under the guidance of Colonel, as he then was, Colin Gubbins on his visits to Poland. It was with this underground movement, the Armia Krajowa (AK), the Home Army, that Polish forces within SOE were able to make contact in the future. The Polish contribution to the allied war effort proved to be of enormous proportions. First, proficiency in the sphere of ciphers had been particularly adept. Before the German attack Poles had captured, and had been able to copy, two commercial Enigma encyphering machines which the Germans had modified to carry their most secret traffic. These the Poles handed to French and British experts who were able to develop the process of decyphering that had already been started; the rest is history.

Secondly, Polish escapees, lifted from their homeland by air to southern Italy, managed to bring out certain key parts of a V 2 rocket. FANY house-keepers looked after their needs. But this is anticipating. At first the training of Polish agents took place in England. There were a number, eventually more than ten, of holding and training stations scattered over the country, catering solely for Poles.

A Polish government-in-exile was set up in London at the beginning of the war and by the early months of 1941 some 24,000 Polish servicemen had reached England. This number was to increase ten-fold when certain of their fellow-countrymen managed to extricate themselves from Russia as the result of the Polish-Soviet Pact, also from France and elsewhere. All Polish service personnel were under the jurisdiction of the Sixth Bureau in London, answerable to their Commander-in-Chief, General Wladyslaw Sikorski, their President Wladyslaw Raczkiewicz, and their government. This was so whether they were part of the regular fighting units or the smaller, but still significant, contingent being trained by SOE for return to Poland as agents.

Flights to Poland from the United Kingdom were possible only in the winter months on account of the longer hours of darkness; the return journey of at least fourteen hours in an unheated plane, where much of the load needed to be fuel, presented enormous difficulties. Nevertheless, from early 1941 until the autumn of 1943 SOE organized 103 operations in support of the Polish secret army, of which 72 were successful; 194 agents and 80 tons of stores were dropped, at the cost of ten aircraft.[1]

By the third quarter of 1943 circumstances worsened; during two nights in September, six aircraft were lost. The shortest route to Poland passed over the German night fighter and anti-aircraft zone which protected Berlin, then under serious British attack. A suggestion came from the Air Ministry that attempts be made to reach Poland from the south; Sidi Amor airfield near Tunis was a possibility. The Polish Flight of three Liberator and three Halifax aircraft (later known as 1586 Flight, although the Poles liked to keep their old number 301), which had formed part of 138 Squadron, left England for Tunis towards the end of the year. There the first group of FANYs joined them. In time improved plans were made and the eventual destination became some small villages in southern Italy, with the use of Brindisi airfield, newly adapted to accommodate larger planes.

The creation of an operational station, a holding unit and possibilities for further training for the Polish agents, who were known as *Cichociemni* (those who come stealthily), was a major logistical exercise. In addition, Polish forces had their own signals outfit for traffic between bases and Poland, and did not share the SOE network. A third Polish signals unit, extra to the two already established in the United Kingdom, was set up near Brindisi.

Which FANYs should be chosen for the highly secret and potentially hazardous job of running these unusual sectors in unfamiliar surroundings was a delicate decision. Christine Hoon (Kolczynska) recounts the events that led to her selection. A South African, she came to hear of the FANY Corps in a way that was shared by many others, through a chance encounter with a member. In 1938 Christine and her mother were in the Austrian Tyrol on a ski-ing holiday. A fellow guest at their hotel described the history and aims of the FANY to which she belonged. In August of the following year mother and daughter were in Jugoslavia when the threat of war made them decide to take the train to England. In their carriage were five young Poles who were escaping to France in the hope of joining Polish forces regrouping there, a meeting which foreshadowed the shape of things to come. Once in England, Christine enrolled as a FANY driver and spent the next three years on various locations in the southern counties. In October, 1943, a summons took her to SOE headquarters in Baker Street where she was confronted by Lieutenant-Colonel H.B. Perkins, head of the Polish Section, Captain Jessica Aldis, FANY, his assistant, and later, most intimidating of all, by Commandant Marion Gamwell, head of the 'free' FANYs, who posed the most direct questions. Was Christine keen on creature comforts? She replied that she would not like to be parted from her eiderdown. Did she feel that her long hair would be difficult to manage where there was little running water? Christine turned her 'bun' into an advantage; she did not need hairdessers. No destination was mentioned, but there were warnings: a hot climate and associates with 'razor-sharp nerves'. She passed the test and went on ten days' leave before embarking for the unknown.

Barbara Legge (Kwiatkowska), daughter of the Earl of Dartmouth, joined the FANY as a driver in January, 1939, together with her sister Josceline (Donegall) who was later to follow her to Italy. On the outbreak of war Barbara, with others, was absorbed into the ATS and served in the ranks for the next three years, at which point she was given the option to be released. This she took and reverted to the FANY, who put the suggestion to her that she might join the group who were to serve abroad in the Polish Section.

Pammy Leach (Dyboska, later Niven), from Lyminge in Kent, became a FANY straight from school in the autumn of 1942 and served in various SOE Polish units as an orderly. Station XIV, in common with many others, was a requisitioned stately home, currently home to a group of expert Polish forgers, whom Pammy served and washed up meals; she kept the house clean and tidy and arranged flowers. The FANY cook was Olive, sister of Lieutenant-Colonel Dodds-Parker of MASSINGHAM. Lord Aldenham, the owner, who still lived on in part of the house, had for some time no inkling of what was being carried on under his roof, until one Christmas the printed decoration round the edge of a card presented to him by his 'guests', he, as a banker, recognised as similar to that on foreign bank notes. Documents to carry agents in the field past the closest scrutiny, money, ration cards, railway tickets, were all painstakingly produced at Station XIV, since lives depended upon their apparent authenticity.

On 12 November, 1943, twelve FANYs, selected for their reliability and cool heads, embarked at Liverpool on the *Monarch of Bermuda*, a former Caribbean cruise ship, sailing as part of a convoy. In command was Lieutenant Jean MacLachlan (Lindsay), formerly a don at Girton College, Cambridge. She was very regimental, took her duties seriously and insisted that her charges should carry their own luggage, her favourite expression 'being booted and spurred'. On board was Peter Ustinov, en route for Algiers to play in a film *The Way Ahead*, also members of the Rifle Brigade who showed themselves only too ready to carry FANY luggage. One of them, Raleigh Trevelyan, in his book[2] written many years later, commented 'The FANYs . . . couldn't be more charming, so we are not lonely'. Almost more exciting even than the Rifle Brigade were the large bowls filled with sugar and great slabs of butter on tables at meals, a family's rations for a month at home.

Sue Ryder (Cheshire and later Baroness Ryder of Warsaw), who had served on various SOE Polish stations in England, became a member of this FANY draft. Her wartime association with Polish soldiers was to lead to her memorable work among the sick and suffering in post-war Poland and elsewhere. Her 'Sam Browne' leather FANY belt is now preserved in the museum of the Sue Ryder Foundation in Cavendish in Suffolk, signed on the reverse by Peter Ustinov and Raleigh Trevelyan, as a memento during this voyage.

At the beginning of December the *Monarch of Bermuda* docked at what turned out to be Algiers. The bright sunlight and rows of white houses in terraces, rising up to a mountainous background, gave a false impression of cleanliness. The FANY group divided, an advance party of five to a sleazy hotel (with the unsuitable name of Oasis) in the town where some troops had been ill on the stairs. The first job in Africa was to clean this up. After a few days, they were driven to ISSU6, as MASSINGHAM was known, SOE's unit fifteen miles outside Algiers, where lunch was provided with the large contingent of FANYs. Then on to Blida, MASSINGHAM's airfield, where Major Krol was waiting with his Liberator of the Polish Flight to fly them to Tunis. Their temporary base and airfield was at Sidi Amor, twelve miles outside the town on flat countryside near the coast, surrounded by palm trees, olive groves and cacti. The crews were housed in tents and it was in the mess tent that the five FANYs were entertained to supper when they landed. Christine Hoon, as a driver, was shortly busy transporting aircrew; Pammy Leach and Sue Ryder catered for a house of Czechs, as they all waited for the extensions to Brindisi airfield and the move to Italy. The first operations to Poland from Sidi Amor were flown on 15 December, but they were forced back by bad weather. A further attempt, with the same three aircraft, was a success on 18 December, which was regarded as a good omen for the new southern route.

Tunis itself, an attractive town with wide boulevards, had a light-hearted atmosphere and a mixture of races after the battles of the North African campaign, recently over. Captured German vehicles were on the streets and Italian prisoners of war put to mend the badly churned-up roads. The FANYs received a good deal of hospitality. Such simple pleasures as a hot bath has remained in the mind after over fifty years, a German prisoner of war was detailed, in the absence of running water, to fill the bath from jugs.

Another recollection was tea in the British Air Force mess in a villa with decorated tiled floors in a grove of eucalyptus trees near the beach. A visit to nearby ancient Carthage followed, where the ruins stand on green hills and outcroppings of red sandstone with views of the Bay of Tunis below and the mountains of Cape Bon peninsula behind. In the great deserted Carthage amphitheatre, one of the RAF hosts recounted the tragic story of Dido, legendary queen of Carthage, and a strange pink light shone over the sea, followed by a brilliant orange and red sunset. Here was the home of the great Carthaginian leader Hannibal, who threatened the power of Rome in the Second Punic War of 218–201 BC and who crossed the Alps with 90,000 infantry, 20,000 cavalry and forty elephants. Strangely enough, his farthest port of call in Italy had been Tarentum, present day Taranto, a few miles only from the destination of the five FANYs who left Sidi Amor next day (22 December 1943) in a Polish Liberator for the airfield of Campo Casali at Brindisi.

An operational station, codename TORMENT, for the transfer of men and stores to Poland by air, was still in the throes of completion when the first FANYs arrived at Latiano, ten miles from Brindisi. They were taken straight to the Rose Pink Villa, a single-storied house of two inter-leading rooms at each side of a hall, with kitchen quarters down a passage at the back. There was no electricity or running water, which had to be drawn from a well; small oil lamps gave a mild glow. Behind the villa among orange groves was an earth closet. Later a makeshift shower was installed outside the kitchen. The only furniture was a table, some chairs and handmade beds which a Polish carpenter had created from the only materials at his disposal – timber from packing cases and grey army blankets nailed on to the frame. After a few nights, the weight of the FANYs caused distinct sagging towards the tiled floors; their camp beds had not survived the journey and eventual replacements seemed to be designed for wolf-cubs. A signal to London folk-memory records as having read: FANYs IN TORMENT BEDS TOO NARROW.

Close by was another villa, white this time, which housed the signal station and the Polish wireless operators and coders. The operational headquarters was in a building named the Admiral's Villa. Lieutenant-Colonel Terence Roper-Caldbeck was in charge of the advance party, with Major A.M. Morgan as Senior British Officer at Latiano. Polish officers were Captain Oranowski and, later, Major Jazwinski. Former primitive cooking arrangements in a field kitchen for these officers were soon improved.

On Christmas Eve Christine Hoon drove the British CO into Bari to collect a truck. In the late afternoon they broke their return journey at Ostuni where a training unit for Polish parachutists, code name IMPUDENT, was being set up in a building half-completed by Mussolini as a sanatorium. It was not thought reasonable to transport the many volunteers from Polish forces in the Middle East to England, only to bring them back later for their drop into their own country. About fifty men had arrived in the inhospitable shell, with sacking across glassless windows and oil lamps. But the atmosphere was warm for the ceremony of *Wigilia* or traditional Polish Christmas Eve: a Mass, supper and Christmas tree. The soldiers sang familiar carols unaccompanied, followed by the best that their cooks could do with army rations. Two days later the crews of the planes from Brindisi airfield joined the FANYs in the signals villa at Latiano, bringing with them an accordion, guitar and banjo to accompany dancing and singing.

The worst winter weather to hit Italy for many years persisted well into the spring of 1944; there was thick snow, driving rain and wind. Early in January two planes, with these same crews, carrying supplies to Poland, crashed at dawn on their return after a night of severe storms, one at Brindisi and the other into the harbour at Taranto. All were killed. Brindisi was undoubtedly a dangerous airfield, exposed to crosswinds, only one runway, and at that time no flare-path. The effect on the FANYs can be imagined. Any illusions as to their present assignment being purely an adventure were soon dispelled. To be of help to the *Cichociemni* and to assist them to bear their heavy burdens of isolation and fear would call for great personal strength. Early in February the first thirty *Cichociemni* arrived, together with the remainder of the FANY party who had remained temporarily in North Africa.

The days on the outskirts of Algiers at Sidi Ferruche had not been easy. The houses that had been rented for them and the Polish parachutists soon to arrive were dirty and needed to be scrubbed. Cooking for nearly forty people was done on two oil stoves. The drains blocked frequently, partly because leaflets designed to be dropped for propaganda purposes, and printed *Courage et Espoir*, were the only available sources of loo paper. The landlord was unsympathetic: '*Tirez, tirez, tirez, tout le temps*'. That was the trouble. On Christmas Eve the first of the Polish parachutists arrived by sea. Barbara Legge drove down to Algiers harbour with a truck late at night and it was a long time before she was able to find them. Hasty preparations were made for Christmas.

After several weeks the party left Algiers railway station on an ancient French train, bound for Philippeville, a journey of three hundred miles, but of thirty hours' duration. A new CO had joined them, Captain Mary McVean, who, after a year of coding at MASSINGHAM, hankered after the more pastoral life of domestic administration, the main work of a 'Polish' FANY; also two other MASSINGHAM girls, Sheila Burton and Joan Cutbush (Slominska), considered sufficiently mature. No one has forgotten the horrific nature of the next two days and nights. There was no food, no heating, though the nights were bitter as the train wound its way slowly through snow-covered mountainous country, no water, no sanitation. Stops were made at icy stations during the night. The FANYs lay across their luggage and tried to sleep. At least their carriages were covered; soldiers in open trucks burnt holes in the floors by lighting fires. Mary McVean had filled her water bottle with brandy; even girls who did not drink alcohol, which was many of them, were glad of it. Rumours that ships leaving Philippeville were often torpedoed did not prevent relief at being on board the *Ville d'Oran* which was to take them to Taranto. Cabins, mattresses, sheets and hot water awaited, and an OC troops who allowed them to come on board two nights early and not spend more time in the railway station. Malta was the first port of call, where no one was permitted to land, but Molly Pocock was able to go far enough to telephone her brother in the Royal Air Force who had just returned from a flight and was soon on the ship. The approach to Taranto was through a minefield. Jessica Aldis, who had flown from London, was at the port to meet them. A fifteen cwt truck took them to Latiano where the unit was reunited, experiences shared, and, best of all, there was mail from home. Thirty parachutists needed to be fed, so Sheila Burton and Diana (Dippy) Portman (Manning) began preparations immediately in the kitchen.

The original five FANYs, Christine, Pammy, Sue, Milly Price and Jean Robertson, had moved from Rose Pink Villa in anticipation of this arrival to a very large building of a type particular to the region, called a *masseria*, a fortified farmhouse, built against marauders from the sea, of which there had in times past been many. This one, called *La Capieri*, was two-storied with a flat roof, enclosing a spacious courtyard with palm trees. Accommodation for humans was on the first floor; formerly animals had been kept below. Rooms for FANYs and parachutists were in separate wings,. There was a small chapel, but still no electricity, heating or piped water. The kitchen was the centre of activity and of problems, principally for the two FANYs in charge of the catering. With the help of three local Italian women, one of whom they named Screech-owl, because of her shrill voice and style of singing at work, with her plain but cheerful daughter Rosaria and her beautiful, gentle niece Francesca, reasonable meals for fifty were produced from army rations.

The bitter weather of the first three months of 1944 caused great disappointment operationally. There were only three nights when conditions were suitable for reaching to Poland and out of twenty-three operations attempted, success was achieved on only one in January and one in March, with the loss of two aircraft. Because of the delays, men became disappointed and dispirited, and the girls' concern to maintain good morale increased. To try to counteract boredom, especially in the unfinished Ostuni building, a club was set up, run by the FANYs in a large house just above the ramparts of the town, with various forms of recreation.

With the spring of 1944 came more comings and goings, at first mostly comings. As already recorded, with the setting-up of the various branches of

HQ Special Operations (Mediterranean) in Italy, Lieutenant-Colonel Henry Threlfall came out from Baker Street to form the headquarters at Monopoli of the Polish and Czech sections, which were known as Force 139. Lord Selborne, Minister for Economic Warfare, paid the FANYs at Latiano a visit as part of his tour of units in Italy, as did Commandant Marion Gamwell. She arrived in a storm of torrential rain, when the house was at its coldest. Lunch was prepared for her and a brazier lit behind Gamwell's chair in order to try to raise the temperature. Two metal plates needed to be swung backwards and forwards to ignite the charcoal. Gamwell was busy talking when there was a loud explosion. The brazier was flung several feet into the air, along with charcoal and fragments of tiles. The heat had cracked the floor. Fortunately, neither she nor any of the others were injured and the FANYs were commended for their fortitude in the face of the austerity of their living conditions.

For the visit of the Polish Commander-in-Chief to the Latiano unit lunch was held out of doors on a balcony in sunny weather. Christine Hoon spent the morning gathering wild flowers to decorate the tables, while the iron railings were entwined with palms and shrubs. After speeches and modest feasting, the General awarded military decorations to four of the parachutists. On Easter Day a group of the men had managed to find a pig which was slaughtered and eaten for breakfast, plus cherry brandy and cognac, a change from the usual diet of dehydrated vegetables, spam and dried egg provided by army rations.

As more parachutists arrived from England, it became necessary to form a second holding unit at Laureto, near Fasano, ten miles north of Ostuni. the FANY group broke up to be able to run both it and Latiano. Just at the right moment FANY reinforcements arrived, also from England, in the shape of Sheilah Muriel (Buzuk) and Barbara Matheson. Barbara provided another driver, while Sheilah, with her domestic science diploma and cooking experience at Grendon, was invaluable, for the Laureto girls were now preparing meals for eighty men. Three more FANYs followed: Barbara Yardley, Jean Randall and Francine Agazarian. The last-named was a Frenchwoman married to an Englishman; she had been in the field with him in France. On 17 June, 1943, they had been transported home by Lysander. M.R.D. Foot writes:[3]

> Three doomed women [all FANYs] climbed down the ladders of
> a Lysander into the meadow grass on a particularly fine moonlight
> night in the Loir valley, seven miles north-east of Angers.

They were Cecily Lefort (ALICE), courier to JOCKEY, Diana Rowden (PAULETTE), courier to ACROBAT, and Noor Inayat Khan (MADELEINE), wireless operator to CINEMA. All died in concentration camps. Jack and Francine Agazarian were waiting to be evacuated, and made the return journey in the Lysander to England. On a second operation, Jack Agazarian returned to France without Francine, was captured and sent to a camp.

The additional help meant that gradually a more ordered system replaced the *ad hoc* arrangements of earlier days. More Italian cleaners were trained and officers no longer rummaged for their laundry; it was marked, washed, ironed and sorted into eighty neat piles. Barbara Yardley typed letters and kept accounts. Barbara Legge would leave at 5 a.m. to be at the head of the queue each week to collect rations from an army depot, a journey of 38 miles; she also supplied two holding units of Czechs and Jugoslavs. Laureto was a hill village of small traditional houses which were requisitioned for the new inhabitants: some were *trullis*, small, round, whitewashed, buildings with conical roofs. peculiar to the region. With the coming of spring, the FANYs were able to appreciate the beauty of the Puglian countryside, the contours, vegetation and wild flowers: cyclamen, freesias, orchids and lupins.

On a country walk Sheilah Muriel and others came across two young German soldiers, obviously deserters, who had been hiding in a cave. Driven out by hunger, they were begging food from Italians. They were able to see them taken into custody. She describes the daily routine:

> Sue Ryder and I cooked on a traditional Italian cooker in the big kitchen of the mess villa. A high, wide, pretty blue and white shelf with charcoal-fired frying and boiling areas and a large deep pasta cauldron. Outside we had an oil and water drip-fed cooker for baking, very dirty and unreliable, blowing up from time to time, covering us in choking black smoke.
>
> The Italian servants loved to make fresh pasta for us, draping it to dry, before cooking, on all available chairs and tables. A boy who was meant to help wait at table spent much of his time playing the guitar and singing in a high tenor voice. We taught him 'Where my caravan has rested', which he loved. One of our jobs was to arrange distractions, excursions, parties, etc, for our Polish 'boys' who were under great strain during the waiting period. There was relief and hectic excitement when operations were on, and often terrible dejection and depression when they were cancelled or perhaps went wrong. We tried to make the surroundings and atmosphere as normal and pleasant as possible, which wasn't easy.

One talent which not all the FANYs possessed was marksmanship. Mary McVean records:

A FANY who was turning towards an instructor and pulling a revolver's trigger said, 'Look, it won't go off'. He replied, with obvious restraint, 'Thank goodness'.

A change in the weather in the spring of 1944 allowed operations to begin again. One hundred and thirty-two operations were attempted in April, of which half were successful; the total for May was considered equally good.

Antoni Nosek, Secretary of the Polish Home Army Parachutists Association, writes:

> I was dropped into Poland with five others on the night of 4/5 May, 1944. We never knew when our turn would come. At lunchtime they would tell us, 'Get ready. It will be tonight'. We did not need much time to get ready. We put on our civilian suits, made specially for us, a heavy belt with money, two Colt pistols, poison tablet, flask with brandy (it was not my favourite Remy Martin) and on top of that a special boiler suit and helmet. In the evening an army lorry, with blinds down, took six of us to Brindisi aerodrome and straight to a waiting Halifax. In no time we disappeared into a dark night and flew into the unknown.

They took with them 'memories of those lovely times we had in Italy, being looked after by FANYs; they were all lovely girls'.

In the two months 104 parachutists were dropped into Poland and 172½ tons of stores, more than twice the amount which had been sent from England in the previous three years. Five aircraft were lost. The Polish unit had its own packing station and packers, near the airfield at Brindisi. On one occasion, in an emergency, FANYs were brought in to help pack the containers to be dropped into Poland. They heard on the airfield that the possibility of re-fuelling on Russian soil had been refused. Some senior officers made the parachute descent despite their age. One such was General Leopold Okulicki whom Christine Hoon and Pammy recall in particular; he joined the Secret Army from Latiano on 26 May. In order that the younger parachutists should not be aware of their presence and be in a position to reveal it, if captured, some of the more senior officers were kept apart from the rest in separate houses in the hills, with catering by FANYs. This was true, not only of those who went into the field, but those whom it had proved possible to extricate.

Three daring operations, code name WILDHORN I, II and III, by specially adapted unarmed Dakota aircraft of 267 Squadron, took place on 15 April, 29 May and 25 July. Each took a few passengers into Poland and brought out five, three and five respectively – certain significant political and military figures whom it was important to evacuate. The crews were British with a

Polish co-pilot. They were on the ground for three and seven minutes on the first two occasions, and although the Polish forces guarding the landing sites had heavy losses on the May operation, the exchange of passengers was made and the plane arrived back safely in Italy. On 25 July the Dakota KG 477 became stuck on boggy Polish land and efforts to take off appeared of no avail. The situation was desperate. Josef Retinger was on board, aged 57, having previously dropped into Poland, and now on his way to see Winston Churchill. Another passenger was a courier carrying vital parts of a V 2 rocket which had been found unexploded in Poland, and also plans for its manufacture in a Polish factory, rescued by the Underground.

After an hour and ten agonising minutes (while Polish soldiers kept the enemy at bay) and the aid of ropes and horses, the Dakota's pilot, Flight Lieutenant S.G. Culliford, a New Zealander, managed to take off. Pammy Leach remembers providing food, on their welcome arrival at Latiano, for the evacuees. Among them on the three flights were Tomasz Arciszewski, a future prime minister of Poland, General Tabor, Deputy Commander-in-Chief of the Home Army (both of whom moved on from Italy), and Lieutenant-Colonel Hancza CBE, who was hidden in part of the complex of houses at La Selva near Fasano, with a FANY custodian. When the war was over he took command.

During the light evenings of June, 1944, operations needed to be suspended. Parachutists and FANYs were given leave. Rome, now liberated, was a favoured option, especially as it involved an emotive drive past the ruins of Cassino where the Polish Second Corps had incurred such losses. The trees on the hillside were reduced to matchsticks and a few thin cats cried in the rubble. Mary McVean visited a cousin with the Argylls at the School of Mountain Warfare at Sepina, near Benevento, before they went up to the front line. She found the garments of the village people patched with tartan.

Back at the unit, the worst experiences of the year in Italy were approaching when, on 1 August, 1944, the Polish Home Army in Warsaw, joined by the civilian population, rose against the Germans. After some operations and high aircraft losses, it was declared that flights with supplies of arms and ammunition must cease. The discussions between Henry Threlfall and top-level military and air force chiefs have already been described. Further talks changed dropping zones and squadrons, but losses continued to be so serious that few were attempted. A daylight drop of supplies from London was made by American Flying Fortresses on 18 September, but the outcome, as far as Warsaw was concerned, was not affected. The sixty-two days of the Warsaw rising, and the consequent almost complete occupation of Poland by both German and Russian troops, led to a bitter autumn at Laureto and Latiano. Reports of the street battles came direct to the Latiano radio station; sympathy with the parachutists who had left so recently was strong. Those who could no longer get there felt guilty at their absence in their country's hour of need. FANYs remember heartrending messages from Poland, pleading for help. *La Capieri* was closed, as the water butts were found to be breeding malarial mosquitoes. A temporary move to San Vito heralded the eventual break-up of the unit. Several Polish officers were transferred to the Second Corps. FANYs and the remainder were concentrated at Laureto.

One last attempt to send in an operation into Poland was made on the night of 26/27 December. A largely British group of five, code name FRESTON, dropped fifty miles north of Cracow on their fourth try from Bari which revealed sharply and for the last time what had always been known – quite how difficult flights to Poland from Italy could be. On the first endeavour mist like milk rose up and the aircraft returned to Brindisi at four a.m. after hours of cramp and cold. The next two attempts were no better. The second was on Christmas Day. Eventually, the following morning at ten thirty a.m. they were off once more. Fires were seen on the ground and the men made a dangerous landing from a low level. Their leader, Lieutenant-Colonel 'Marko' Hudson, had been in Jugoslavia with Mihailovic, as had Major Peter Solly-Flood. Major Peter Kemp had previously dropped into Albania. Their Polish companion was Captain Antoni Pospieszalski, with the pseudonym 'Captain Currie'. The wireless operator was Sergeant Galbraith. Their intention, to make contact with remaining segments of the *Armia Krajowa* and to report on their condition, was hardly possible, as the party spent its time evading German attack and eventually were incarcerated by the Russians. After a series of bad experiences, lousy and transferred to Moscow, they eventually reached Cairo via Tehran in March, 1945.

By this time the FANY 'Polish' unit was beginning to disperse. Led with sensitivity and skill by Mary McVean in a manner worthy of her cousin, Colin Gubbins, they had acquitted themselves with honour. Menial, often tiring, jobs had been carried out without complaint under difficult circumstances. Discipline, especially self-discipline, had been accepted. This had been laid down in regard to relationships with their Polish colleagues under wartime conditions. That there were romances and marriages, especially in the years that followed, was hardly surprising. There were two weddings in February, 1945: at Latiano, Barbara Legge married Adam Kwiatkowski in the Catholic chapel on 3 February. Flowers and a buffet lunch were arranged by her friends. Sue Ryder managed to make a wedding cake, despite the curious stoves; that it began to lean over on one side in the primitive tin was considered entirely appropriate. On February 11 Dippy Portman married Flight Lieutenant Guy Manning in a ceremony in the chapel of a private house at Laureto, an equally happy occasion. They flew to Florence for their honeymoon. Eight days later, taking off on the return flight, the engine of their aircraft stalled and the plane struck the ground vertically. The New Zealand pilot and all four passengers were killed. FANYs attended the military funeral, with shots fired over all the coffins. Dippy Manning's corner of a foreign field is grave 2/C/18 in the Florence British Empire Cemetery. Dippy, from Florence, had telephoned Julia Cope at No. 1 Special Force HQ in Siena the day before the accident. She suggested that Julia should hitchhike to a party and return on their plane the following day. Julia, ever conscientious, refused regretfully, as she had mountains of work for Dick Hewitt. It saved her life.

So the sojourn in southern Italy ended on a tragic note. But the record stands. A Polish officer has written:

> You couldn't have found a finer type of Englishwoman anywhere. Cultured and friendly, hard-working and smiling, they created the relaxed happy atmosphere so necessary before the coming adventure. In the daytime they would cook, or sweep, or drive cars, and in the evening . . . they would join the parachutists in dancing tangoes, waltzes and *Kujawiaks*.

Future visits to Poland rekindled friendships made long ago. Christine Hoon, by then Kolczynska, and her son, made a journey in 1990. They attended a church parade in Warsaw of the survivors of the *Armia Krajowa*, with banners flying. Later some of the remaining *Cichociemni* gathered to meet them with bouquets of red and white flowers. 'Of course we remember you; we remember all the FANYs.'

Chapter Seven

SOUTHERN ITALY – III

BARI	**FORCE 266 – LATER FORCE 399**
TORRE A MARE	**HQ SO(M) ADMIN. ECHELON.**
MOLA DI BARI	**HQ SO(M)**

The Italian section of MASSINGHAM moved quickly to Italy after the allied landings and the Italian armistice (as already related in Chapter Three), thereby shortening the distance between base and missions in the field. The visit of General Gubbins to SOE Cairo in the autumn of 1943 set in motion the removal of the Jugoslav and Albanian Country Sections from Egypt to the Adriatic coast of Italy for the same reason. The objective was not only to reduce the span covered by radio communications and improve their quality, but, more importantly, to shorten the journey by air and sea taken by the supply of stores to the partisan armies in the Balkans, for such they had become.

After his part in securing the services of General Stawell to command Special Operations in the Mediterranean, General Gubbins appointed Jack Beevor[1] to help him. With the title of GSO I (Plans and Ops), Beevor's knowledge of SOE since 1940 would supply the experience of the organization which Stawell lacked. Jack Beevor arrived in Cairo in January, 1944, and the two men were engaged in the immediate problem of what elements of SOE Cairo should remain there to handle operations in Greece and Bulgaria and which should be moved forward to southern Italy, and, moreover, where SOE units in that country should be located. They flew, after a rough passage, to

Algiers for consultations at AFHQ, and later to Caserta, whence AFHQ was to move into the huge palace of the former Kingdom of the Two Sicilies.

After the war Jack Beevor recorded his experience of this visit on a tape at the Imperial War Museum. A decision had to be made:

> Whether to have the SOE headquarters for the Mediterranean in Caserta which was going to be AFHQ as soon as they could move forward from Algiers or on the other side of Italy, at or near Bari. When we were at Caserta some cynical but sensible friend said that there was no room at Caserta for another organization unless we were prepared to go on the fifth floor; and if we were on the fifth floor as much out of touch with the important people on the first floor, as if we were on the other side of the Apennines. We decided, I think rightly, on a suitable site a few miles south of Bari, which worked out well.

From April, 1944, HQ Special Operations (Mediterranean) occupied a sizeable building, the *Palazzo Albertonza*, in the small Adriatic port of Mola di Bari, some thirteen miles out of Bari itself. Here General Stawell assembled his immediate staff, headed by Jack Beevor and Phil Macpherson,[2] with various assistants. FANY secretaries joined soon from Cairo. (My own arrival came in June.) A second unit, HQ SO(M) Admin Echelon, Military Establishment 57, was created at Torre a Mare, five miles north of Mola. A signal office was set up there, with Royal Corps of Signals wireless operators. Eventually FANY operators who had been at MASSINGHAM outnumbered and largely replaced them. FANY coders arrived from Cairo and later from North Africa (and a few from England). A new supply base and parachute packing station was established at Torre a Mare, under the supervision of Brigadier (Bonzo) Miles. Lieutenant-Colonel Peter Ashton was the dominant figure at Torre, as AA and QMG, handling personnel.

Bari, as a reasonably large port, though nothing as large as it has become, was considered the best site for the Jugoslav and Albanian Country Sections which moved swiftly from Cairo in October, 1943, to a series of requisitioned flats. The size of the SOE contingent in Bari increased considerably during the course of 1944 and included a large group of FANYs. Lieutenant-Colonel Lord Harcourt was in charge of the SOE unit which graduated from being named Advance MO 4, later Advance Force 133, to Force 266 and eventually Force 399.

For the first six months after November, 1943, the girls who arrived from Cairo to work in Bari were all civilians. Most of them later became members of the FANY Corps, as requested by the authorities; a few declined to do so. Although a certain amount of pressure was placed upon them, this small group succeeded in maintaining their independence and wish to live a less regimented life in their own flat in Bari. Since they were all fairly senior secretaries who had been in SOE Cairo almost since its beginnings, their services were valuable from an operational point of view. On this account they had their own way, (under the mistaken impression that this was a FANY edict, whereas it was made at a high military level).

Annette Crean[3] was one such and was among the first to arrive in Italy by air in mid-November, 1943. She became secretary to Brigadier Miles. Annette was accompanied by Nina Tamplin, a Latvian, widow of Guy, whom he had married during his service in the Baltic. Much to the surprise of all on the airfield at Taranto, Nina descended the Dakota and kissed the ground, much in the manner, later, of Pope John Paul II, and murmured 'Europe at last'. They were met by Bill Harcourt, placed in a flat in Bari vacated by an Italian family, and although conditions were primitive and army rations sparse, they were provided with a cook and a maid. They were soon hard at work in a nearby office in Bari and presently joined by a small group of other civilian girls from Cairo. The menage endured for over a year, while everything and everybody became military around them.

A bizarre happening that winter concerned an American aircraft containing twenty United States nurses and eight male stretcher bearers which lost its way over the Adriatic and crash-landed on the borders of Albania and Jugoslavia on 8 November. No one was injured. Fortunately there was a British SOE mission nearby. The British officer burned the plane and arranged for the evacuation of the nurses from one British mission to another, escorted by Partisans. After a good deal of walking, they managed to reach the coast where a British Motor Torpedo Boat brought them to Bari. The aforementioned SOE girls went down to the harbour to greet them on 8/9 January, 1944, with whatever comforts they could muster. The American servicewomen put on brave faces after their ordeal; one of the worst features had been the acquisition of lice. They were flown directly back to the United States.

On the evening of 2 December, 1943, a lone reconnaissance pilot, Oberleutnant Werner Hahn, flying over Bari harbour in his Me 210 at 6.10 pm on the final stages of his flight, could see not only that the port of Bari was jammed with ships, but was able to count that there were over thirty. He flew rapidly to his base in north Italy and by 7.25 a wave of *Junker* 88 aircraft flew in from the sea to drop their bombs. They carried flares to bathe Bari harbour in brilliant light. Seventeen ships were totally destroyed and eight others badly damaged. More than a thousand military personnel were killed and a large number of Italian civilians.

Most of the ships were American merchantmen, carrying vital supplies from the United States for the British Army, including ammunition and trucks, filled with 'gasoline', also medical supplies. The most serious consequence of the raid was later revealed. According to the account of Glenn Infield,[4] a Major in the United States Air Force, and Italian sources[5] many casualties had unexplained symptoms and injuries, reports of which survive:

> Hospital personnel treated the survivors for shock and exposure, not realizing that they had been subjected to a chemical agent. It wasn't until many of the patients died without obvious cause that an investigation was launched and the true reason for the deaths learned.

The American merchantman *John Harvey* carried a top-secret cargo of one hundred tons of mustard gas. The ship had received a direct hit. Glenn Infield explains:

> In August, 1943, President Roosevelt, alarmed by the reports of imminent use of chemical agents by the Axis, issued a statement outlining allied policy on the matter of poison gas. Its use would not be initiated, but if the enemy were to do so (signs of which had been reported) retaliation would follow.

A consignment was sent to Italy on the *John Harvey* as a precautionary measure. After the explosion, military experts in chemical warfare were called in and all reference to the mustard gas injuries marked MOST SECRET. So the episode remained for many years. In the British cemetery at Triggiano, a few miles inland from Bari, lie the bodies of countless victims of the raid.

The newly-arrived SOE secretaries dived under their desks and tables when the noise began. The town rocked with the explosions, while the flares produced a brilliant light. All the glass blew out of the windows of the office. The girls were later escorted to a house inland for the night, since one of the ships, still burning, and towed out to sea, might explode. There was no electricity for a week. Eleanor Hodder, a coder at No. 1 Special Force at Monopoli, thirty miles from Bari, recalls hearing a series of 'terrible bangs as the lights failed and the shutters blew off the windows'. Peter Lee, head of security, temporarily at Monopoli from his Bari office, drove there quickly. He found Ruth Hermon-Smith, the sole FANY then in Bari (having come there with him a month before from MASSINGHAM) showing a great deal of *sang-froid*. She was sweeping up broken glass from a skylight on his arrival. During the attack she had taken herself to the cellar, down three flights of stairs with a glass roof overhead.

Ruth's responsibilities in the security section were considerable. She was PA to Peter Lee and two other officers who interviewed a mixed collection of

Italian and other nationalities who crossed the lines from areas occupied by the enemy. The search for spies and agents planted by the Germans was continuous. Ruth ran six flats, five of them for various bodies who appeared in Bari and under interrogation. Some were considered 'hot' and needed to be kept apart from the rest:

> At one time, in the flats I was running were General Zervas and staff, General Serafis and his retinue, two Romanian millionaires, an Armenian archaeologist, a Hungarian ex-cabinet minister and of course the odd Italian or two . . . Furnishing the flats was always a problem and there never was enough room.

A few girl coders arrived in Italy from Cairo during the early part of 1944, all of them becoming FANYs. Among them was Jean Gibson, later Heller, and Peggy Prince, one of the South African recruits. Jean had worked as a coder in Baker Street before leaving for Egypt in the summer of 1943, mostly on main-line traffic between large stations, not the field, and therefore entirely in figures, for which she had a special aptitude. Both worked in the signal office at Torre a Mare, in a purpose-built series of huts. At this early stage girls would walk a short distance along the shore to their shifts, past rocks off which they could swim. Torre before the war had been a seaside resort for dwellers in Bari with a handful of villas and almost no shops. More and more villas were requisitioned as FANYs began to arrive. Jean shared a villa, Peggy a flat. Neither had furniture except for camp beds. It was extremely cold, with no heating or hot water. They wore men's battledress and their pyjamas to try and keep warm on night shifts. Jean had become engaged in England to Pat Heller on his embarkation leave for the Middle East. When he was posted to Italy, they decided to get married. Jean hitchhiked to Naples to try and locate her fiancé, but failed to do so. To her amazement, a short time later, coming off night duty, she found Pat walking along the main street of Torre a Mare. They made plans for a date in March.

In the meantime Vesuvius, the volcano near Naples, began to erupt on 22 March and thick dust reached the east coast by 23 March, the date of the wedding, when it was almost pitch dark all day. As the bridegroom needed to travel a hundred miles to reach his commanding officer for his marriage papers to be signed, he arrived with his chaplain for the wedding (in a corner of an allied club in Bari) several hours late, with only half-an-hour to spare. Jean drove into Bari with one of her friends, who advised her to wipe the smuts from her face before the ceremony. When the newly-married pair arrived in Naples on the night of 24 March Vesuvius was providing a magnificent fire-work display, flames and sparks of fire shooting hundreds of feet into the sky. Next morning the mushroom cloud over the peak was similar to the pictures of the first atom bomb. The lava dust on the road to the Sorrento peninsula, where they spent their honeymoon, lay thick on the surface.

Late in April, 1944, Peggy Prince helped Staff Commander Hope Gamwell who had come from England to train a large group of thirty-two potential FANYs (secretaries and coders). They had by that time arrived from Cairo. Two courses, one of eight candidates in Bari and twenty-four in Torre, took place during the following month. There were eighteen sessions, seven outdoors, of drill and so on, and eleven lecture periods of one hour each. The subjects were designed to supply the equivalent of the basic training given to FANYs on recruitment in England. At this point uniforms arrived from Cairo.

The training needed to be woven into shifts and be beyond office hours, and was, therefore, not popular with the potential FANYs nor their military superior officers. It was not repeated. In future civilian girls from Cairo took their places among FANYs and settled down as members of the Corps without further ado. During the spring and summer more FANYs arrived from Cairo, some of them to work in Bari, but the majority in Torre a Mare, as many were coders. Peggy Prince helped to establish a new FANY mess there for meals and spare time. It was a large hut, with kitchen premises, a spacious dining room and adjacent sitting room with an open fire. The building, though covered with foliage and inside locked gates, was still standing when I visited Torre in the autumn of 1996.

Jean Outram (Argles), a coder and FANY from Cairo, came to Torre in April, 1944, when she remembers the countryside was covered in almond blossom. Her first billet was at Villa Anna I, on the road inland to Noicattaro. There was a wood-burning boiler for which driftwood could be gathered on the shore. If the water ceased to flow (a periodical happening, also affecting the electricity supply) the result was a red-hot stove. Excursions were made into Bari to attempt to penetrate one of the top floors of the Imperiale Officers' hotel. If successful, a hot bath was the ultimate luxury. Jean Outram moved to Villa Anna II by the seashore, where one dark downstairs room, with cock-roaches, was served by a cold tap. She and Jean Heller would hitchhike over the Apennines to Naples during a break of thirty-six hours after a spell of night duty and go to the enormous San Carlos Opera House, where Gigli was the most famous singer. Tickets in a sixth-tier box cost one shilling and six pence, and it was almost possible to touch the painted ceiling. On one return journey a driver allowed them to take turns in handling the vehicle over the mountains, all highly irregular. On another trip, when the golden broom was full out, the steering wheel on a truck came adrift in the driver's hands.

I was relieved to find, when I landed at the airfield at Bari on the afternoon of 4 June, 1944, that a van had been sent to meet me. An army driver took me the thirteen miles south to the town of Mola di Bari on a road which led along the rocky coast with the sea on our left. We drove through the village of Torre a Mare, but with no FANYs visible. On the outskirts of Mola, a beautiful, delicate, white Baroque tower, with three tiers of windows, gleamed in the sunlight, which seemed softer and less glaring than the light in Egypt, and the air fresher. Olive trees were the prominent vegetation, but there were a few fields of corn on land cleared of rocks. Round Mola's main square were grouped a large church and the eighteenth-century Palazzo Albertonza, which had been requisitioned to become HQ Special Operations (Mediterranean). Small white houses, all joined together, flanked the main street which led south towards the harbour.

In the harbour a stone mole stretched out towards the sea for the landing and protection of small fishing vessels. There was nearly always a pretty bad smell of rotting fish in this area, the discarded heads and tails of fish, no doubt. The inhabitants of Mola were short of food in 1944. They lived in narrow streets and alleys, no gardens, but one saw occasional balconies and court-yards. Two houses, 250 yards apart, in the main street, had been requisitioned for FANYs. One was the mess where all meals were cooked and served by Italian servants, and there was sleeping accommodation for six. The second house, where a space had been provided for me, held five girls in three rooms. A bathroom, where water usually trickled out of a tap, was an unusual facility in Mola, but it was, of course, cold. Heating it up required finding wood for the boiler which was in the bathroom, as was a lavatory with intermittent flushing potential.

On my arrival, there was a warm welcome from Daphne Sears, PA to General Stawell, and Blossom Spicer, a South African who worked in the Operations department, both of whom I had known in Cairo. After supper I wrote a quick airmail-letter-card to my parents (which is now before me, number fifty), fixed up my camp bed and soon fell asleep. I had been up virtually all night since leaving Cairo the previous day. It had been too uncomfortable to do other than doze on the plane in tin bucket seats.

As in the case of my arrival in Egypt, the timing of my coming to Italy was also momentous. The news broke that Tito had landed in Bari unexpectedly the day before. On 5 June Rome fell into allied hands and shortly after 6 June we heard of the landing in Normandy. Operation OVERLORD had taken place at last. Harold Macmillan's *War Diaries* give a vivid account of his reception of the news that Tito's headquarters at Drvar in Bosnia had been overrun by the Germans. Maclean's second-in-command, Lieutenant-Colonel Vivian Street (who later married Annette Crean), had noticed on 22 May a small German reconnaissance plane hovering over the British Mission. He warned Tito of the danger and moved out of the town. Enemy parachutists followed and Tito was fortunate to escape capture by penetrating deeper into moun-tainous country. Captain Hilary King, signals officer of the British Mission, had destroyed his ciphers and wireless equipment at the height of the alarm, but managed to put a radio set together from spare parts. Vivian Street made contact with Bari to arrange for Tito's obviously necessary hasty departure for Italy. He gave a map reference and requested a pick-up operation for around a hundred men. They were all successfully brought to Bari by C 47 aircraft of a US Air Force squadron, operating under RAF command. General Stawell and Jack Beevor, alerted at HQ SO(M), drove into Bari to meet Tito. They found that he had arrived in a United States C 47 aircraft made available under the lease-lend programme to the Soviet Mission under General Korneyev. It had taken off, without orders, and without waiting for the US squadron. A staff car provided for the Soviet Mission was waiting to take Tito to the latter's villa in Bari.

On hearing of the attack and knowing how Winston Churchill would be worried, since his son Randolph was at Tito's headquarters, Harold Macmillan sent the Prime Minister a telegram. Winston Churchill replied that Maclean (temporarily in England to report) would soon be returning and how he wished he could come himself. 'But I am too old and too heavy to jump in a parachute'.[6] On Sunday 4 June Harold Macmillan was wakened in the night by the arrival of a MOST IMMEDIATE telegram, telling him of Tito's arrival at Bari. He wrote in his diary[7] that he felt it imperative that Tito should leave as soon as possible for the Island of Vis, then in Partisan hands, having been captured by a mixed bag of Commandos and Jugoslavs. This was, in fact, what happened, but not before Anne Butler, FANY PA to Peter Ashton, had been sent to the NAAFI in Bari to purchase toothbrushes. The move also had repercussions in the office of the Chief Signals Officer at HQ SO(M), as I was to discover.

The liberation of Rome filled every FANY in Italy, by that time over 150 in number, with a determination to go there, and as soon as possible. Permission for leave had been closed over a busy period, but was re-opened by the middle of July, when two friends and I were to make our way there by a variety of means. In the meantime I settled down to work in HQ SO(M). In front of the Palazzo Albertonza stood the unit's vehicles, three-ton and fifteen-cwt trucks, 'public utility' vans (known as PUs) and jeeps. A sentry was permanently on duty at the large entrance doors. On the ground floor were the service departments: drivers, Camp Commandant's office, and his staff, MO and so on. Offices were on the *piano nobile*, the first floor, at the top of an imposing staircase. The Chief Signals Officer, Lieutenant-Colonel Rollo Seddon, was a pleasant, quiet man. His G II was 'Jimmy' Grice and G III 'Pat' Riley, both of whom had been in the Cairo office. I was to work for them all. We had our appointed places at a series of trestle tables in a huge room with painted walls and doors and great long windows. Outside in the corridor sat two NCOs with quantities of files: red-haired Sergeant Muir and a young corporal who had in peacetime played a trumpet in a Salvation Army band. Marshal Tito having been duly conveyed by sea to the island of Vis, it was of importance that the enemy should not realize that he and his headquarters had left Bosnia. Jack Beevor had the brilliant idea that a scheme of signals deception should take place. Heavy signal traffic should be sent to a set in Bosnia. A wireless operator was despatched by air to one of the Partisan brigade headquarters with instructions to operate his set heavily at regular intervals. FANY coders were required to encode quantities of bogus messages in his direction. I seem to recall that this included nursery rhymes. Meanwhile messages to Vis were dropped by parachute. The details of this scheme were worked out by Colonel Seddon's office and I typed them. Jack Beevor's book[8] describes how the success of the operation became clear.

> Before long, enemy aircraft started to overfly the area [in Bosnia, where the false trail was lodged] and the local Partisan commander soon interpreted the situation correctly. So our radio operator was forbidden to operate his set and had to return to base. But the deception worked for a time.

None of this, of course, could be relayed to my family. My letters contained news more domestic and mundane – details of what happened in free time (all FANYs were entitled to a complete day off each week unless there was a flap), parties and descriptions of those with whom we went to parties. HQ SO(M) was a friendly unit. There was a short break for everybody at eleven am (we began work at eight-fifteen) when officers and FANYs, of whom there were never more than eleven at one time, would congregate on a landing and tea would appear in an urn. Soon we became acquainted with one another. General Stawell was invariably courteous and knew us all by name.

Two FANYs normally arranged to take their day off together. We might hitchhike along the coast to places where it was possible, with so many rocks, to get into the sea for a swim. On my first excursion of this kind, Blossom Spicer and I stopped a truck going in a southerly direction and, as we climbed into the front seat, the driver told us that he was the vanguard of a long convoy, all of which we had brought to an abrupt halt. British soldiers were always keen to give lifts to servicewomen (they were forbidden to carry Italians) and proved very reliable. It is interesting, in retrospect, to recall, in the climate in which our grandchildren live, how safe we felt. Although we were often escorted by friends who were male on expeditions to swim or walk or eat somewhere, there were many occasions when FANYs would be un-accompanied. Walks along the coast in the evening in the dark after the office and supper, to get a breath of air and some exercise, were frequent. Often were the times when we would hitchhike in an army vehicle alone. We were more isolated at Mola than the FANYs at Torre a Mare, or at Bari itself, although, as time went on, officers from various regiments and units came to know of our existence and we received a large number of invitations.

The next arrival in Mola, after my own, was Commander Margery Hume Henderson, formerly a senior commander in the ATS, on secondment. In her late thirties, she had been in the FANY Corps for several years in peacetime, had been absorbed into the ATS, completed a staff training course and obviously had a good deal of experience of administration. She was placed in overall charge of all FANYs in the Mediterranean area, probably around 400 at the peak period, in units in North Africa and Cairo, as well as Italy. Trained as a scientist at London University, she was a woman of intelligence, but highly strung and nervous in the presence of senior officers. It was generally agreed after the war that she had done a good job, although there were situations that she did not handle wisely, as was made clear when the experiences of some former FANYs became told. Captain Peggy Minchin, who was also an older woman, had been a despatcher of women agents to France and had undertaken parachute training with them. She arrived in Mola to be second-in-command to Hume Henderson.

As secretary to the FANY administrators, Elizabeth Abraham (Ward), a young Princess Elizabeth look-alike with the same splendid complexion, came from England to live at Mola. She suffered from an old back injury, was in constant pain and was forced to return to London for hospital treatment. Before her departure she was allowed a visit to Rome by air in a plane set aside for troops' recreational purposes. The pilot invited her into his seat to fly the aircraft, which she did with varying degrees of success. She found it difficult to keep it level. Over what remained of the village of Monte Cassino, she saw a line of white washing; life was being carried on.

On my first visit to Bari during a day off Daphne Sears and I rang the FANY mess there to ask ourselves to lunch (there was a field telephone between all our offices and sleeping quarters). A domestic crisis caused them to have no food, so we ate at the YWCA and, since the weather was windy and there was dust blowing everywhere, we went to the garrison cinema to see Humphrey Bogart in one of his heroic roles in pursuit of the Japanese. Bari FANYs, probably around fifty in number, had a hectic life. Several of them worked in the Jugoslav and Albanian Country Sections. The newly constituted Balkan Air Force Headquarters had been set up on 7 June, 1944, to coordinate the work of the regular forces in the Balkans with those of special operations. It included supply-dropping sorties, infiltration of personnel, bombing and fighter support, coastal raiding actions of Land Forces Adriatic, Commandos and naval units. Its head was Air Vice-Marshal William Elliot.

With the establishment of Balkan Air Force HQ, the FANY coders who had previously worked in the signal office at Torre a Mare were now brought to Bari for each shift by open truck, although still sleeping at Torre. They worked in the basement of the Balkan Air Force HQ building near the harbour. On days in the winter they could arrive soaked to the skin. With such a large military presence in the town, entertainment possibilities were considerable: the Imperiale Officers' hotel, the Allied Officers' club, the opera, garrison cinema, YWCA, YMCA, and many others. Lynette Jooste (Croudace), writing from South Africa, recalls her days in the map room of the Albanian Section. She was hardly ever in for dinner in the FANY mess. Life was not all rosy, however, as there was an epidemic of polio in Bari, which she contracted. An officer in the Albanian Section, Captain James Harrett, died in an iron lung. Lynette had a long spell at the Red Cross convalescent depot at La Selva and recovered, though she continued to suffer from headaches. Missions to Albania had a high casualty rate. In addition to the death of Arthur Nicholls and capture of Brigadier Davies, already mentioned, there was another very sad loss. Major Philip Leake, head of the Albanian Country Section in Bari, dropped into the field in May, 1944, and was killed a month later. Major Elliott Watrous became head of the Section, at the age of twenty-two. FANY Lieutenant Nora Galbraith, a South African in her forties, was welfare officer to the British Liaison Officers in Albania, she wrote letters to their families and saw to their needs.

A considerable source of interest in Bari was the *va et vient* of officers from the field in the Balkans, with accounts of their exploits, the most colourful of them being Fitzroy Maclean who came regularly in and out of Jugoslavia. He liked to represent himself as a ladies' man, which sources in his biography[9] maintain was somewhat of a pose. He frequented the flat of the civilian girls, such as Annette Crean, whom he had known in Cairo, and liked the company of various Bari FANYs, whom he named 'the dolls'. He would send messages to them in his signals from the field, especially to a good-looking coder, Alice Holland, who had done nothing to draw his attention upon herself. To her embarrassment, one of his personal messages was not expunged at an early stage, and reached the office of the Prime Minister, since Maclean was his personal envoy.

Randolph Churchill became attached to Maclean's mission and arrived in Bari for the first time on Boxing Day, 1943. He accompanied Maclean to Marrakesh a few days later, where the Prime Minister was convalescing after a bout of pneumonia. He reappeared in Bari on 10 January, 1944. Though a brave soldier, a flawed reputation preceded him. He and Fitzroy Maclean dropped to Bosnia during the same month before Randolph could do much damage, but he was profoundly bored and wrote a number of signals on which he put a high priority, such as 'Decode by officer only', when he was merely asking for personal replacements of various kinds, which much annoyed FANY coders. He came out in the rescue plane with Vivian Street, but did not return to Jugoslavia with Tito, but flew to London. Later came the decision that Evelyn Waugh was to be his companion for some months, with a view to forming a bridge with fellow Roman Catholics in Jugoslavia. Their flight to Croatia in a Dakota on 16 July made a bad landing: lights had been perceived on the landing strip, but, once having lost height, the aircraft shot upwards before crashing to the ground. The British officers in the tail emerged less injured than others. Of the nineteen passengers from Bari, ten (including a girl Partisan) were killed, including Randolph's batman. Randolph's knee was hurt and Evelyn Waugh suffered some burns on arms, legs and face. The following day they were flown back to Bari and admitted to the 98th General Hospital. Randolph later went by air to Algiers with a view to being nursed by Lady Diana Cooper. Her letters to her son describe what a trial this had been. Evelyn Waugh's diaries declare that Force 399 in Bari had been 'absolutely useless' in giving help. Alas, both men had been so rude and demanding to the secretaries that they had forfeited the chance of further assistance.

Another figure seen frequently in Bari was Major Donald Hamilton-Hill, a veteran of the Auxiliary Units and an early SOE recruit. He was ordered by General Gubbins to gather up captured enemy equipment in Sicily, at the suggestion of the Joint Chiefs of Staff, and have it conveyed to Bari for shipment to the Partisans in Jugoslavia. In his book *SOE Assignment*[10] he describes the scene in the Hotel Imperiale in Bari, ostensibly in October, 1943. Apart from the fact that no FANYs arrived in Italy until November, and then only to Monopoli, with the exception of Ruth Hermon-Smith, he provides a vivid picture of the cross-section of service personnel present:

> The distaff side was also in evidence and indeed much sought after. Officer status, but 'other ranks' paid – First Aid Nursing Yeomanry Service [sic] were surrounded and outnumbered by their escorts by at least seven to one. FANYs were allowed to wear silk stockings – a big attraction.

At Mola the last members of the British Mission to Mihailovic, who had made their tortuous way down to the coast and across the Adriatic, came to see General Stawell during June. I just caught a glimpse of them. Brigadier C.D. Armstrong, head of the Mission, had not seen Mihailovic for some weeks before his departure and they had not been on friendly terms. Major Jasper Rootham, who accompanied the Brigadier, had maintained contact until the end, according to the account he gave Harold Macmillan.[11]

FANY lives at Mola were taking shape. Two girls were posted away, which left only three of us in our small house. The weather became much warmer during July and office hours changed to the pattern we had experienced in the

Middle East 0815 to 1315 and 1630 to 1930. The afternoons could be spent swimming along the coast in the hottest part of the day. Officers from the Raiding Support Regiment, who seemed to be able to lay their hands on transport and time off between raids across the Adriatic, often descended on our mess from their unit a few miles inland. We went swimming with them a good deal and sometimes with one of their number to the Allied Officers' Club in Bari, for dinner and dancing to a violin and accordion. Crewing for a friend who could lay his hands on a dinghy was an occasional treat.

A group of men who worked for PWE (Political Warfare Executive), a propaganda organization, lived in a villa on the shore beyond Torre a Mare. They gave good lunch parties on Sundays where there were nearly always interesting guests: Douglas Dodds-Parker, Lieutenant-Colonel 'Barty' Pleydell Bouverie (who was a prominent member of SOE in the USA) and, most fascinating of all, Lord Birkenhead, who spent some time in Jugoslavia. On the beach, he was a curious figure in a 'twenties' striped bathing suit with legs, but he was one of the most riveting conversationalists I had ever met. After dinner we would sit round a table in the candlelight (there was no electricity at the villa) drinking wine while he recounted stories of his father, the celebrated lawyer F.E. Smith, and his own ancestry.

The possibility of a change of work cropped up, which had been mooted in Cairo in view of my knowledge of German, also the chance of leave, since it was over six months since my visit to Jerusalem. This became a reality on 18 July, when Daphne Sears and I left Mola at six a.m. for Bari and the daily courier plane to Naples. Our destination was, of course, Rome. Three separate vehicles gave us lifts into Naples from the airfield, to the YWCA where we booked our beds for the following week on the Island of Ischia. Vera Aungiers and Leo Railton, now established in a villa as Douglas Dodds-Parker's staff at HQ SO(M) Liaison with AFHQ, provided lunch, transport to the airfield and news of a plane to Rome during the afternoon. A large hole in the fuselage presented itself as we climbed aboard; the aircraft had been used for parachute training. It did not, fortunately, fly very high, but was still draughty. A jeep on Rome airfield took us all the way to the YWCA, only opened nine days before and our names were on the first page of the visitors' book. Its former existence had been as the German Hotel Victoria at the Porta Pinciana. Instructions as to behaviour during an air raid, written in German, still hung in the bedrooms. Best of all was lashings of hot water.

Blossom Spicer appeared next day to join us; a replacement had suddenly been found to enable her to have leave. What was more, she had flown direct from Bari. There was no public transport in Rome (and almost no cars). Only military transport could be seen on the roads of Italy at this period. The SOE security section under Peter Lee had established itself just off the Via Veneto, with its posse of FANYs. There I met for the first time Prue Willoughby, who was to become a life-long friend. A jeep and driver materialized to take us to St Peter's which would otherwise have been a long hot walk. After seeing the Basilica, we were swept into an audience chamber, where Pope Pius XII was carried in on his *sedia gestatoria* in order to address members of the allied forces, of whom there were a great assortment. The Pope spoke in English, then in French. We were a long way from home, he said, and from those for whom we cared. As there were so few women, we three FANYs were pushed to the front and the Pope shook us each by the hand. Some Americans stood on chairs to get a better view, which was not very pious. The greatest piety was shown by the Poles.

During the following days we staggered round Rome to see the sights, dazed but exhilarated by the Pantheon, Colosseum, Forum, Palatine – an experience shared by most of the FANYs who were at one time stationed in Italy. Our tour ended with mass at St Peter's on Sunday 23 July, with singing by the Sistine Choir. That afternoon we left the YWCA to cover the 170 miles to Naples. A jeep took us to Highway Six, where an RAF truck containing three airmen took us on board and we drove through villages recently devastated by fighting. After fifteen miles the truck began to act strangely; one of the tyres had burst and was on fire. The truck carried an extinguisher, but no jack. During a wait for rescue the airmen poured petrol on the earth at the side of the road and brewed very strong tea in a tin can, without milk, but with plenty of sugar. The army called such a drink 'char'. They shared one tin mug, we another. Soon a passing vehicle lent the necessary equipment to change the tyre and we entered Naples just after seven. Since the YWCA was full, we stayed in a primitive officers' transit hotel. It was the site of several FANY adventures.

(Margaret Brown and Hazel Greenwood, having arrived in Naples, in a Mitchell bomber from Bari, were awakened in this hotel during the night, since the house on the opposite side of the road was on fire. The sleep of Vera Long and Julia Cope, in the same premises, was interrupted on another occasion by SAS revelry in rooms on the floor below. When the sound included that of shots being fired, despite Vera's cautions, Julia went down to complain.)

Permits from the Navy were acquired on the subsequent morning of our leave, in order for us to travel in the afternoon to Ischia, which was under naval control. Two hours in a launch brought us to the dreamlike island. The colours were like those of a technicolour film: bright blue sea, yellow sand, grey rocks, green mountains and trees and white villages connected by dusty winding roads and a brilliant YWCA in a house distempered in pale blue. On a veranda overlooking the sea we ate all our meals. Naval officers in jeeps, with a motor boat and seemingly endless spare time, appeared from nowhere. Our companions for the next few days, they took us swimming and all over the island. It was a short but blissful existence; the only material lack was drinking water. The naval vessel which brought us carried great demi-johns of water on board.

My leave permit was a day shorter than that of my friends, so at half-past seven on 27 July I left the YWCA by truck for the harbour and over to Naples once more. The news regarding my onward journey was not good. An American pilot had crashed with some British servicewomen on board. Until further notice no one was to fly without movement orders, pending a directive on future policy. In other words, no casual hitchhiking. I would need to proceed by road. One possibility was the truck which took copies of the forces newspaper, the *Union Jack*, for the following day across to the east each night; the other was the blood-transfusion van. Neither worked out. Eventually I rang a local motor transport depot and was picked up at four o'clock in the afternoon by a driver in a jeep. Fortunately it had a hood, because the road was dusty. The back was crammed with freight and the driver had been on duty for many hours without sleep the previous night. It was an eventful ride in the growing darkness across the Apennines, with frequent warning notices put up by the army: 'Mines', 'Suicide corner', 'Do you want to make your wife a widow?', 'Do your brakes work? Others have thought so too'. The tired soldier driving the jeep made the usual fire to brew tea and put his head under the fountain in the main square of Benevento to try to keep himself awake. He began to nod and tear along at a fast pace, only to turn at the last moment to his side of the road in the face of oncoming headlights. Alarmed, I began a series of inane conversations. Fortunately, the driver was destined for Brindisi, so passed the very front door of our mess at half-past eleven. There were sixteen letters awaiting me, one of the most precious elements in our lives. I read them all before going to sleep, but I was in the office next morning by eight. My friends returned next day, having been re-vaccinated for smallpox which had broken out on Ischia, a serpent in paradise.

Soon after my return from leave, there came an interview with Major John Humphreys of the Intelligence Department of HQ SO(M), with a view to my joining his staff. As a way of whetting my appetite, he showed me a signal which had recently come in from London, marked MOST SECRET, revealing the plot on the life of Hitler on 20 July, 1944. There was no news at that time as to the outcome, which was in the end bitter and tragic. My move was agreed and, following a replacement in the Chief Signals Officer's department, in the shape of Isobel Hatfield, a red-haired migrant from Cheltenham Ladies' College, I was released to join the 'I' branch. Assistant to John Humphreys was Captain Ronald Preston,[12] a Cambridge graduate in French and German who also spoke Russian. He had been born in Ekaterinburg at the time of the murder of the Tzar Nicholas II and his family in 1917, since his father was the British Consul in that town. A corporal by the name of Cuthbert completed the team.

My job was to deal with what was called 'enemy order of battle', to learn all there was to gather about the German forces: where they were, their movements, and try to calculate their intentions; also to collect as much information as possible on the terrain which the enemy occupied, its political system, indigenous forces and tensions. The information upon which these assessments were made came in daily from a variety of sources: aerial reconnaissance, intelligence reports on the ground and from other agencies. Every morning, except Sunday, at 0815 the 'I' staff produced a 'situation report' on enemy activity during the previous twenty-four hours. This was a verbal report, given in around fifteen minutes, by John Humphreys, or Ronald, or eventually, sometimes, me. Benches were assembled each morning in the War Room adjoining our office, where the walls were covered with maps and flags representing various units, to be moved when there was cause to do so. All the officers of HQ SO(M) from the General downwards would come daily, plus FANYs, to hear the report. Another member of the 'I' staff other than whoever was producing the information would point with a long pole at the relevant area on the maps where activity was taking place.

It was interesting work with a great deal for me to learn. But the autumn of 1944 was a good time to be learning it. The Germans were beginning to withdraw from the Balkans, starting from Greece, following the Russian attacks on Hungary in the north and the collapse of Bulgaria. It was important to try to gauge how they proposed to do so. Various units in Bari, such as the Commandos, Long Range Desert Group, RSR and Special Boat Section, went into action to help partisans harass the departing German forces. An advance guard, code name FOX FORCE, arrived on the island of Kithira in mid-August, and on the mainland of Greece at Patras on 3/4 October. The allied landing of General Scobie and his regular troops of 3 Corps, took place on 17 October, 1944. British Liaison Officers returning from the field arrived at HQ SO(M) for de-briefing, with interesting tales to tell. More equipment was being poured in: Margaret Graydon, a FANY secretary in the Balkan Air Force HQ building, writes from Zimbabwe: 'I recall typing many detailed lists of packages which were dropped into Jugoslavia'. In the opposite direction, Partisan wounded were transported into Bari military hospitals in increasing numbers. A New Zealand surgeon, Lindsay Rogers, set up a field hospital in Bosnia, hidden in a forest, where he worked sixteen hours each day. A redeeming feature was 'a FANY in the base office in Bari who tried to send us what we wanted'.[13]

At Torre a Mare signals traffic was heavy. More FANY wireless operators and coders were arriving in Italy after the closing down of MASSINGHAM. Alice Holland describes how double transposition as part of a code for field traffic, based on poems or books, had been largely replaced by a fresh system called

One-Time-Letter-Pad, sadly for her, because she had enjoyed the unravelling of 'indecypherables':

> As before, the agent and coding office had identical pads which were simply pages of randomly selected groups of five letters . . . Unlike the code we previously used, this was unbreakable because the actual letters of the message were substituted by others and never appeared . . . There was still a challenge – speed.

Word association helped. 'To this day, if I am following a car, I often try a word association with its number'.

Hazel Greenwood worked in Signal Distribution at Torre. Each morning she sorted out the signals which had come in from agents in the field and 'was one of the few people in Force 399 who knew what was going on everywhere'.

Dagny Grant (Holland Martin) flew out from England via North Africa, to replace Elizabeth Abraham as secretary to the FANY CO. The Movements department had omitted to arrange for her to be met at the airfield at Bari. Aged nineteen, she was somewhat dismayed until, having made her way to Torre, Anne Butler greeted her on the threshold of the FANY mess with the words, never to be forgotten, 'Have a Marsala'. Anne was a good 'fixer' who made all the arrangements at a week's notice for the wedding of the FANY signal planner Gwen Johnson, to Captain Michael Lees. He had been in the field with Mihailovic. Since he was a Roman Catholic, the ceremony took place in the Cathedral in Bari. It was followed by a splendid supper and dancing at the Allied Officers' Club. Two of the Torre FANYs had been recommended for commissions by their colonels since they were undertaking Staff Lieutenant's work and held against appropriate vacancies. Anne Butler was one, a vital part of Peter Ashton's department, and the other was Margaret Brown, whose duties included taking minutes at important meetings. Hume Henderson refused these requests. She tried to restrict commissioned rank to those who were in charge of others, i.e. administrative officers who were more senior in age. (It was some time before she gave in to pressure from the security section to raise Ruth Hermon-Smith to the rank of Lieutenant, as she was only twenty-one, in spite of all her responsibilities.) The Torre girls expressed their disappointment in their letters home, but took the decision fairly philosophically. Anne wrote that comfort lay in their interesting jobs and the appreciation shown in that quarter. The disparity of treatment accorded to women, as opposed to men, still required the shake-up it was to receive in the next generation but one.

Reinforcements in the form of FANY administrative officers arrived from England in the autumn of 1944, in view of the increasing number of girls in Italy. All the officers who came had originally been members of the FANY

Corps who were absorbed into the ATS, and now were seconded back. They were exceptionally pleasant and efficient: Lieutenant Antoinette Budd took charge of the FANYs in Bari, Lieutenant Josceline Legge helped Captain Joan Prechtel who was the CO at Torre and Captain Ann Mann became an assistant to Hume-Henderson, the overall Commanding Officer. Captain Barbara Amos, as already described, went to be in charge of the FANYs at No. 1 Special Force at Monopoli.

Deep sadness in the Torre mess followed the deaths of the husbands of two FANY coders. Gillian Johnson, from South Africa, had been married in Cairo less than a year before to Miles, a Rhodesian Wing Commander. He was killed in September, 1944. Ten days later the husband of Carmen Farrer died in action at the Italian front. Letters home describe how grievously the news affected everyone.

Back at Mola, an interesting assignment fell to my lot: a visit to AFHQ at Caserta on 6 September, 1944. John Humphreys had been asked to supply information for false papers being prepared for an Austrian national who was to drop into his German-occupied country. While a prisoner-of-war in British custody, he had undergone an operation in a British military hospital. An entry in his papers needed to be made to support this having taken place in a German *Feld-Lazarett*[14] which had been captured with all its documents, so that it would not be possible for the enemy to check the details. My duties were to trace such a *Feld-Lazarett*.

I left Bari on the daily courier plane to Caserta and entered the huge AFHQ building with amazement at its enormous size. Built in 1752 by Charles III of Bourbon and completed by Ferdinand I in 1774, it is 247 metres long and thirty-six metres high. I presented my request to the intelligence Records department who were expecting me and was told to go and have lunch. This was served in the vast dining hall reached via an impressive staircase. The painted ceiling was one of the largest I had ever seen. Later, I made my way back to Bari by plane, armed with the information that had been sought – altogether an extraordinary day.

John Humphreys' suggestion that I be given a commission as I was holding an officer's vacancy and doing such work was turned down by Hume Henderson on account of my age (twenty-two), but she agreed that I be promoted to sergeant. Up to then I had been a corporal, so my pay increased from 4s. 7½d to 6s. 1½d a day. He also asked that I should take the parachute training, which Ronald Preston had just completed. Needless to say, this was rejected also. I had been wondering how to convey this information to Palestine, without being insecure. When John Humphreys was posted away from SO(M) at Mola, Ronald and I carried on without a major but with a new corporal, Jack Ashdown, a tall, broad, athletic man, later made sergeant. Ronald called us 'Father, Mother and Alfie', though Alfie was larger than either of us. It was now Ronald who presented the morning report on enemy activity and it would be I who pointed the pole at places on the maps.

There came occasions when Ronald was called away for various duties, or leave, and the responsibility for the daily 'waffle', as he called it, on the activities of the enemy, fell to me. Although nervous at the outset, it became more familiar to search for the information daily and spell it out at 0815. 'Alfie' wielded the pole. Much worse was giving the weekly talks on current affairs to the 'other ranks' of the headquarters, which Ronald did on Wednesday mornings at 0715 in the basement. The idea was to keep them in the picture with the general progress of the war. On other mornings the programme was weapons drill or compulsory PT. A senior NCO would shout for all to stand up at my entry with a clipboard. On one occasion three men on a bench stood up suddenly and precipitated the fourth on the ground, a very old trick which caused the planned diversion, but I was determined not to flinch. One of Ronald's absences led to my having to present the talk he gave periodically on the progress of the war to the FANYs at Torre a Mare. I was sufficiently unnerved to leave behind the pole we used to point to places on maps (I had brought some with me) and needed to improvise with a piece of firewood. The electricity failed that afternoon and my words were accompanied by the hissing of a tilly lamp.

As a result of this activity, Hume Henderson was forced to give in on my commissioning, though again stressing my age. On 8 November I became an Ensign and an intelligence officer. Some wag in the HQ coined the phrase, 'The nearest approach to an intelligent FANY'. It was mildly irritating, but perhaps better than being called 'a doll'; increase of pay was to 7s. 4d. per day, plus a Mediterranean allowance of 4s. 6d. per day. Some minor administrative duties were allotted to me in connection with supervising the Italian servants in the mess, examining the state of the cloths used for washing and drying up, etc.

The hot summer weather began to fade during September and gone were our bathes in the afternoons and evenings when our limbs left phosphorescent trails in the dark water. I helped to organize games of basketball in the afternoons; there was a pitch at Torre a Mare. FANYs, officers and soldiers all piled into a truck to take us there. Sergeant Ashdown was far the best player. As the weather deteriorated further, with cold, wind and rain, electricity failures were many and often lasted several days. The authorities were driven to change our working hours so that we were not free in the afternoons and used the hissing tilly lamps and candles in our free time, rather than at work. As information for the following day's report often came in late, it meant working on after five-thirty if it were my turn to prepare it. There were constant water problems, either none or a flood. Members of the Camp

Commandant's department would come tramping in with lanterns through our swamped second floor.

Some FANYs became ill. We at Mola had endured boils, ringworm, athlete's foot (and Blossom, trench mouth, on marked cutlery). Isobel and Margery Hume Henderson and a large number of FANYs at Torre developed jaundice and were admitted to hospital in Bari; others succumbed to amoebic dysentery. Margaret Brown, who was one of them, wrote to her parents that she was away from her work for nearly three months. Elizabeth Fooks, having arrived at Torre from MASSINGHAM, was ill again and spent Christmas at La Selva. She was, however, well enough to play the leading role as queen of the fairies in the topical performance of Sergeant Cinders.

A letter from J announced that he was coming in my direction from Palestine. On his way to the front, he called for a couple of hours. It was six months since we had said goodbye in Cairo and so much had been written in the meantime that conversation was rather stilted.

During the autumn of 1944 a situation had arisen in Greece which is of importance in the context of this book since it directly involved seven FANYs. As the German forces withdrew from the Greek mainland, although it was considered unlikely that the various guerrilla groups would seize the opportunity of filling the power vacuum thereby created,[15] it was decided to take no chances and send in a British force. Small Commando units had already, as mentioned, established a foothold in the islands. On 28 September, 1944, an agreement was made, in the presence of General Maitland Wilson and Harold Macmillan, between the guerrilla leaders, Generals Zervas of EDES and Serafis of EAM, who had been flown to Caserta from Greece. The terms provided that all their forces would be placed under the Greek government, which was to return under the leadership of George Papandreou as Prime Minister, and be subject to the orders of the British General commanding allied forces in 3 Corps, for the liberation of Greece, Lieutenant-General Ronald Scobie. Furthermore it was agreed that general demobilization of guerrillas would then follow. The Greek Generals returned to their country to continue to harass the German withdrawal.

General Scobie arrived at Piraeus on HMS *Orion* on 17 October, 1944, followed by Papandreou the next day. At first they found general jubilation at the liberation from the Germans. The re-entry of British troops, code name MANNA, was carried out on a peaceful basis. As food shortages were acute, by the middle of November 130,000 tons of supplies had been unloaded. This became a monthly average. There was unfinished business to be carried out by SOE, having infiltrated a large number of men into Greece during the previous three years. An SOE Special Force detachment took up its position with 3 Corps in Athens. Lieutenant-Colonel Hugh Penman of the Royal Army Medical Corps ordered the immediate despatch to Greece of his FANY secretary Betty Bailey (in her nineties – 1999). She had experienced some adventures since leaving her native East Africa, including forming part of the escort of a German pilot shot down in Cyprus while she was there on leave. She left Bari in the daily aircraft carrying blood. She was the only passenger; it was bitterly cold. A member of the crew lent her a fur-lined jacket. Flying low over the Corinth Canal, she saw it crammed with damaged German ships. Her brief was to set up an office in Athens to which SOE agents were to report for de-briefing, baths and clean clothes. She wrote letters to their families. 'Old ladies, seeing my uniform, fell to their knees, grasping hold of me and praised their deliverer.' Other FANYs joined her: Prue Willoughby, Joan Cutbush, Joan Rigby, Betty Maxwell from Cairo and Betty Gray have been identified.

It soon became clear that the left wing EAM/ELAS party and KKE, the extreme Communists, showed no inclination to demobilize. On 3 December revolution broke out. The previous night General Scobie had forbidden all demonstrations, but a long procession of EAM and KKE supporters, half a mile long, appeared in the main street. The police fired and left several dead. By lunchtime British armoured cars appeared, but, as they had orders not to fire, the crowd did not disperse. A general strike followed. This caused the disappearance of servants at the *Grande Bretagne* hotel where the SOE party were staying with the entire Greek Cabinet, General Scobie and his staff, newspaper correspondents, the Bishop of Gibraltar, workers in the YWCA, Toc H and so on, in luxurious surroundings, but with inadequate army rations. There was no electricity or hot water. Prue Willoughby wrote in her report to Commandant Gamwell:

> In the office events were moving so fast that before a document was out of the typewriter it was out of date.

EAM/ELAS was more heavily armed than during the German occupation and had a considerable store of guns and ammunition in the city. It was obviously their intention to seize the whole of Athens. Prue continued:

> When it was too dangerous to go to the office, we collected dust-pans and brushes and tried to tidy up the hotel . . . There was tea and doughnuts at Toc H where food went on being served throughout the battle. At night the shooting died down a bit, for there was a curfew . . . By the middle of the week the situation had become far more serious with great concentrations of ELAS troops practically surrounding the city . . . Beaufighters were brought into action . . . One morning we saw great balls of fire streaming from the planes as they flew over the mountains strafing the ELAS concentrations.

One night there was a search through the hotel for a sniper who was thought to be trying to sabotage the generator and water supply. The whole set-up was alive with German agents who had been left behind to stir up revolution and civil war; many of these were captured while we were still in Greece.

A decision was taken at HQ SO(M) to evacuate the FANYs. Prue again:

> All this time air travel, though badly disorganized, had continued. The journey to the airport was dangerous and hand-grenades were sometimes thrown at the three-tonners, but we got through safely. While we were waiting for the plane, we saw Beaufighters taking off every few minutes to go into action. Even when we had taken off, our trip was not without incident, for the plane was carrying mail and had to come down at another airfield which was a hot-bed of EAM/ELAS activity. As we landed, a crowd of ELAS surged round the plane, but a jeep with a tommy-gun enabled us to take off safely.

During the five weeks that the insurrection lasted ELAS brought up mortars and artillery, but eventually admitted defeat. The outcome was never assured. In late December Winston Churchill, General Alexander and Harold Macmillan converged on Athens in appallingly cold and stormy weather.[16] An effort to achieve peace in Greece was attempted by bringing General Plastiras from France to be Prime Minister and appointing Archbishop Damaskinos as Regent until a plebiscite could be held to determine whether or not the King should return, something that SOE officers in Greece had suggested in the early autumn of 1943. Even so, complete demobilization of ELAS hung fire for many months, while British troops occupied Greece.

The weather became bitter during December. Our sleeping quarters, with their stone floors and walls, were like a sepulchre. A colleague on a visit to Cairo bought me a hot water bottle which I would fill in the mess kitchen after dinner and carry along the main street under my greatcoat to bed. Eventually a stove arrived for the mess sitting room, but the office was still unheated and arctic. We wore battledress trousers, jumpers, scarves and boots. On 12 December Captain Ian Macpherson of the Ops branch came into our office holding the ribbon of the Military Cross. General Stawell had just told him of the award for his work in Bulgaria into which he had dropped in the autumn, and from whence he had recently returned. He asked me to sew it on his service uniform. I did not make a very good job of it, for all I had in my 'hussif', with which all army personnel were issued, was a bodkin and some khaki wool. It was a propitious moment for Ian, for General Alexander had turned up at the SO(M) senior officers' mess that afternoon. His plane to Caserta had been grounded at Bari on account of the bad weather. He made a speech at dinner during which he congratulated Ian. General Stawell came to dinner with the ten Mola FANYs in our mess just before Christmas. He had been far from well since the spring, and returned to England early in the new year. (He lived to be ninety-two!)

General Stawell's place at HQ SO(M) was taken by Colonel Louis Franck, a Belgian banker who had prevented a large quantity of his country's gold falling into German hands by his swift action after the German invasion. That, and later exploits in West Africa and New York in the service of SOE, were good examples of his acute mind. Electricity was restored before Christmas and with it Middle East hours of work, which meant free time in the afternoons. Louis Franck would turn up for the games of basketball at the pitch at Torre a Mare with FANYs, other officers and other ranks, and join in with enthusiasm. From time to time he would draw out of his pocket various items of totally unobtainable make-up (probably from the United States) and give them to FANYs at Mola. I was the fortunate recipient on more than one occasion of this continental chivalry.

Christmas at Mola was an exhausting time. Since there were so few girls in the unit as a whole, we felt obliged to attend parties for all ranks. The festival started with a church service at Torre a Mare on the morning of Christmas Eve. A shortage of padres in the area meant they were all booked up on Christmas Day itself. The ten Mola FANYs gave a party that evening to the SO(M) other ranks (around fifty) in our own mess. We had borrowed a piano from the garrison cinema. It badly needed tuning, so during the afternoon I hitched to Torre a Mare where, it was reported, a piano tuner lived. He was nowhere to be found, but it proved possible to draw pencils and paper from the stationery store, so it was not a totally fruitless journey. The party began at eight-thirty with several of our guests in an inebriated state. It was Sunday and some of the men who had been off duty had begun to celebrate. They regarded the local wine as much as beer. Within a few minutes we had quelled a fight between two soldiers; a third fell down the stairs and cut open his head on the stone steps, while another put his hand through a pane of glass. The door of the bathroom was wrenched off its hinges. The temperamental drain chose that evening to overflow and the floor was ankle deep in water, which I cleared up at one o'clock in the morning. Although the activities and games we had prepared were rather superfluous, all the food was eaten and we were assured that the evening had been a great success.

On Christmas Day two teams of officers, men and FANYs took part in a comic football match. Officers dressed up in a range of odd garments. Stirrup pumps were positioned behind the goal posts, drenching anyone aspiring to shoot a goal. The locals greatly enjoyed the game which was played on one of their pitches, but became alarmed after half-time when a smoke screen was let off and some of the neighbourhood assumed it was a German landing. Most of the FANYs were faster on their feet than the men. I chose to play rugger and managed to score a try; my team won. Officers and FANYs served Christmas lunch, a British Army tradition, for the men in the garrison cinema. Trestle tables had been set out with white cloths and decorations. Some roast turkeys were provided, also pork and heaps of vegetables. My job was to ladle gravy from a bucket. After our own lunch in the FANY mess, we listened to the King's speech round our new stove and later responded to the suggestion from members of the officers' mess to go for a brisk walk. The day ended with a formal dinner in the FANY mess at Torre a Mare, with around sixty FANYs. Captain Joan Prechtel, their company commander, proposed the loyal toast: 'Ladies, the King'.

Parties continued into the New Year at units all along the coast. Travelling to them in open jeeps and trucks was agony, in view of the bitter weather. At a sergeants' dance at Torre I struck a lucky ticket for a partner in the shape of a young man who had attended his local Mecca ballroom in England every Saturday night. He danced better than any man I had met during my service abroad. At an RSR party on New Year's Eve a kilt came my way and it was possible to perform a sword dance to celebrate my Scottish ancestry.

Leave was due again later in January, six months since my last, but the snow on the Apennines made the mountain crossing unlikely. J reappeared one evening in a jeep with a colleague on a short assignment north of Bari. I had agreed on the telephone to remain at the office until his arrival. The Camp Commandant said they could both stay the night in the officers' mess and we managed to deliver the colleague and have some time on our own. The only privacy was in the open air and we walked for miles and sat together talking on the stone mole of the harbour in our greatcoats until we were nearly turned to stone ourselves by one o'clock in the morning. Next day the Camp Commandant sent for me. J had been very angry with the sentry at the entrance of the HQ the previous evening. The sentry had said that everyone had gone back to their billets; J maintained that I was still inside and became rather heated. It was not a good way to repay hospitality according to the Camp Commandant; he was not pleased. Neither was I, but I allowed my heart to rule my head and continued with our correspondence, and meetings and meals in Bari with J until his posting to Greece a few weeks later. The opera house produced a season of well-sung performances, which we enjoyed.

Blossom and I took our leave by way of Rome to Florence. A series of trucks with chains took us over the Apennines, wearing masses of clothes and covered in blankets. We stayed again in the YWCA and visited sights which we had missed previously, including a remarkable collection of pictures in the Palazzo Venezia that had recently been brought out of hiding during the

German occupation. An airlift took us on to Florence, where we, in company of countless other FANYs, were enchanted by that beautiful city. We returned with some delectable silk underclothes which, alas, we had purchased with our cigarette rations. The journey back to Naples was a nightmare in a series of trucks. 'Good God,' we heard a voice exclaim at one juncture, 'do you know there are *women* in there?' Being late back from leave was a major offence, so we were grateful for all offers.

Late in February came some sunny afternoons. Anne Burrill, who had been a good friend in Cairo, appeared at Torre a Mare as a FANY coder, hoping that this would prove a good way to join her husband in India, in which she succeeded. We would meet sometimes. A pleasant walk in Torre was along a dried-out river bed. Curiously enough, many years later, I found a description of it in Mary Bosanquet's *Journey into a Picture*.[17] Even more curiously, I had met Mary Bosanquet in Frankfurt in 1930 where her father was British Consul-General and my parents, my sister and I went to lunch. She, in 1944, had been working in the YMCA in Bari:

> The river bed can have had no water in it for many years, for wild plum trees grew among its rounded stones and blackthorn and broom came down to its banks and beyond, while small, hardy plants ventured out towards the faint breath of moisture where the bed of the stream had been.

Rumours during the end of February, 1945, reached the FANY mess that we were all, the whole of HQ SO(M), on the move to join No. 1 Special Force at Siena. Ronald had received a posting to the north where his knowledge of Russian would be useful. An option of taking his place or being posted elsewhere was offered. I chose the former. The morning report had fallen to me more often in recent weeks and had lost its terror. Eventually on Thursday 7 March we were told that our sleeping quarters were to be vacated on Saturday 10 March. We had acquired a large number of possessions and made some home-made furniture in the previous nine months. On 10 March we moved to Torre a Mare into temporary quarters. We found it noisy in the Torre mess after our little house in Mola. Hot showers had been built in the village, but the earth floor was swampy with mud, which it was hard to remove. So it was with pleasure and anticipation that we heard on 12 March that we were to fly next day to Siena.

Chapter Eight

CENTRAL ITALY

The first FANYs to be posted north from the coast of southern Italy were members of Peter Lee's Security Section. He arrived in Rome within six days of its liberation (5 June, 1944), as the number of people crossing the lines, with their various personal histories and aliases, had greatly increased; it was easier to interrogate them on the spot. Three FANYs followed on 1 July. Page Willoughby was one of them. Captain Peter Cooper, an excellent linguist who carried out most of the interviews, accompanied them with an NCO and a driver in two vehicles, a 15 cwt truck and a small Fiat saloon. (Ruth Hermon-Smith remained in the Bari office to administer the 'safe houses' for the accommodation of 'hot' personages. The Bari office dealt with the more domestic issues of security: the constant crimes, cases of suspected sabotage of SOE installations, thefts of stores, imprisoned suspects escaping, and so on.) The journey was accomplished in one day, but, since the front line was only thirty miles north of Rome, the nearer they grew to the city the more crammed were the roads with convoys.

They drove through several heavily bombed places, the worst Cassino, still mined up to the verges of the road, with no houses still standing in their entirety. The FANYs' billet in Rome was in the villa of a bed-ridden ninety-year-old contessa who still lived in the basement with her cook and maid. A bargain had been struck that, in return for their services and the accommodation, the army should feed the household as well as the FANYs. Unfortunately the contessa, two nun-nurses permanently in residence and the servants, all with extremely healthy appetites, left very little food for the FANYs by the time they had fed themselves. After several fruitless attempts to stabilize the position in regard to the rations, it was decided that to move was the only answer. A basement was the next residence which was dark, dirty and dingy. The next move to the turrets of a high building on the outskirts of the town provided a terrace where the FANYs could sleep in hot weather, with beautiful views. The onset of winter made this place unsuitable also, as well as the fact that the Fiat saloon in which the girls travelled the two miles to the office was stolen, in spite of being immobilized and the garage locked. Although it was eventually recovered, this method of transport was too precarious and another move was made to a flat nearer the office.

The first office allocated was far from commodious: four small rooms for all the equipment and records, three officers, three FANYs and three NCOs. Accommodation in Rome for all the organizations that poured in was at a premium. One of the rooms on the top floor had enormous glass windows and was uninhabitable in hot weather; another had no window at all. Eventually new premises were requisitioned on the Via Buon' Compagna, near the Via Veneto in the most salubrious area of Rome – seventeen rooms, recently vacated by the Italian Ministry of Popular Culture.

Prue Willoughby writes of her early days in Rome:

> The city seemed to us the most beautiful place in the world, with its elegant buildings, its gardens with their pine trees, and even the glorious weather – all part of our daily experience. One of my colleagues had passed a year in Rome in the 1930s with an Italian family and such free time as we had was often spent in their house, where the two teenage sons had been confined for two years, fearing to be press-ganged into the army if they ventured out of doors.

It was considered in the best interests of security that the section's staff should have an office and billets for its personnel apart from other SOE officers and FANYs. Gerry Holdsworth, who always positioned himself as close to the action as possible, had relinquished his office at the Monopoli base in the early autumn of 1944 and set up another in Rome in the Parioli district. His FANY PA, Gundred Grogan, and the girls who followed subsequently, took up their positions in a villa of Fascist architecture in the nearby Via Barnaba Oriana, the owner of which had made his fortune manufacturing uniforms for the Italian army. A signal office had been established in the basement with Corporal Wadkin as chief wireless operator, in civilian life a trader in buttons. Rosemary Dawe, a FANY wireless operator from Monopoli, joined him there in November, 1944. The work was tedious mainline traffic to other bases, she recalls; no messages from the field, and therefore all in figures. She also carried out some decoding until two FANY coders arrived and more wireless operators in the shape of Mary de Fonblanque and Edna Hewitt. Rosemary writes:

> We slept in an icy flat, trudging in the snow up and down the Via Parioli. I sometimes slept in all my clothes, including my great-

coat. We had meals in the Villa dining room, unless there were important visitors; then we were relegated to a humbler place.

June Mecredy and Ishbel McKenzie, both secretaries, flew to Rome that autumn from Monopoli. June worked for Major Eric Tulloch who commanded the Rome unit, and, as well as her secretarial duties, acted as a driver. She still possesses a permit to drive to an area outside Rome to collect firewood to counteract the bitter weather. She later became the first, and for some time the only, FANY in Siena with an SOE forward unit, billeted in a private house, in extreme cold and little time off, her bed warmed by a pan filled with glowing embers. She was joined by Trudi Ornstein, secretary to Major Pat Gibson,[1] before they both moved on to Florence to work at Charles Mackintosh's Tactical Headquarters. These isolated postings, full of interest for the FANYs concerned, made them necessarily remote from their colleagues. Other friendships claimed them. June, Ishbel and Trudi all met their future husbands during this period and later became Mrs Wilmers, Mrs Orme and Mrs King.

The No. 1 Special Force FANYs were well pleased with their new surroundings when they arrived in Siena in January and February, 1945, after journeys 'staggered' to maintain radio communication with the field. Patricia Wilson wrote to her parents on 20 January:

> We left our 'old home' at six am. We had an awful lot of fuss and bother about weighing in at our orderly room. We were allowed to bring only 250 lbs, including bedding, ourselves, luggage, tin hats and greatcoats. Luckily, I weighed 143 lbs all told, but some fools had so much they had to leave cases behind, and the rest of our stuff is coming by road. We drove off in four trucks to the airport.

She continued on 29 January:

> The billet we have now is a hotel . . . It is definitely the best FANY billet I've ever had, but cruelly cold. We have wonderful spring beds with thick mattresses. There are two big wardrobes with long mirrors and a dressing table and three small tables, also a wash basin with sometimes luke-warm water. You probably have some idea how cold it is here, but believe me it's colder than that. We have radiators in the rooms which are sometimes warm . . . There are Italian staff to do all the work and waiting etc and we have also brought our old army cook who is doing miracles with *very short* rations.
> The town that we are in is quite unique, almost every street is

narrow, cobbled, winding and steep . . . We have quite a long walk to the office from our billet. The office is an old hospital. We started work this morning amid bags of chaos, mechanics and hordes of men rushing all over the place.

Patricia, with other wireless operators and coders who worked shift hours, were housed in the *Pensione Chusarelli*, near the huge church of San Domenico. At night they were given transport, but during the day they walked through the town to the headquarters building, for many years the prestigious grammar school, the *Istituto Tolomei*, which had educated many of Siena's notable citizens. Their names were displayed on boards on a first floor landing. During the war much of the accommodation on upper floors was taken over by the elderly sick; doctors and nurses would hang out of the windows overlooking the courtyard. More than one wireless operator has commented that the dead would be wheeled out of the building in the small hours while they were on night duty. FANY secretaries and other daytime workers secured (temporarily only) splendid quarters in the *Palazzo Ravizza*, a former hotel located in an old house with decorated ceilings and walls, a terraced garden at the rear, views over the countryside and close to the office.

Within a few days FANYs made their way, during gaps between night shifts, to Florence, only about forty miles distance. The officers' hotel, the requisitioned *Savoia*, and the YWCA offered comfortable rooms, hot water and adequate food. The splendours of the Renaissance were in every street, if somewhat overlaid by piles of rubble left by the retreating enemy. Officers on leave from the front who had long been starved of female company gave frequent parties and dances.

Josceline Legge, with considerable daring and enterprise, made a highly irregular visit to the front on seven days' leave in order to see her cousins. She hitched a lift in a Red Cross truck. She wrote to her mother.

> I actually managed to get to my destination which was surprising, to say the least. Tim [Llewellyn Palmer] took me off to stay with his regiment . . . I lived in a billet and fed in about four different messes, as I had to go round to them in turn . . . We rode every day . . . The trip was too thrilling for words, as Tim explained everything so beautifully and we saw places that I never dreamed I would see in my wildest dreams.

While at the front, Josceline met her future husband, Dermot Chichester, later 7th Marquess of Donegall. They married in 1946.

The situation at the front had been static since the end of October, 1944, and was to remain so until April, 1945. The Germans had been able to build a strong defensive position, called the Gothic line, in depth across Italy, twelve miles south of Bologna. Field Marshal Alexander found himself unable to take the initiative. He had given up six divisions to the campaign in France and the weather had become atrocious. For the Partisans in northern Italy, snow conditions hampered their organization. Charles Mackintosh received permission to set up a forward unit to co-ordinate activity between regular and special forces and provide intelligence from SOE missions in the field. At a house overlooking Florence near Fiesole he established Tactical Headquarters, No. 1 Special Force, with a small group of officers and FANYs June Mecredy and Ishbel McKenzie.

Charles travelled over frighteningly bad and frozen roads, often in an open jeep, and observed the state of the front-line troops. There had been heavy officer casualties. Rain and snow fell continually. There was little shelter on the muddy slopes of the sharp hills. Men were wet through, sometimes for days on end. Influenza and dysentery were rife. With the lack of front-line activity, the enemy was able to spare more troops for attacks on the Partisans. Having failed to persuade them to surrender, German *rastrellamenti* of a particularly brutal kind swept over the countryside, killing both Partisans and peasants indiscriminately.

On 18 November, 1944, Field Marshal Alexander issued a proclamation which suggested that Partisan activity should be put on hold in order to save lives. This did not suit their outlook, and so SOE missions continued to be sent in to step up the level of organization and efficiency. Published accounts of some of these missions give graphic descriptions of the difficulties and dangers. Sergeant William Pickering, MM, a twenty-year-old wireless operator, had, as previously recorded, been on an earlier mission in the Salerno area; he then became a base operator at Monopoli. Together with a group of officers (two of whom were killed on the mission), he dropped to a snowy hillside south of the River Po on 5 February, 1945.[2] Their intention, in company with the Partisans, was to prevent the enemy from operating a scorched-earth policy as they withdrew from Italy. Germans were close by. While he was using his radio set, he was obliged to cease transmitting during an ambush and narrowly avoided capture. He quickly sent the group QUG in the Q code: 'I am forced to stop transmitting owing to imminent danger,' and made a dive for the bushes. He realized how anxious he would have made the FANY wireless operators at base who 'would have been wondering what had happened to Sergeant Pickering', until he was able to make another transmission twenty-four hours later to tell them that he had survived.

Michael Lees, after his marriage to Gwen in Bari in the summer of 1944, took part in two missions into northern Italy. On the second in January, 1945, he dropped into the Emilia region and was engaged in putting the local Partisans on a disciplined active footing in the Secchio area.[3] Gwen had been forced by her superiors to return to England. During an attack on a German headquarters, Michael was badly wounded and hidden by Partisans at considerable risk. He was eventually lifted to hospital and safety from a small landing site in the mountains, in a plane captured from the Germans, on the initiative of TAC HQ in Florence.

The contingent of FANYs of which I was a part left Bari for Siena at 7.30 am on 13 March, 1945, in a Dakota DC3. On board were eleven girls, five officers (male) and the crew. The plane circled round the projected airfield a couple of hours later to find it shrouded in fog, so flew on to an American airforce base near Florence. During the three-hour wait, although warned it was a make-shift affair, we were provided with what seemed to us an exceptionally good lunch – chunks of spam cooked in white sauce, sweet corn, beans, fruit salad and cream, all out of tins, but nevertheless excellent. The aircraft took off again when news came that the fog had lifted and we landed near Siena just before two o'clock. It was now bright sunlight as we drove in a truck into the town.

The impact of my first sight of this delectable place was one that has never left me. Deposited at the *Pensione Chusarelli*, a companion and I signed off for the rest of the afternoon and made our way through the narrow, pavementless streets. Tall houses, often six or seven storeys high, rose up on either side. At the fan-shaped *Campo*, the market place, we gazed spellbound at the *Palazzo Pubblico*, the crenellated town hall, flanked by the tall slender *Mangia* tower with its enormous iron-framed bell at the summit. Buildings reflected a radiant pink light which was quite unforgettable, turning everything into shades of terracotta. The cathedral, in contrast, was faced with marble in black and white stripes, its *campanile* also. Beyond the city walls were glimpses of the countryside, in shades of green and dark blue. We walked back to the *Chusarelli* along streets light at one moment, then dark under arches overhead, quite stunned by the beauty around us.

Next day and subsequent days were spent setting up the new War Room of HQ SO(M) in Siena. The former *Istituto Tolomei* provided spacious accommodation for the combined staffs of the former No. 1 Special Force and the original HQ SO(M) at Mola. I had been allocated a large, stone room on the ground floor, with french windows on to a courtyard. Offices and the signal station for wireless operators and coders were linked by a series of immensely long tiled corridors. By the time we from Mola arrived the weather was beginning to improve and offices were not so cold as endured by the earlier arrivals from Monopoli. The walls of the War Room needed to be covered with boarding on which to fix the huge maps of the areas where campaigns were being waged – the western and eastern fronts, our own front in Italy and the Balkans, where the German retreat continued in Jugoslavia. Once the boards were in place, Sergeant Ashdown and I stapled on the maps and then sheets of perspex, to be covered by a myriad of flags and pins denoting enemy formations, Partisan units and SOE missions.

All the new FANY arrivals were placed in the *Pensione Chusarelli* as a temporary measure. Thereafter it would be for shift workers only. Colonel Louis Franck, with customary initiative, had appropriated the *Palazzo Ravizza* as a senior officers' mess, thereby displacing the No. 1 Special Force secretaries, all of whom, with others of us who worked office hours, were to go to a new mess in the country. We lost our free time after lunch through the move. This was inevitable, because of the electricity shortage and the curfew which operated in Siena for all ranks from 11 pm. Later working hours would mean no evening activities.

Siena had marvellous off-duty facilities: an American cinema with films changed frequently and a NAAFI one (it also had a canteen which we called the 'nafe'). The Church Army provided a series of wonderful services: a lending library, dry cleaning of uniforms, a hairdresser and a canteen. An Allied Officers' Club was set up in grand surroundings, an old Sienese *palazzo* with chandeliers and a parquet floor for dancing (we had been accustomed to dancing on tiles). A Church Army van came to our headquarters each day at 10.30 am and 3.30 pm with tea and cakes in the courtyard outside my office. There were no baths at the *Chusarelli*, nor at the mess in the country, but a building in the town taken over by the military, which was called 'AREA', provided bathrooms and hot water for servicemen and women: women officers on Monday, Thursday and Saturday from 2 until 3 in the afternoon. FANYs could be seen walking through the streets carrying towels and a sponge bag.

My twenty-third birthday on 22 March, 1945, was a time to remember. My alarm clock went off at 6.30 am. All our belongings needed to be stacked up in the hall of the *Chusarelli*, since this was the day for our move to the country mess. My blankets and sheets I folded into a bundle with string and, this complete, I rushed to the office. The past days had been spent slaving to prepare the War Room for the first morning situation-report on the progress of the war since our arrival in Siena. Louis Franck had ordered fifteen benches to seat the members of the augmented HQ SO(M). Masses of intelligence information had built up and I remained glued to my RB 2 set to hear what was being reported by friend and foe. As I stood waiting to speak and deliver my account of the recent activity of the enemy, there seemed an inordinate number of expectant faces: a full Colonel, six Lieutenant-Colonels and a mass of lesser fry, senior FANYs and so on. Ten minutes went by eventually, with Sergeant Ashdown pointing to the areas under review with a pole, with the same resolution that I am sure he had shown under fire at the battle of Alamein. He was nervous too.

At lunchtime a large converted van, with benches fixed inside, conveyed me and my colleagues to our new home – an eighteenth century Tuscan villa, formerly a hotel, called the *Scacciapensieri*, three miles into the countryside beyond the northern perimeter of Siena. Here we had our meals and some slept. There was a second empty house a few yards away for sleeping only, where I shared a room with two others. Eventually there were forty-four of us in the two houses. Views on all sides were stunning. 'Our' house was called *Paradiso* – well-named – though it had no running water and a generator provided the electricity. As it was Thursday, a hot 'area bath' seemed a good idea on my return to the office to calm my shattered nerves. That evening my bedroom was filled with flowers given to me by members of the office to cele-brate the events of the day. I began to unpack. The bells of Siena's towers tolled across the valley that separated the house from the city; the light and colours in the dusk were magical. I wrote briefly to my parents: had I not earned my day's pay (seven shillings and four pence)?

All FANYs were working at full stretch. Secretaries thought the office day too long – over ten hours, with only a short break for lunch. Margaret Brown told her parents that, after taking shorthand notes for three hours on end, she was finding it difficult to write a letter. Many of them, needing the exercise, walked to the HQ in the mornings instead of travelling on the van, on which some wag had painted HMT *Romantic*. It made a circuitous route, as the road led near the bombed station and blown railway bridge. We descended into the railway cutting and up on the other side, bumping up and down to avoid the shell holes. There was dust everywhere. Wireless operators and coders dealt with heavy traffic during February and March. SOE was making strenuous efforts to prepare the Partisans for the forthcoming offensive, hoping to drive the enemy from Italy. The British Liaison Officers spread throughout the north with missions to Partisan units did their best to organ-ize groups in a military fashion and increase efficiency. One hundred and twenty-five British and ninety-two Italian agents had been infiltrated behind enemy lines; some escaped ex-Prisoners of War were there already and proved themselves good leaders. Stores, arms, ammunition and explosives were dropped. There was some opposition to the wholesale dropping of weapons in view of the political complexion of some Partisan formations and a fear that those of a Communist persuasion might use them against a legitimate regime in the future. British Liaison Officers who had experienced a similar scenario in Greece and Jugoslavia were well aware of the problem. The provision of intelligence concerning German troop movements also added to the flow of signals from the field to base.

Olaf Brann's replacement as intelligence officer to the Partisans, Captain Louis Melotte, back in Siena, became inundated with material. A summons came to me from Colonel Peter Ashton, head of personnel, with a request for help in the collation of these reports. It was impossible not to agree. There was no possibility of a day off anyway, because of the 8.15 morning meeting, which was daily except for Sundays, but that afternoon needed to be devoted to preparing for Monday.

1 April, 1945, was Easter Day. Some of us walked into Siena early over the fields, conscious of the warning about mines. The small Anglican church had been built forty years before by an English woman and her daughter whom we met later and came to know well. An army padre officiated. It was the day which saw the beginning of Field Marshal Alexander's long-awaited offensive in Italy. A brigade of commandos of the (British) Eighth Army started preliminary operations, to be followed by an (American) Fifth Army attack on 5 April. News came in thick and fast in the succeeding twenty-nine days from a variety of sources. Colonel Franck sent for me to tell me to listen to the German news bulletins. Mercifully, I was doing so already. By a careful turning of knobs on my radio set, it was possible to hear the voice of a news reader of the *OberKommando der Wehrmacht*. The set was contained in a haversack to be carried over one's shoulder. It had earphones, so sleeping companions were not woken in the early hours and it was possible to listen to broadcasts on journeys in and out of Siena on HMT *Romantic*. The German forces were, so it was continuously reported, 'making a brave fight' for some place to the north of one previously mentioned. It helped, with other sources, to piece together the state of affairs. The enemy was in retreat. It was tremendously exciting.

Ronald Preston reappeared for a few days on his way to join a unit in the north. He gave a dinner party for some of his friends at HQ SO(M) and we all went on to dance at the Allied Officers' Club. Next morning, to my horror, he turned up at what he had been in the habit of calling the 'Waffle'. Only he wasn't giving it this time. We had lunch at the NAAFI in the *Campo* and then climbed the *Mangia* tower of the *Palazzo Pubblico*. We came to the conclusion we were the first members of HQ SO(M) to do so. The 331 feet took some effort. The first part, twisting round a central column, was steep and dark. Then suddenly came light, with our arrival in a chamber with open slits on four sides, containing two reasonably large bells and notices *Defence de Sonner*. The next stage of the climb was hair-raising, up an iron ladder to a wooden platform. Above it was slung a bell of huge proportions, suspended by iron hoops and visible from the ground. I touched the bell as a sign that I had been there and Ronald took photographs. The view was sensational. Part of the sensation was that on the roof of the office of HQ SO(M) I recognized the 'Vatican protected sign', a large rectangle painted half in grey and half in yellow. These signs were placed earlier in the war on buildings which were used as hospitals and children's homes in an attempt to prevent their being a target for bombing. It would have originated during the time when the former school had been turned into a hospital for old people.

Exciting international incidents alternated with domestic ones: a present of black market eggs for my breakfast; the water supply at the *Scacciapensieri*, which was always fickle, failing for five consecutive days. A water-carrier came out from Siena and every available vessel was filled. Our electricity came from a mobile generator parked in the garden at the back of the mess. Being duty officer came round every fortnight when part of the duty, armed with a torch, was to turn off the generator at midnight, as well as locking up. As one turned off the switch the machine would give a loud sigh like a wounded animal and then be silent. Of course, it meant going to bed in the dark oneself, in my case, down the drive of the *Scacciapensieri* and up to the *Paradiso* to my own room.

At a party in the country there were present some charming Italians who gave an account of the enemy's withdrawal from Siena: 'And after that day, we saw no longer any Germans.' News of the current withdrawal now came in hourly, although fighting was still fierce. (Field Marshal Alexander was to write later, 'The last battles in Italy were just as bitter as any we had experienced in the Western Desert'.) There were those, however, in the German army who were aware that they had lost the war. Evidence suggests that Lieutenant-General Karl Wolff,[4] military governor of northern Italy and head of the SS there, was of this opinion back in May, 1944. He had had a secret audience at the Vatican with Pope Pius XII on this subject before the Germans left Rome. He claimed after the war to have been prompted then to communicate with the Allies through Cardinal Schuster, Archbishop of Milan.

In February, 1945, Dick Mallaby, hero of the MONKEY episode, was dropped once more into northern Italy with the pseudonym Captain Tucker, his intention to link up with the CLNAI (see p. 85) in Milan. Due to lack of security on the part of his Italian companions, he was captured by Fascist militia, but managed to secure an interview with General Wolff. He maintained that he was the bearer of a secret message from field Marshal Alexander to the Fascist Marshal Graziani, Minister of War.[5] Mallaby and General Wolff spoke for two hours on 26 February, when the former encouraged the General (who acknowledged that anyone could see the impossible position of Germany) to speak to Allen Dulles, OSS representative in Berne. Wolff, who was already putting out feelers towards the Allies through other intermediaries, caused Dick Mallaby to be escorted to the Swiss frontier at Chiasso. Field Marshal Alexander sent a British and an American general to meet Wolff in Switzerland; the latter had secured Field Marshal Kesselring's authorization to start talks. Kesselring, by order of Hitler, had been sent to command the western front His successor in Italy, General Karl von Vietinghoff, did not take up his post for a fatal fortnight.

Meanwhile, on Monday 11 April Field Marshal Alexander had issued a Special Order of the Day to all soldiers and airmen of the allied Forces in the

Mediterranean theatre. Everyone received a copy. I sent mine home to my parents for safe keeping and it is before me now. It was an exhortation 'to play our decisive part'. 'Final victory is near,' it began. 'It will not be a walk-over; a wounded beast can still be very dangerous'. During the following fortnight at HQ SO(M) thrilling news came in thick and fast from missions with the Partisans. Leave was closed; FANY wireless operators and coders were at full strength and stretch, since nearly everyone who had been at Bari and Torre a Mare (except a small number still employed on Balkan affairs) was now in Siena. Traffic from the north was busy.

Massimo Salvadori[6] jumped with Captain Keaney and Sergeant Pickering into the snow in Piedmont on 4 February, 1945. His object was to reach Milan as soon as possible; this he achieved. He had discarded his uniform and relied on his carefully prepared false documents to pass as a civilian. Although stopped at a road-block, he was not arrested. His brief was to act as head of the missions in Lombardy and as liaison officer between the regular forces, Fifteen Army Group and the CLNAI. Among the details set out in his duties was to maintain harmony among the parties of that organization. For more than two months he moved from one set of sleeping quarters to another, telling few friends where he could be found, while he made contact with the members of the Resistance. One of them was General Cadorna. He acted with considerable courage, for it became known to the secret police that an allied officer, in close touch with the central leadership of the resisters, was living in the city. A courier from AFHQ at Caserta informed Salvadori that he was now a Lieutenant-Colonel. On 25 April he was present at a meeting of the CLNAI when a proclamation was issued ordering a revolt in all towns of northern Italy. As a result, the Germans mounted guard inside the barbed wire of their Milan headquarters. Salvadori spoke on the radio. When the first American patrols arrived on Sunday 29 April, the city was under CLNAI control. The same scene was repeated elsewhere. On 28 April a FANY wireless operator received a signal in plain language from the field: MUSSOLINI KILLED TODAY.

Allied troops had entered Bologna on 21 April. Partisan forces had been active inside and outside the town from the previous day and handed over captured weapons. J.G. Beevor[7] writes that Partisans liberated over one hundred towns and took some 40,000 German and Fascist prisoners. The most spectacular surrender took place in Genoa, where, due to a great extent to the efforts of British Liaison Officers Peter McMullen and Basil Davidson,[8] the German garrison surrendered to Partisans. Moreover, the port had not been dismantled by the retreating enemy.

Official histories written in the 1950s tend to underestimate the part played by special operations and resistance forces and diminish the German fear of Partisan activity, a fact that was to be disproved by an officer of HQ SO(M) a short time after the end of hostilities (see p 154).

When General von Vietinghoff took up his post as commander of the German forces in Italy he realized that the German cause was lost. He agreed to sign an unconditional surrender provided he could do so 'with honour as a soldier'. He nominated two German officers as his plenipotentiaries and asked for a draft instrument of surrender to be sent to Berne. This was refused on the Allied side. Signing could only be done at Caserta. This took place between General William Morgan, Chief-of-Staff, in a ceremony at 2 pm on 29 April. Both German officers wore civilian clothes. The terms were to take effect at midday on 2 May, 1945.

Back at their headquarters in Bolzano, the German generals feared execution, as they had been told by Hitler to fight to the finish. (Such had recently been the fate of a German general in Berlin.) There was also the possibility that the surrender document would not be honoured and troops in the battle zone not made aware of the cease-fire. Hitler's death was announced on the evening of 29 April. At the same time commanders in the field declared they had insufficient ammunition to fight the Partisans. After some delay, Wolff was eventually able to persuade Kesselring (who had on 28 April been placed to command the Italian front also) to agree to the surrender. When Alexander heard the plain language messages going out to German units to cease-fire, he announced at 6.30 pm on 2 May the surrender of all German forces in Italy.

General Gubbins, to quote his biography, had promised himself a lightning visit to Italy before the German surrender 'which was now expected daily'. He just made it and turned up at my morning survey of enemy activity at HQ SO(M) on 3 May, together with a bevy of officers who were accompanying him. It was an excitement to add to the triumphal news. Next morning, since there was no longer an enemy, I delivered my last report. We all felt quite dazed. The war, for many of us, had lasted for over a quarter of our lives. I spent a day tearing up papers and another having my first complete day off since arriving in Siena.

Anne Butler wrote on 4 May to her aunt in Northumberland, commenting on the two events – the reception of the end of the war and the arrival of General Gubbins:

> The news is really terrific . . . Last night all the lights have been on in the streets and it looked quite enchanting . . . lamps high up on the buildings giving the effect of making everything floodlit. Flags were hanging above all the doors and the streets were thronged with people dressed in their Sunday-go-to-meeting clothes and singing. It was most romantic and lovely . . . We have a distinguished visitor here today and we are all standing by for him to come round the offices. He is only a few hours late and everything

is so clean and tidy that no one likes to begin any work in case they spoil the effect.

As HMT *Romantic* with its consignment of FANYs drew up in the courtyard of HQ SO(M) in Siena early in the morning of 4 May, we were aware of some drivers putting finishing touches to the servicing, cleaning and polishing of a staff car and a jeep and trailer. They told us that they had been instructed that, whatever happened, the vehicles must spring to life immediately on the first pressure on the self-starter. We were later to learn that these were the vehicles which were to carry Lieutenant-Colonel Henry Threlfall, former head of Force 139, and Captain Louis Melotte, both fluent German speakers, to the headquarters of the former German army in Italy. They were accompanied by two drivers, a batman and two wireless operators (alas, FANYs had not been chosen) with their radio equipment which would enable them to communicate with base.

The report of Colonel Threlfall of the visit makes fascinating reading.[9] He was part of a joint venture of SOE and OSS, acting as a liaison mission of the Allied Fifteenth Army Group, charged to make an immediate visit before the arrival of regular forces. Its prime concern was to investigate the enemy's attitude to Partisan problems and to supervise the Germans' implementation of instructions consequent upon the surrender. Threlfall described the entry into still German-controlled territory in dramatic terms. As they drove through Rovereto to Bolzano and General Vietinghoff's headquarters, armed German patrols were still at their posts along the road. German troops stared from the pavements and German anti-tank guns still pointed in their direction. Next day they began conversations with various officers, including General Wolff in person, also with the head of the local Partisans, Dr de Angelis. The Allied party was anxious to know which part of the German forces, the army or the SS, had been responsible for activity against the Partisans. Questions were asked as to reports of atrocities against the Resistance and in relation to members of the Italian civilian population. Enquiries were also made as to the whereabouts of various allied servicemen who had disappeared in the field. That they were met by a certain amount of evasion and lack of information was not unexpected. The matter of disarming German troops was waived aside with the counter-question, when were the Partisans to lay down their arms?

Some of the most important discoveries made by Colonel Threlfall were among the documents that he discovered and was able to translate. They showed the substantial fear instilled into the German forces by the Partisans and how much harassment and impediment in regard to communications they had caused. Reference was made to the destruction of bridges: 'supply traffic is severely handicapped'. Other examples included 'The Partisan bands possess an excellent intelligence service'; '5 April 1945: A large number of vital supply routes are now only useable in convoy and are to some extent completely in partisan hands.' Kesselring himself signed a telegram on 26 February, 1945, that 'The execution of partisan operations shows considerably more commanding leadership'. He called for several large-scale operations which 'will nip in the bud the increasing activity of the partisan bands in Northern Italy'.[9]

Vera Long and June Stanley recall processing Henry Threlfall's report and findings and, most especially, the quantity of French champagne from the German headquarters which he brought back from Bolzano on his return on 14 May.

President Roosevelt had died on 14 April and a party which should have been held in the Senior Officers' mess at the *Ravizza* was postponed until the following week. But it was nothing like the party for General Gubbins on 7 May. He danced with me for nearly half an hour and remarked, 'Dancing is like riding. You know when you've a good partner.' Words which I have not forgotten after over fifty years.

'A Service of Thanksgiving for Victory' took place in the courtyard of HQ SO(M) the following day. The weather, which had been reasonably warm at the end of April, suddenly turned cold and wet, so we were still in our winter uniforms and the order to put on khaki drill had not been issued. 8 May was suddenly extremely hot. Everyone sweltered, being required to wear service dress with gloves. There was a parade first, an inspection and a good deal of 'front rank this and rear rank that' until the whole of HQ SO(M) filed into the courtyard to sit on chairs and benches, formed up on three sides of a square. On the fourth side was a table with a Union Jack upon it and the officiating army padre. The service followed a printed leaflet and it crossed my mind to wonder when it was drafted and at what stage it had become certain that the Allies would win, though I don't believe that the possibility of not doing so ever crossed our minds.

An out-of-tune piano had been carried out to the courtyard. Despite being so out-numbered, the soprano singing of the FANY predominated over that of the tenors and basses. General Gubbins gave an address. Perhaps it was because many of us had cause to remember countless friends and relations who had not survived to this day, that the ceremony did not appear particularly joyful. I heard one senior officer remark, 'You'd think we'd lost the war, and not won it.'

A sad piece of news had come to the office a few days before the end of hostilities. Pat Riley, with whom I had shared an office in Cairo for nine months, was killed in an aircraft accident when on a brief liaison job in the south of Italy. The plane on which he was travelling hit a mountain in the fog. He had come into my room only days before to ask for the latest news. A sad blow for his parents, who must have considered him safe now. A sudden recall that he had borrowed my tennis racket made me wonder whether it would appear heartless to ask for it.

There were others for whom peace did not bring comfort. When the Allied armies reached the German former concentration camp at Flossenberg they discovered that several prisoners had recently been hanged. Among them was the Lutheran pastor, Dietrich Bonhoeffer, and Jack Agazarian, husband of Francine. It was an act of pure vindictiveness, for it was at that stage abundantly clear that the war was lost. Francine slept in a room directly below the one I shared at the *Paradiso*. After she heard the news we would see her in the garden in the evenings kicking the gravel in an attempt to come to terms with it.

A problem now faced FANY administrators. Many girls, having been so busy, no longer had any work. FANY secretaries were fairly well occupied as the departments which had despatched missions had weeks of winding and clearing up, resolving problems in the field, and reports. But the sudden reduction of signals traffic meant that many wireless operators and coders were at a loose end. It was obviously impossible to secure immediate passages back to England for such numbers when servicemen had been abroad for longer periods.

Some girls offered themselves for service with SOE in the Far East; volunteers were still required. Dagny Grant was posted to a unit in Austria. Since it was under the jurisdiction of the Eighth Army and not SOE, when it was discovered that she was under twenty years of age, she was required to return to Siena. SOE's more flexible regulations had served us well. Leave to a host of interesting towns in Italy claimed many FANYs. Margaret Brown had asked her parents to send out some ancient copies of Baedeker, so her sightseeing was on an informed basis.

My long-term future had an uncertain quality. To my amazement, J had appeared at the office on 2 May on his way from Greece to a posting in Austria. How he found HQ SO(M) in Siena was a mystery. It was forbidden to reveal either our location as to town, or the address, in letters. We spent two hours talking together and then did not meet for a year, when he came back to England for demobilization. By that time we had grown apart and, although we met as friends for a couple of years, as a romance, it was over.

My immediate employment was a far more pressing problem. The War Room was no more, with the absence of a war. Margery Hume Henderson sent for me and presented some alternatives. There was the possibility of an Intelligence post in the Far East. The one she recommended was that the post of FANY Education Officer be created for me. To this I agreed. Twelve FANYs would be handed over into my care for a fortnight. The object would be to keep them occupied in some pursuits of a vaguely 'educational' nature until arrangements were made for them to travel back to England. By that time another twelve would present themselves and so on. Two former wireless operators, Ann Bonsor and Lorna Green, were made up to sergeants as assistants. (They had been corporals and had in recent months completed a three-week instructors' course at the Army School of Education at Perugia.) I was to be a Lieutenant. The irony of the situation struck me. First, I had been promoted having discharged my heaviest responsibilities; secondly, my education at that point had finished at school and I had not then been anywhere near a university; neither had the other two. But we had only a few days in which to prepare for the arrival of our first dozen pupils. We became busy once more.

Our overall problem was shortage of resources. We had few books, only those collected during our service abroad, a wind-up gramophone, the promise of the transport we needed, a small float of cash and our own slender experience. Lorna was musical; Ann had a knowledge of English literature (we were to meet again at Oxford eighteen months later), and there was my smattering of information on current affairs. We had barely a week to prepare for our first arrivals on 14 May.

During our first months in Siena we had made the acquaintance of Signora Bruchi, an Englishwoman married to an Italian banker and senator. Her mother had built the English church. Signora Bruchi had lived in Siena since her marriage forty-five years before. German officers had been billeted on them without knowing her original nationality. She introduced us to Miss Helen Josephine Robins (always in full), an elderly American lady who had spent a lifetime in a house on the Via Sapienza with a superb view over Siena from her terrace at the rear. In view of her age, the Italian authorities had not bothered to intern her. Both these friends put us in touch with people who might help. We visited a convent which taught needlework, an art school, the University of Siena where I had an interview with the Dean in French, the *Biblioteca Communale* (Public Library), a teacher of Art History who spoke English, and so on. A journey by jeep, circumventing potholes and fought-over roads, covered in dust to Perugia proved well worth it. Members of the army School of Education produced the loan of books, gramophone records and much encouragement.

The three of us devised a 'course' with a daily programme and joining instructions. In the morning came an introductory session, followed by needlework at a convent or drawing at the art school. Italian lessons, visit to galleries, swimming in a river eighteen miles away, play-reading with records, musical appreciation, talks by the three of us, and excursions further afield took place in the afternoon. Siena had a considerable musical tradition; some FANYs had already taken piano and singing lessons. A remarkably fine pianist was discovered, who agreed to give recitals. An invitation had come to me earlier to lunch in the mess of members of the United States Women's Auxiliary Army Corps, stationed in Siena. They were charming, courteous girls and we admired (and envied) their several changes of uniform and bedroom furniture, all flown from the USA. They readily agreed to come to a joint debate with our 'students'. This went well and was repeated.

Members of our courses were required to sleep at the *Scacciapensieri* mess, to keep everyone under one roof. They and their bedding needed to be collected beforehand, transport and meals ordered for the newcomers. by the end of the first week we three were totally exhausted. There had been some minor crises. The first concerned the visit to San Gimignano. Miss Robins had found for us Louisa, a plump Italian teacher of art history, in her thirties. She was a member of an illustrious family which had provided a pope and numerous ecclesiastics over the centuries. She gave a good talk in English on the subject of San Gimignano which was to be followed by a visit to that delectable town. Unfortunately neither she nor Emma Nardi, who taught the Italian lessons, had been there since the outbreak of war.

We set off in an open three-ton truck with benches fixed in the back. It was soon apparent why San Gimignano had remained one of the most perfect examples of mediaeval architecture, since it certainly was off the beaten track. When we arrived at a 'blown' bridge, some local people showed us a diversion which was a track straight up a mountain side, a one-in-ten gradient, on the left a steep slope, on the right a deep ravine. We negotiated the bends with the wheels near the edge of the road. The visit to the town itself was greatly enjoyed as there was much of beauty to see: the cathedral with its frescoes of Ghirlandaio (a favourite of mine) and the Benozzo Gozzolis in San Agostino. The thought of the return journey was bothering me not a little. Enquiries as to an alternative route were negative. Bridges in this part of Italy had been systematically blown by the retreating Germans. Coming down the mountainous route was infinitely worse than the ascent. Half our girls closed their eyes, while others clung to the sides of the truck. Louisa sat, pale, but calm. The driver was thought to have enjoyed himself. At the end of the week Lorna took the group to Assisi, with the night spent in Perugia. They were late in returning, a cause for alarm. A FANY had mislaid her military pass. My energies had been directed towards planning for the next week.

Our daily events begin with a description of an anniversary. Ones that fell to me were the birth of Montrose, the death of Voltaire and the accession of Queen Victoria; the rest are beyond recall. Tracing enough information was a nightmare. The *Biblioteca Communale*'s stock was mostly in Italian and beyond our competence. I asked about a French encyclopaedia. The librarian offered me *Larousse*. 'Oh Russian isn't any good to us,' said my companion.' Though never more than a couple of days ahead, and there being only a Sunday between courses, we survived the first month. We had made some good excursions: to Assisi again and to Florence where we saw trucks of German soldiers, officers and men, *en route*. It had become very hot. One of our students fainted at her easel in the art school and another on a visit to the WAAC mess, from 'heart trouble'. Then, at the end of June came the exciting news that the third and last course would include a five-day visit to Venice.

Paper-work included movement orders all round, FANYs and drivers, communication with the Town Major at Venice, as leave there was strictly regulated. With two trucks and two drivers, sixteen FANYs set off on 21 June. Everyone had been woken at 4 am by me; breakfast was at 4.30. There was the usual hitch about filling waterbottles. Also, it was found that one truck was empty. Nothing had been provided to sit upon for a journey of 250 miles. With the help of the mess staff, we hauled two iron garden seats into the back of the truck. The other, fortunately, had benches. As there was no accommodation on the way, the whole journey needed to be made in one day.

We left at 5.20, passed the outskirts of Florence and on towards Bologna and the Futa Pass where so much fighting had taken place. The scenery was mountainous and spectacular until the plain of Ferrara. We stopped for lunch under some trees and cut bread and opened tins. The mess only possessed one tin-opener, which we were not allowed to take away, so dangerous improvisation took place with a clasp knife belonging to one of the drivers. We suggested they should have an hour's sleep, while I went to a cottage with a tin of our own water (and tea bags) and a request for it to be boiled. It was certainly the liquid on which the British army survived the war. Flat and dusty roads led to the River Po. Tangled wreckage of steel girders and bricks of an older bridge lay beside a new one. It had been built, so notices informed us, by Sappers who had left their own messages as to the ingenuity of the construction on pontoon floats, and a drawing of a large chamber pot. We passed through Padua and reached Venice around 7 pm. The trucks were parked as near to the centre as possible and we proceeded by gondola. To glide through the water was a relief after bumping about in a truck for fourteen hours.

FANYs had been placed in two sets of accommodation, eight in the YWCA on the Lido and eight in an officers' leave hotel in Venice itself. Ruth Hermon-Smith and I shared a room at the latter.

The next few days were pure delight. Some friends from Siena came up to join us and we were able on that account to be more adventurous. Louis Franck was in Venice. We met him quite by accident and he took Ruth and me out to dinner, an event which sticks in my memory because he sent the wine back as corked, always an act of mastery. It characterized him. On Sunday 24 July (we were due to leave for Siena the following day) an older FANY rang me from the Lido. One of the girls at the YWCA was ill. A sweltering journey on the iron deck of a tank landing craft (they were plying backwards and forwards in the Lagoon) to the Lido and sight of the unfortunate FANY made me realize that in no way would she be able to travel next day. She was clearly suffering from sunstroke. Although her rigors and delirium had improved and her eye symptoms had calmed down, she was still far from well. A doctor from the RAMC who appeared at my request was somewhat dismissive. He had no accommodation at his Field Dressing Station for women and the patient's condition was a result of personal folly from lying out too long in the sun on the beach. But she was not fit to travel. The YWCA kindly agreed to keep her and I made a visit to the Town Major's office to ask for permission to extend my own stay.

Next day at 7 am the two trucks departed for Siena with fourteen FANYs, two short. Although extra days in Venice might sound a bonus, they were largely filled with attempts, mostly unsuccessful, on an army telephone system to reach base, or other sources of transport. At last, on Thursday 28 June, the MO having pronounced the patient fit to travel, a jeep from Milan came to take the two of us to Siena. We arrived at five in the evening. Anxious and fed-up because of all the trouble she had caused me, I had placed the FANY on a charge for self-inflicted injuries. Everyone had received constant warnings as to the strength of the Italian sun. The charge was heard on the following morning before Margery Hume Henderson with her hat on and other FANY officers with their hats on. The FANY in question, in her defence, pleaded that she had been told, with others, that allowing oneself to be made liable to sunstroke was an indictable offence, but not individually. Awareness of the trouble she had caused and the undesirable exposure of stupid behaviour before the doctor and Town Major brought sympathy in my direction and a reprimand in hers.

Helping with the arrangements for the despatch of FANYs to England now fell to me: heavy luggage was required to be sent ahead. There was a general longing to be back with our families. Anne Butler wrote to her aunt: 'I want to come back very much now and see you all again . . . Everything is closing down in Siena and there is not much work to do . . . I feel the sooner I can get home and get cracking on some post-war employment the better.' A struggle with mess accounts was followed by counting handed-in garments of those FANYs in the departing drafts. A letter to my parents describes 952 small sleeve buttons, 310 tunic buttons, a forgotten number of greatcoat buttons, and so on. But there were still some good parties, including an excellent twenty-first birthday celebration for June Stanley and Anne Butler whose birthdays fell close together. Some of the British Liaison Officers were back from the field. Charles Mackintosh, whose looks were stunning, and Adrian Gallegos, back from prison camp, were among those I remember.

(The appreciation and gratitude felt by Partisans towards the Allied officers and men who came to help and support them during the war years has even now (1999) not waned. Their Italian sons and grandsons continue the friendship forged in those days. To return to receive the freedom of towns and the naming of streets in their honour is a humbling experience. In the autumn of 1998 a group of present-day FANYs travelled to the Dolomites to traverse the route in the mountains covered by H.W. Tilman and his companions in 1944. Their reception from the descendants of those among whom he had lived fifty years earlier was heart-warming.)

Fencing became an interest of mine in Siena. Dick Mallaby, who had known Maestro Barbera in his years in Siena before the war, introduced a group of FANYs to his fencing school and gallery of arms. I was among them. We began to have lessons. It was a taxing and strenuous sport which took a hold and, as work grew less, more time could be spent upon it, feeling like D'Artagnan, but probably looking more like Jack the giant-killer. The last weeks were a brief period of almost pure enjoyment: wonderful expeditions into the Italian countryside, Sunday at Lake Trasimeno, swimming in a mill stream near San Gimignano, visits to the Siena Pinacoteca which had opened its gallery of primitives and to the Bruchis' home. The Palio, Siena's famous horse race, took place on 2 July for the first time since the war. The preparations had filled the city with flags of the various *Contrade* (districts) which were entering their horses. HQ SO(M) had booked a series of balconies in the *Campo* overlooking the race.

Finally the *Scacciapensieri* mess had to be vacated. It had been so beautiful there, with the views and colours and the fireflies in the evenings. All remaining FANYs were to live in the *Chusarelli*. A draft for England was consigned to me – eleven girls. June Stanley was the other officer. After a nostalgic leaving dinner party with a group of friends, and an inspection next morning in the courtyard of HQ (M) by Lieutenant-Colonel Archie Fynn, then in command, we piled into two three-ton trucks with our luggage. We said goodbye to Siena, which has continued to tug at my heart, on Saturday 11 August, 1945.

A seven-hour drive brought us to Rome and an overnight stay at the YWCA. A treat was in store. It became possible to secure tickets to a performance of *Aïda* in the open air at the Baths of Caracalla with excellent singing and, of course, the spectacular setting. It began at sunset when all the surrounding buildings became blood-red in the fading light.

A nightmare existence awaited us in Naples at an ATS Transit and Holding Camp where over three weeks were spent awaiting further transportation. Daily visits to Movements were extremely frustrating. After a week we were joined by the final FANY draft. This meant that Hume Henderson took over some of the arguing, but she was not much more successful than I had been. Morale became very low, so brief sleeping-out passes were issued and, since one of the trucks had been retained, FANYs were able to stay at Positano and other places on the Sorrento peninsular, at leave hostels. It was not until later that news was brought to me that one of my flock had gone by air to Athens. The San Carlos Opera House was an attraction with good performances of *La Bohème* and *La Traviata*. Otherwise life was misery, with poor conditions and great heat. Several of the FANYs became ill. Joan Tapp was admitted to hospital with quinsy.

At last, on 3 September, after endless false alarms, the FANY party of thirty was brought to the Naples quayside. The troopship *Franconia* was already very full and countless troops hung over the rails. Hume Henderson insisted on my drawing up the FANYs into some kind of order for her to inspect. As I shouted words of command, my voice was copied by high-pitched echoes from the soldiers on the ship. At least I had my back to them! The poor FANYs had to face the barrage of mockery. We staggered up the gangway with out kitbags to our quarters. We were ten to a cabin in two-tier bunks, with insufficient space on the floor to dress (or undress) simultaneously. The two small portholes needed to remain closed, as the water was close. Inadequate blowers produced a certain amount, but nothing like enough, air. The journey was calm and uneventful. The weather, at first hot and sunny, grew grey and overcast as we sailed north west towards the Irish Sea. The brides of British servicemen from various foreign countries huddled on deck looking increasingly miserable and apprehensive.

Everyone longed to see the first glimpse of England. As we passed the Scilly Isles on the last night of the voyage, all on deck, we saw a winking light. Quick as a flash, one might say, Diana Thatcher, one of the FANY wireless operators, read out WHAT SHIP ARE YOU? I felt proud in the presence of such competence. Francine Agazarian was standing by the rail. I asked her if she had plans for the future. She told me she would be going back to France to find out who it was that had betrayed her husband.

Next morning a band was playing on the quay as the *Franconia* docked at Liverpool; *Welcome back to Dear Old Blighty*. As all on board had moved to that side of the vessel the OC Troops quickly urged over the loudspeaker that we should disperse or there would be an accident. The order of leaving the ship took hours to arrange. At last came the FANYs' turn. We filed down the gangway; we were home.

General Gubbins was generous in his tribute to FANY association with SOE in a letter which he addressed to Commandant Gamwell on 5 January 1946.

> I am left tongue-tied when I try to tell you what the FANYs have meant to the organization and to me. I say to me because I took the original decision and had the idea to use them to the utmost, and I am personally sufficiently human to be glad to find my

judgment proved right. But to the organization they were every-thing, as you well know, and without them we just couldn't have done it. In every theatre they have become a household word for efficiency, guts, cheerfulness, persistence, tenacity and comrade-ship in difficulty, and I am proud to have been the means of their proving their great qualities, they have been magnificent, and invaluable.

I know that what they have themselves learnt will be of ines-timable and permanent value to their country.

In the meantime, FANYs who had served in the Mediterranean had been dispersing and nearly all of us had been demobilized by Christmas, 1945. But friendships have endured to the present day.[10] At regular intervals some of us meet to recall the experiences we shared with laughter and incredulity. Were we really part of that extraordinary set of circumstances? No one put it better than Dickens: 'It was the best of times, it was the worst of times.'[11]

NOTES

Chapter 1

1 Putnam, 1937.
2 Later Major-General Sir Colin Gubbins, KCMG, DSO, MC.
3 Later Lieutenant-Colonel Sir Peter Wilkinson, KCMG, DSO, OBE, who joined the Foreign Office after the war; his last posting was British Ambassador in Vienna.
4 Colonel Sir Douglas Dodds-Parker, for many years a Member of Parliament.
5 See David Lampe, *The Last Ditch*, Cassell, 1968.
6 Later Colonel Andrew Croft, DSO, OBE.
7 After the establishment of SOE, it became Station XII.
8 ed. Oonagh Hyndman, *Wartime Kent, 1939–40*, Meresborough Books 1990 p. 103.
9 *The Fateful Years, Memoirs 1931–45*, Frederick Muller, 1957, p 288.
10 *Foreign Fields*, IB Tauris, 1997, p 147.
11 Major Alfgar Hesketh-Pritchard MC, Royal Fusiliers, an officer of exceptional brilliance, killed in Carinthia, December 1944.
12 From A History of SOE Signals, still among classified material; reproduced with permission from the SOE Adviser to the Foreign Office.
13 Archives, FANY HQ.

Chapter 2

1 Chatto and Windus, 1996.
2 Later Mme Cosyn and headmistress of the British School in Paris.
3 Lieutenant-Colonel Bickham Sweet-Escott, long-standing member of Sector D and SOE, in Cairo, London and elsewhere; author of *Baker Street Irregular*, Methuen, 1965.

4   Colonial Civil Servant Nigeria 1921–60. Speaker of the Assembly of Northern Nigeria, Kt Bachelor 1959.
5   See Brian James Crabb. *Passage to Destiny – the Sinking of SS Khedive Ismail,* Paul Watkins, 1997.

Chapter 3

1   Report of 28 December, 1943, SOE Archives; reproduced by permission of SOE Adviser at the Foreign Office.
2   KCMG, DSC, later British Ambassador in Saigon and in Greece.
3   1894–1986, Minister Resident at AFHQ 1942–45, Prime Minister 1957–63; OM 1976, Earl of Stockton 1984.
4   See his book *Happy Odyssey,* Jonathan Cape, 1950.
5   *Setting Europe Ablaze,* Springwood Books, 1983.
6   *The Central Blue,* 1956.
7   *War Diaries,* Macmillan, 1984.
8   *The Jedburghs. A Short History,* Privately printed and revised 1995.
9   Life Peer 1990. I am indebted to Baroness Park for her permission to recount these experiences of hers at MASSINGHAM in 1944.
10   See A.L. Funk, *The Hidden Ally,* Greenwood Press (USA), 1992 Madeleine Masson, *Christine,* Hamish Hamilton, 1975.
11   Free translation taken from his book *Tutti le Strade conducono a Roma,* il Mulino, Bologna, 1983.

Chapter 4

1   Frank McLynn, *Fitzroy Maclean,* John Murray, 1992
2   Lord Moran, *Winston Churchill, The Struggle for Survival 1940–65,* Constable, 1966, p. 48 nl.
3   General Gubbins' report of 28 December, 1943, SOE Archives, op.cit.
4   Frank McLynn, *Fitzroy Maclean,* op. cit. pp 173, 256.
5   My thanks to her daughters Fiona Mackay and Helen Roberts for permission to reproduce extracts from Evelyn's diary.

Chapter 5

1   From his book *From Cloak to Dagger,* Kimber, 1982.
2   Free translation from *Tutte le Strade Conducano a Roma,* op.cit.
3   *War Diaries,* p. 164.
4   He later moved to Ravello and the government to Salerno.
5   *Baker Street Irregular,* op.cit. p. 214.
6   *When Men and Mountains meet,* CUP, 1946.

7   SOE Adviser at Foreign Office 1982–88.
8   Lieutenant-General Sir James Gammell, KCG, DSO, MC.
9   Wife of the Earl of Ranfurly; personal assistant to General Maitland Wilson at AFHQ. Possessor of a parrot named Coco.
10 *The Drums of Memory*, Leo Cooper, 1994.
11 *From Cloak to Dagger*, op.cit.
12 *Recollections and Reflections*, Bodley Head, 1981, p. 197.

Chapter 6

1   Josef Garlinski, *Poland, SOE and the Allies*, Allen and Unwin, 1969.
2   *A Clear Premonition*, Leo Cooper, 1995.
3   *SOE in France*, HMSO, 1966, p 292–5.

Chapter 7

1   Lieutenant-Colonel John Grosvenor Beevor, OBE, 1905–95.
2   Colonel George Philip Stewart Macpherson, CBE, Allied Control Commission to Austria 1945–46.
3   I am very grateful for being allowed to read her privately printed book *Long Ago and Far Away* of 1990.
4   See *Disaster at Bari*, Robert Hale, 1971.
5   See Pasquale B. Trizio. *Bombardamento del Porto di Bari di 2 Dicembre 1943* Adda di Bari.
6   Harold Macmillan *War Diaries*, p 448.
7   ibid, p. 454.
8   See his *Recollections and Reflections*, p. 122.
9   Frank McLynn, *Fitzroy Maclean*.
10 William Kimber, 1973, p. 67.
11 *War Diaries*, p. 462.
12 Later Sir Ronald Preston Bt, died 4.5.99.
13 *Guerrilla Surgeon*, Collins, 1957.
14 Field hospital.
15 Christopher Woodhouse who had led the Allied Military Mission was of this opinion, as expressed in his book *Apple of Discord*, Hutchinson, 1948, p. 213.
16 Comments by the Prime Minister's doctor, Lord Moran, who accompanied him, are of interest; *Winston Churchill, The Struggle for Survival*.
17 Hodder and Stoughton, 1947, p 54.

Chapter 8

1   Life Peer 1975
2   *The Bandits of Cisterna*, Leo Cooper, 1991.
3   *Special Operations Executed*, William Kimber, 1986.
4   Pre-war Chief-of-Staff to Himmler.
5   See Richard Lamb, *The War in Italy*, John Murray, 1993.
6   See *The Labour and the Wounds*, Pall Mall Press, 1958.
7   *Recollections and Reflections*, p 143.
8   *Special Operations Europe*, Victor Gollancz, 1989.
9   SOE Archives; reproduced by permission from SOE Adviser to the Foreign Office.
10 The FANY continues to thrive, with a London HQ. In the spring of 1999 it changed its sub-title to 'Princess Royal's Volunteer Corps'.
11 Opening sentence of *A Tale of Two Cities*.

BIBLIOGRAPHY

Amery, Julian, *Sons of the Eagle*, Macmillan, 1948.
—— *Approach March*, Hutchinson, 1973.
Astley, Joan Bright and Peter Wilkinson, *Gubbins and SOE*, Leo Cooper, 1993.
Auty, Phyllis and Clogg, R. *British Foreign Policy towards Wartime Resistance in Yugoslavia and Greece*, Macmillan, 1975.
Battaglia, Roberto, *The Story of the Italian Resistance*, G. Einaudi, 1964.
Beevor, J.G., *Recollections and Reflections*, Bodley Head, 1981.
Bosanquet, Mary, *Journey into a Picture*, Hodder and Stoughton, 1947.
Brown, Arthur, *The Jedburghs*, privately printed, 1995.
Carton di Wiart, Adrian, *Happy Odyssey*, Jonathan Cape, 1950.
Collier, Richard, 1940 *The world in Flames*, Hamish Hamilton, 1979.
—— 1941, *Armageddon*, Hamish Hamilton, 1981.
Cooper, A.R. *Adventures of a Secret Agent*, George Mann, 1957.
—— *Born to Fight*, William Blackwood, 1969.
Crabb, Brian James, *Passage to Destiny, The sinking of the SS Khedive Ismail*, Paul Wilkins, 1957.
Croft, Andrew, *A Talent for Adventure*, Hanley Workshops, 1991.
Dalton, Hugh, *The Fateful Years, Memoirs 1931–45*, Frederick Muller, 1957.
Davidson, Basil, *Special Operations Europe*, Victor Gollancz, 1989.
Deakin, William, *The Embattled Mountain*, OUP, 1971.
Dodd-Parker, Douglas, *Setting Europe Ablaze*, Springwood Books, 1983.
Fielding, Xan, *Hide and Seek*, Secker and Warburg, 1966.
Foot, M.R.D., *SOE In France*, Stationery Office, 1966.
—— *SOE* Mandarin, 1984.
Funk, A.L., *The Hidden Ally, The French Resistance, Special Operations and the Landings in Southern France*, Greenwood Press, USA, 1992.
Garlinski, Josef, *Poland, SOE and the Allies*, Allen and Unwin, 1969.
Gleeson, James and Tom Walden, *Now it can be Told*, Paul Elek, 1952.
Hamilton-Hill, Donald, *SOE Assignment*, Kimber, 1973.

Hastings, Stephen, *The Drums of Memory*, Leo Cooper, 1994.

Hoggart, Richard, *A Sort of Clowning*, Chatto and Windus, 1996.

Hyndham, Oonagh (ed.), *Wartime Kent 1939–40*, Meresborough Books, 1990.

Infield, Glenn, *Disaster at Bari*, Robert Hale, 1971.

Ivanovic, Vane, *LX, Memoirs of a Jugoslav*, Weidenfeld and Nicolson, 1977.

Kemp, Peter, *No Colours, no Crest*, Cassell, 1960.

Lamb, Richard, *The War in Italy*, John Murray, 1993.

Lampe, David, *The Last Ditch*, Cassell, 1968.

Leeper, Reginald, *When Greek Meets Greek*, 1951.

Lees, Michael, *Special Operations Executed*, Kimber, 1986.

Lett, Gordon, *Rossano*, Hodder and Stoughton, 1955.

Macintosh, Charles, *From Cloak to Dagger*, Kimber. 1982.

Maclean, Fitzroy, *Eastern Approaches*, Jonathan Cape, 1949.

Macmillan, Harold, *War Diaries 1943–45*, Macmillan, 1984.

McLynn, Frank, *Fitzroy Maclean*, Jon Murray, 1992.

Masson, Madeleine, *Christine*, Hamish Hamilton, 1975.

Maule, Henry, *General Scobie, Hero of Greece*, Arthur Barker, 1975.

Peter, King, of Jugoslavia, *A King's Heritage*, Cassell, 1955.

Pickering, William, *The Bandits of Cisterna*. Leo Cooper, 1991.

Pimlott, Ben (ed.), *Second World War Diaries of Hugh Dalton, 1940–45*, Jonathan Cape,
    1986.

Roberts, Brian, *Randolph, A Study of Churchill's Son*, Hamish Hamilton, 1984.

Rogers, Lindsay, *Guerrilla Surgeon*, Collins, 1957.

Rootham, Jasper, *Missfire*, Chatto and Windus, 1946.

Salvadori, Massimo, *The Labour and the Wounds*, Pall Mall Press, 1958.

Slessor, John, *The Central Blue*, Cassell, 1956.

Smiley, David, *Albanian Assignment*, Chatto and Windus, 1984.

Stafford, David, SOE and European Resistance 1940–45, Macmillan, 1980.

Sweet-Escott, Bickham, *Baker Street Irregular*, Methuen, 1965.

Tilman, H.W., *When Men and Mountains Meet*, CUP, 1946.

Trevelyan, Raleigh, *A Clear Premonition*, Leo Cooper, 1995.

Trizio, Pasquale B, *Bombardamento del Porto di Bari di 2 Dicembre 1943*, Adda di Bari.

Valiani, Leo, *Tutti le Strade conducano a Roma*, il Mulino, Bologna, 1983.

Ward, Irene, *FANY Invicta*, Hutchinson, 1955.

Wheeler, Mark, *Britain and the War for Yugoslavia*, Columbia Univ. Press, NY 1980.

Williamson, Henry, *Goodbye West Country*, Putnam, 1937.

Wilkinson, Peter (and Joan Bright Astley), *Gubbins and SOE*, Leo Cooper, 1993.

—— *Foreign Fields*, IB Tauris, 1997.

Wilson, Charles (Lord Moran), *Winston Churchill and the Struggle for Survival 1940–65*,
    Constable, 1966.

Woodhouse, Christopher, *The Apple of Discord*, Hutchinson, 1948.

INDEX

D section, 5–6, 20
Dalton, Dr Hugh, 6–7, 165
Damaskinos, Archbishop, 138
Darton, Maj James, 101
Darton, Mrs – see June Stanley
Davidson, Maj Basil, 52, 55, 100, 152, 168
Davies, Brig E F, 55, 127
Davies, Lt Paddy RNVR, 39
Davis, Lt-Col William R, 42
Dawe, Rosemary (Mrs Newman), 82–83, 95, 143–144
Dawes, Daphne (Mrs Iles), 14
Deakin, Lt-Col William, 54, 64, 100
de Angeles, Dr, 154
de Gaulle, Gen Charles, 30–31
de Guélis, Jacques, 31
de Haan, Maj Edward, 39, 74, 77, 86
de Haan, Mrs – see Pauline Ratsey
de Fiori, Silvio, 76
de Fonblanque, Mary (Mrs Duncan), 82–83, 95, 143
de Zoete, Mrs – see Gillian Grant
Denario, Carlo (Leo Donati), 76
Dido, 108
Digne, 48
Direction-finding, 11
Dixon, Jacqueline (Mrs Tucker), 90–91, 96
Dodds-Parker, Col Sir Douglas, 5, 9, 15, 28, 37–38, 42, 49, 79, 129, 165–166
Dodds-Parker, Olive, 106
Dodecanese, 70, 87
Donegall, Marquess of (Dermot Chichester), 145
Donegall, Marchioness of – see Lady Joscelyne Legge
DRAGOON landing, 29, 44–45, 64
Drau river, 103
DRIZZLE signal plan, 77
Dulles, Allen, 151
Duncan, Mrs – see Mary de Fonblanque
Dunkirk, 3–4, 31
Dury, Christine (Mrs Parker), 14, 91
Duthie, Doris, 82

Dvar, 123
DYNAMO operation, 3

EAM, 55–45, 136–138
Economic Warfare, Ministry of, 6, 111
Eden, Sir Anthony, 36
EDES, 55–56, 136
ÉGLISE, 47
Eisenhower, Gen Dwight D, 16–17, 36, 44, 78–79
ELAS, 136–138
Elliot, Air Vice-Marshal William, 99, 126
Elizabeth II, Queen, xii, 126
Elwes, Aline (Mrs McDonnell), 31, 44
EMERALD signal plan, 78
Emilia, 146
Empson, Sir Charles, 22, 61
Enigma machine, 104
EPHEDRINE mission, 46
Evans, Mrs Dee, 82, 86, 89

Faith, Pam (Mrs Macbeth), 82
Far East, 96, 156
Farida, Queen, 58, 63
Farrer, Carmen, 134
Farouk, King of Egypt, 63
Fascists, 85, 151–152
Fairbanks, Douglas Jnr, 29
Fasano, 111, 114
Fawley Court, 11–12, 17
Fencing, 161
Field-Security, 28
Fielding, Maj Xan, 47–48
Fiesoli, 146
First Aid Nursing Yeomanry (FANY)
    Basic training, 9–10
    Change of name, 8
    Deployment in SOE, 28
    Formation of, 7–9
    Headquarters, 21
    Recruitment for, 13, 68
FANY – East African, 25
Fleming, Peter, 5
Florence, 81, 84, 88, 96, 98, 116, 140, 144–147, 159
Flossenberg, 156
Fooks, Elizabeth (Mrs Way), 27, 136
Force 133 – see also MO4, 52 et seq, 118
Force 139/Punch, 98–100, 111
Force 266, 71, 118
Force 399, 118, 128, 133

Foreign Office, 3, 36, 51, 56, 101
Foreign Legion, 75, 83
Forgers, xii, 83, 106
FOX FORCE, 132
French elements in SOE, 27, 31–33
    'Free' French, 30
    'F' Section, 31, 82
    'AMF' Section, 47
Franchi group, 85
Franck, Col Louis, 139, 148–150, 159
Franconia, 162
FRESTON operation, 115
Fynn, Lt-Col Archie, 161

Galbraith, Nora, 127
Galbraith, Sgt, 115
Gallegos, Lt-Cdr Adrian, 75–76, 83, 160
Gambia, The, 23
Gammell, Gen Sir James, 91, 167
Gammell, Mary (Lady Stormonth-Darling), 91
Gamwell, Staff-Cmdr Hope, FANY, 8, 122
Gamwell, Cmdnt Marion, FANY, 8, 10, 14, 17–18, 68, 106, 111, 137, 162
Garibaldi, 85
Gasperi, Alcide de, 85
Gauld, Mrs – see Margaret Marshall
GHQ Middle East, 20, 52, 57–58, 60, 62, 65
Genoa, 152
George II, King of Greece, 56, 61, 138
George VI, 4, 140
Gezira, 59–62, 66, 70
Gibraltar, 31, 75
Gibraltar, Bishop of, 137
Gibson, Jean (Mrs Heller), 121–122
Gibson, Maj Pat, 144, 168
Gibson, Valerie, 31
Gilfredo, 79
Giraud, Gen Henri, 30–31
Guistizia e Libretá, 85
Gizyc, Kyrstina – see Christine Granville
Glenconner, Lord, 52, 56
Glyn, Francis, 28
Goldsmith, Capt John, 32
Golian, Gen, 99
Gorgopotamos river, 55–56
Gothic line, 146
Grand, Maj Lawrence, 5
Grande-Bretagne, Hotel, 137